Enlightenment Thought in the Writings of Goethe

Studies in German Literature, Linguistics, and Culture

Edited by James Hardin
(*South Carolina*)

PAUL E. KERRY

ENLIGHTENMENT THOUGHT
IN THE
WRITINGS OF GOETHE

A Contribution to the History of Ideas

CAMDEN HOUSE

First published 2001
by Camden House

Camden House is an imprint of Boydell & Brewer Inc.
PO Box 41026, Rochester, NY 14604–4126 USA
and of Boydell & Brewer Limited
PO Box 9, Woodbridge, Suffolk IP12 3DF, UK

ISBN: 1–57113–221–x

Library of Congress Cataloging-in-Publication Data

Kerry, Paul E.
    Enlightenment thought in the writings of Goethe: a contribution to the
history of ideas / Paul E. Kerry.
        p. cm. — (Studies in German literature, linguistics, and culture)
Includes bibliographical references and index.
ISBN 1-57113-221-X (alk. paper)
    1. Goethe, Johann Wolfgang von, 1749–1832 — Philosophy.
2. German literature — 18th century — History and criticism.
3. Enlightenment — Germany. 4. Germany — Intellectual Life — 18th
century. 5. Europe, German-speaking — History — 18th century.
6. Intellectual life — History. I. Title. II. Studies in German literature,
linguistics, and culture
(Unnumbered)

PT2193 .K436 2001
831'.6—dc21
                                                    2001025879

A catalogue record for this title is available from the British Library.

This publication is printed on acid-free paper.
Printed in the United States of America

For our dear daughter, Emma Song Sophia
11 January 2000–30 June 2000

'How many are you, then,' said I,
'If they two are in heaven?'
Quick was the little Maid's reply,
'O Master! we are seven.'

— William Wordsworth,
from "We are Seven," 1798

Contents

Acknowledgements

Not a little ink has been spilt in this book in the attempt to show that Goethe promoted the idea of *Anerkennung* [recognition]. Thus, it would be a biting irony indeed if I neglected the pleasurable duty of recognising at least some of those who influenced its genesis.

Professor T. J. Reed (The Queen's College, Oxford) discussed Goethe, the Enlightenment, the history of ideas, and much more with me on numerous occasions over several years. This book began as a doctoral thesis under his supervision and I appreciate deeply his continued friendship — and the continued discussions.

Professor Eda Sagarra (Trinity College, Dublin) and Mrs. Pamela Currie (Lady Margaret Hall, Oxford) commented on the original manuscript and I profited from their expertise in both history and literature. Most recently Professor James Hardin, general editor of Camden House, and Mr. Jim Walker, managing and production editor, have provided valuable advice in preparing this book for publication.

I am grateful to esteemed associates at the University of Oxford who helped me along the way, including: Dr. David Constantine, Professor R. J. W. Evans, Dr. Kevin Hilliard, Dr. Katrin Kohl, Mr. Francis Lamport, the late Mr. Raymond Lucas, Professor Peter Pulzer, Marie Cabaud, Dr. Jonas Jølle, Dr. Uwe Lang, and Dr. Stephan Wendehorst. Professor Ritchie Robertson, a fellow of St. John's College and my former graduate tutor, was ever willing to discuss ideas at length with me. Encouragement also came from the following kind acquaintances who took time to converse with me during their visits to England: Professors Dorrit Cohn (Harvard), Greg Kucich (Notre Dame), Carlos Piera (Madrid), Judith Ryan (Harvard), and from Brigham Young, John Hawkins, Randall Jones, David Magleby, Paul Thomas.

Able scholars who invigorated my interest in intellectual history in previous seminars and courses include Dr. Glenda Abramson (Oxford Centre for Hebrew and Jewish Studies), and Professors Gerhard Botz (Salzburg), John Boyer (Chicago), Peter Burgard (Harvard), James Engell (Harvard), Johan Galtung (European University Center for Peace Studies), Reinhold Heller (Chicago), Geoffrey Howes (Bowling Green), Samuel Jaffe (Chicago), Anton Kaes (Berkeley), Dovid Katz

(Vilnius), Azade Seyhan (Bryn Mawr), and Frank Trommler (Pennsylvania).

This book was completed in England whilst I was a Visiting Research Fellow in the History Department at the University of Reading, and I wish to express my gratitude to my colleagues there, particularly Professors Anne Curry and Michael Biddiss. I also acknowledge my colleagues in the History Department at Brigham Young University, especially Professors Kendall Brown and Frank Fox, and the Dean of the College of Family, Home, and Social Sciences, Professor Clayne Pope, for their strong endorsement of my research projects.

I have benefited from efficient and thoughtful assistance at several libraries and research institutions. I am indebted to Jill Hughes at the Taylorian Library, Oxford; Professor Friedrich Niewöhner at the Herzog August Bibliothek, Wolfenbüttel; Dr. Regine Otto at the Stiftung Weimarer Klassik; Professor Alois Wierlacher and his assistants at the Universität Bayreuth, not least Rainer Haarbusch at the Toleranzforschungszentrum; Roland Bärwinkel at the Herzogin Anna Amalia Bibliothek, Weimar; Dr. Andreas Merkt at the Institut für Europäische Geschichte, Mainz; and Julie Radle, the senior departmental administrator in the BYU History Department.

I owe thanks to co-operative staff at the following institutions: the Bodleian Library, the History Faculty Library, the Modern Languages Faculty Library, the Rhodes House Library, the St. John's College Library (all at Oxford), the British Library, London; the Institute for Germanic Studies, London; the University of Reading Library; the Centre for Tolerance Studies at the University of York; the Goethe- und Schiller-Archiv, Weimar; the Deutsches Literaturarchiv, Marbach; the Freies Deutsches Hochstift, Frankfurt; the German Society of Philadelphia Library; the Mennonite Historical Library, Pennsylvania; the Moravian Archives and Library at Moravian College; and the Quaker Archives at Haverford College. Grants from the British ORS Awards Scheme, the University of Oxford, St. John's College, the University of Reading, and Brigham Young University funded my research.

My late father, whose namesake I am, cultivated my delight in books early on by reading aloud to me and my siblings, Joseph and Marguerite, as children. The love and devotion to education of my mother, Moon Ja Yi, and Grandmother, Song Hui Pak, have ever inspired me and set me on an academic career. Finally, this book would not have been possible without the faithful support of my dear wife Ruth.

P. E. K.
Reading, UK, June 2001

Citations of Editions of Goethe's Works, Letters, Diaries, and Conversations

Goethes Gespräche	Biedermann/Herwig edition of *Goethes Gespräche*
WA	*Weimarer Ausgabe* of Goethe's works
FA	*Frankfurter Ausgabe* of Goethe's works
HA	*Hamburger Ausgabe* of Goethe's works
MA	*Münchner Ausgabe* of Goethe's works

Goethe's writings and his conversations with Eckermann are cited using the FA; his letters and journal entries using the WA. The MA is used for a few of Goethe's earliest writings (chapter 1) and his letter exchange with Zelter (chapter 6) and for commentary. The HA is used exclusively for commentary. Volume numbers to the editions of Goethe's works always appear first, followed by section numbers, if any, and then page numbers. For example: FA 10, 570–71, or including section number, WA IV/16, 97.

Introduction

IF JOHANN WOLFGANG VON GOETHE (1749–1832) had emigrated to Great Britain's thirteen American colonies in 1775 as he thought to do, he might well have become, like Franklin whom he admired, one of the Founding Fathers, or at least worked to further their cause, speculates Katharina Mommsen.[1] This at first startling suggestion becomes understandable when Goethe is viewed in the context of the Enlightenment.

Historians have tended to view the Enlightenment as a loosely connected European and American movement, which, although spanning years and emphasizing different ideas, was constituted by a common concern for natural law, natural religion, freedom, humanism, and scientific inquiry.[2] Some dissent from this view, of course, and see no "coherent intellectual program" in the Enlightenment.[3] Recent research points in the direction of a series of national Enlightenment movements that shared some intellectual ground, but differed in history because they differed in geography.[4]

This brings us back to Mommsen's provocative thought, for she continues to say that Goethe, while having ideas similar to Jefferson's, could not develop them in the same way in his "Zwergstaat" [dwarf state] of Weimar as Jefferson could in the expanse of the United States of America. The Enlightenment was realised differently in different places.

Rather than explicating the Enlightenment as a static set of factors that form a checklist definition, it is perhaps a little less reductive to understand it as an "attitude of mind,"[5] a "process,"[6] and to recall that the word itself suggests the metaphor of "light."[7] This broader view is crucial to seeing Goethe as an exponent of Enlightenment ideals in the German lands. For unlike William Robertson, John Locke, Christian-Guillaume Malsherbes, David Rittenhouse, Pietro Verri, and many other Enlighteners, Goethe was a poet of the first order. Like other prominent Enlightenment figures, he was involved in government: for years he was an important figure in the administration of the Duchy of Weimar. He also pursued his natural science interests throughout his life, as did other eighteenth-century thinkers. Nevertheless, Goethe's most recognised contribution remains his literary legacy — few will recall that he discovered the inter-maxillary bone or that the mineral iron hydroxide (FeOOH) is named after him (Goethite).

Goethe and "the inheritance of the Enlightenment"[8] has long been the subject of scholarly debate,[9] and this book contributes a specific element directly to that general discussion, namely, that some of Goethe's writings can be seen as a further development of Enlightenment thought. It also seeks to situate Goethe within the wider context of the history of ideas by analysing a corpus of his writings from the viewpoint of intellectual history. The battles of the Enlightenment were often fought for in literary and philosophical texts. Goethe stands in a long line of distinguished forebears — Montesquieu, Voltaire, Rousseau, Diderot, Swift, Sterne, Lessing, to name a few — who wrote novels, dramas, and essays to provoke and entertain, and by doing so to help audiences and the reading public to entertain new, enlightened ideas.[10]

What is particularly intriguing is that Goethe embodies the Enlightenment idea of tolerance in his writing, decade after decade until his death. He understood the Enlightenment meaning of *Toleranz,* and he expanded, transformed, and transmitted the idea into the nineteenth century. The word "tolerance" as opposed to "toleration,"[11] which is often associated with the narrower definition of religious toleration, underscores linguistically his greater anthropological, epistemological, and hermeneutic concerns. If the geography of the Enlightenment is a major factor in the shape it takes in a country, it is telling that Goethe beat the drum of tolerance in Germany. Did he sense that this cardinal Enlightenment virtue was needed more there than in other nations? By tracing this overriding concern in Goethe's writings, further facets of his commitment to the Enlightenment are illuminated. But first it is necessary to review historically the development of the tolerance discussion within the German lands and then place Goethe and his writings in relation to this discourse.

While sixteenth- and seventeenth-century debates about theodicy and theophany contributed to the Enlightenment discussion on tolerance, many eighteenth-century thinkers looked back in horror at the terrible religious wars unleashed during the previous centuries.[12] Contemporary readers must bear in mind that these conflicts devastated Europe, particularly Germany, and contributed to an existential and moral crisis that cracked the bedrock of church authority and scholastic philosophy, as they were often suspected of being linked to religious fanaticism.[13]

Questions about the nature and accessibility of divine truth in the wake of exhausting European religious wars pressed religious toleration to the forefront of deliberation in the German lands.[14] The eighteenth century broke intellectually with previous centuries in that tolerance as such, not only religious toleration, became a central issue.[15] Moses Mendelssohn serves as an eloquent spokesman for Enlightenment thinkers who pleaded with potentates to grant religious toleration:

> Regenten der Erde! . . . Bahnet einer gluecklichen Nachkommen-schaft wenigstens den Weg zu jener Hoehe der Cultur, zu jener allgemeinen Menschenduldung, nach welcher die Vernunft noch immer vergebens seufzet! Belohnet und bestrafet keine Lehre, locket und bestechet zu keiner Religionsmeinung! Wer die oeffentliche Glueckseligkeit nicht stoehret, wer gegen die buergerlichen Gesetze, gegen euch und seine Mitbuerger rechtschaffen handelt, den lasset sprechen, wie er denkt, Gott anrufen nach seiner oder seiner Vaeter Weise, und sein ewiges Heil suchen wo er es zu finden glaubet. Lasset niemanden in euren Staaten Herzenskuendiger und Gedankenrichter seyn; niemanden ein Recht sich anmaßen, das der Allwissende sich allein vorbehalten hat! Wenn wir dem Kaiser geben, was des Kaisers ist; so gebet ihr selbst Gotte, was Gottes ist! Liebet die Wahrheit! Liebet den Frieden![16]

> [Regents of the earth! . . . At least make the way for happy descendants to that height of culture, to that general tolerance of others, for which reason still vainly sighs! Reward or punish no teaching, entice or captivate for no religious opinion! He who does not disturb the public peace, who acts justly towards the civil laws and towards you and his fellow citizens, let him speak as he thinks, call on God according to his ways or those of his fathers, and seek his eternal salvation where he believes to find it. Let no one in your States be a judge of people's hearts or minds; no one presume a right that the Omniscient reserves for itself! If we render to Caesar what is Ceasar's, so give God what is God's. Love truth! Love peace!]

One way to trace the transformation of the idea of tolerance in the German lands is to outline the development of the word itself. Eda Sagarra observes: "During the period 1775–1840 the popular conversation lexicons and encyclopedias reflected changing views in bourgeois German society about the function of the church in the modern world."[17] Similarly, definitions of *Toleranz* mirror changing views about society during this period, and in some instances Goethe's writings from 1770 to 1830, the years covered in this book, reflect these changes, forecast them, or provide imaginative alternatives.[18] Johann

Heinrich Zedler's influential *Universal Lexikon* (1737–1750), one of Europe's first encyclopaedias, an astounding cultural achievement and historical document, alerts modern readers to the risk of anachronism when considering eighteenth-century definitions:

> Toleranz . . . dieses Wort wird insgemein von einer Obrigkeit gebrauchet, welche in einer Provinz oder Stadt geschehen laesset, daß auch andere Religions-Verwandten ausser der daselbst eingefuehrten Religion . . . die freye Uebung ihres Gottesdienstes darinnen haben moegen. Dergleichen Toleranz derer Protestirenden, Dissenters oder Non-Conformisten, so in vielen Stuecken von der Englischen Kirche abweichen, ist in Engelland durch eine Parlaments-Acte verstattet worden.[19]

> [Tolerance . . . this word is as a whole used by an authority that allows other religious groups outside of the established religion in a province or city . . . the free exercise of their religious services therein. Similar tolerance in England of Protestants, Dissenters, or Non-Conformists that differ in many parts from the Church of England has been permitted through an Act of Parliament.]

This suggests that tolerance was a prerogative of rulers, something to be dispensed from the top down. Furthermore, it shows that the 1689 English Toleration Act was known in Germany, and implies that it was seen to be a model.[20] Certainly Voltaire's *Letters Concerning the English Nation* (1733), written while he lived in exile in England, popularised this notion. In Zedler's further discussion it is striking that a potentially devastating criticism of tolerance — that it may disrupt the peace of the land — is deflected by explaining that its practice appeals to "Vernunft" [reason], and by citing the experience, an important precedent in political argument, of Holland, another model nation.[21] Tolerance is thus presented as a public good, a principle that can lead to unity within the political system — reasoning that appealed to German rulers like Friedrich II.

In Johann Christoph Adelung's 1774 dictionary, another influential text in Germany and a major linguistic accomplishment, the word "Duldung" is defined as the sufferance of religions not sanctioned by the laws of the land.[22] Under the entry for the verb "dulden" there follows this example: "die Juden werden im römischen Reiche geduldet, sie werden nicht als Juden bestraft" [the Jews are tolerated in the Roman Empire; they are not punished as Jews].[23] However, religious toleration was still seen in many German lands in the mid-eighteenth century as a temporary measure until conversion to the true faith would occur:

Der Grund der Toleranz, so man den Irr-Gläubigen angedeyhen laesset, muß in der allgemeinen Liebe und Erbarmung liegen, und der Zweck derselben bloß dieser seyn, daß sie den irrenden Naechsten von dem Irrthum seines Weges nach und nach unter dem Seegen GOttes zu ueberzeugen suchet, wozu sie theils alle Evangelische Mittel, doch ohne Zwang anwendet, theils die Hindernisse aus dem Wege raeumet, und der Wahrheit Platz machet.[24]

[The reason for tolerance, such that one allows the false believers to prosper, must reside in universal love and mercy, and the purpose of the same is simply this, to seek eventually, under God's blessing, to convince the confused neighbour of the error of his way, whereby one applies evangelical means — but without compulsion — and removes barriers, and makes place for the truth.]

As the eighteenth century came to a close, Georg Gottfried Strelin's 1796 dictionary defined *Toleranz* as a "menschliche, christliche, bürgerliche und kirchliche Duldung" [human, Christian, civil, and ecclesiastical sufferance].[25] This marks a slight shift in previous usage, as *Toleranz* now associates religious and civic meanings. By 1807 Campe could polemicize against viewing tolerance as an inherently superior attitude: "Die Duldung Andersdenker sollte gar nicht als etwas Verdienstliches angesehen werden" [Tolerating those who think differently should not be seen at all as something meritorious]. Indeed, Kant, like Schubart, had already intimated this attitude in 1784 when he writes ironically about the "hochmütigen" [arrogant] name of *Toleranz*.[26]

This shift in thought is registered in the widely read nineteenth-century Brockhaus *Conversations-Lexicon* (1815), which puts forward an important definition of tolerance that includes "Anerkennung" [recognition]:

Duldung (Toleranz), ist die tätige Anerkennung der Freiheit, die jedermann hat, in Ansehung des Glaubens oder seines Urteils über das Wahre, Gute und Schöne seiner eigenen Überzeugung zu folgen. Diese Duldung ist Pflicht, weil die Denkfreiheiten ursprüngliches, durch kein geselliges Verhältnis der Menschen verlierbares Recht der Menschheit ist.

[Sufferance (Tolerance) is the active recognition of freedom that everyone has, in respect of belief or his judgement about the true, good, and beautiful, to follow his own convictions. This tolerance is duty because freedom of thought is an original right of humanity, independent of societal relationships.]

It is significant that such a broad definition of tolerance had reached this popular reference work. No longer was tolerance confined to the religious realm, but its dimensions now included freedom of thought and aesthetic sensibility. The groundwork for this advance, which would ultimately change the status of art and artists in society, was laid by Kant in *Kritik der Urteilskraft* (Critique of Judgement, 1790) and Schiller in *Über die ästhetische Erziehung des Menschen in einer Reihe von Briefen* (On the Aesthetic Education of Man in a Series of Letters, 1795). Yet the necessary precursor for this aesthetic re-evaluation was the freedom of belief. T. J. Reed discerns the order of this important causal connection:

> The principle of artistic autonomy, great advance though it was, had nevertheless its own antecedents. . . . They lie in the Enlightenment struggle for intellectual and religious toleration. . . . For the artist's liberty to obey only the inner laws of his own work is an extension of the individual's liberty to hold his own beliefs; the requirement that each individual artistic approach be appreciated in itself, regardless of how it stands to orthodox beliefs . . . follows from the idea that we must consequently practise a "suspension of belief" with regard to the content of other men's thinking in order to recognise the value of the common human activity of thought.[27]

Pierer, writing in 1826, connects tolerance explicitly to human rights:

> Duldung (religiöse Toleranz), beruht auf dem Grundsatze, daß ein jeder Mensch das Recht habe, seines Glaubens leben zu dürfen, und äußert sich in der gegenseitigen Zugestehung desselben. Das Recht, eine eigne Überzeugung haben und derselben folgen zu dürfen, gehört zu den unveräußerlichen Menschenrechten.

> [Sufferance (religious tolerance), rests on the fundamental principle that each person has the right to live his beliefs, and expresses itself in the reciprocal recognition of the same. The right to have a personal conviction and to follow the same belongs to the inalienable rights of man.]

This decisively shifts the argument from a top-down concession to a bottom-up claim, thus this statement represents a decisive change in the justification provided for tolerance: instead of citing it as something decreed from on high, it is here considered to be an innate human right. And by 1830, the *Rheinische Conversations-Lexicon* trumpets: "Die Glaubens- oder Gewissensfreiheit ist ein unveräußerliches Recht des Menschen, in dem ihn niemand beschränken oder zwingen darf" [The freedom of belief or conscience is an inalienable right of human beings, in regard to which no one may limit or compel him]. German literary and philosophical interest in tolerance thus bears directly on the socio-political debate in German society[28] about not only the status of religions to each other and to the State, but more penetratingly to the freedom of belief generally.[29]

The history of the Germanic lands is one of conflict over religion:[30] the Reformation, the Thirty Years' War (1618–1648), and the Siege of Vienna (1683) are only the more obvious flash-points at which *Heilsgeschichte* [salvational history] collides with *Zeitgeschichte* [contemporary history]. Tolerance, at least the actual use of the word in a legal sense, is rather modern.[31] Schreiner notes: "Weder im Toleranzedikt von Mailand (313) noch im Toleranzedikt von Nantes (1598) ist von 'tolerantia' oder 'tolérance' die Rede" [Neither in the Tolerance Edict of Milan (313), nor in the Tolerance Edict of Nantes (1598) is there any mention of 'tolerantia' or 'tolérance'].[32] By the seventeenth century economic prosperity and *pax et concordia* [peace and concord], something quite different from rationality and rights, could be served by some measure of tolerance. "Staatsräson" [reasons of state] would play an increasingly key role in its establishment during the eighteenth century. Imperial cities such as Ulm, Ravensburg, and Augsburg were excluded from the *cuius regio, eius religio* [in a (prince's) country, the (prince's) religion] clause of the Peace of Augsburg (1555) so that they could prosper economically. Meanwhile, they had become, to some degree, quietly bi- or pluri-confessional.[33] Goethe took a keen interest in Bohemia, where the spark of the Thirty Years' War was struck, and came to know the history of religious strife involving Wycliffe and Huss.[34] But the first legal reference in the "Reichsrecht" [laws of the Empire] to tolerance occurs in the 1648 Treaties of the Peace of Westphalia and is a negative one — a reminder to all that tolerance was forbidden ("nulla alia religio ... recipiatur vel toleretur").[35] In fact, the Papacy issued a Bull condemning formally the religious clauses of the Peace.[36] Sagarra, however, draws attention to a different aspect of the Empire, noting that a relatively wide variety of religions could be found in the German lands and that this eventually led to mutual acknowledgement between them.[37]

As a direct result of Louis XIV's Revocation of the Edict of Nantes (October 1685), Friedrich Wilhelm, the Calvinist Elector of Brandenburg, responded within a month with his Potsdam Edict, which invited the persecuted and expelled French Huguenots to his lands. Cassirer suggests that Pierre Bayle (Goethe knew his *Dictionnaire*),[38] who fled with other French Protestants to Holland, was among the first to make the intellectual breakthrough to the modern idea of tolerance as a general principle.[39] "Acts of Toleration" passed in the English colony of Maryland (1649) and in England (1689) were narrowly conceived and implemented, but they do prefigure the pattern of state-sanctioned tolerance that continued in the eighteenth century. By the beginning of the century there also existed a strong literary interest in the controversies over tolerance, thus transforming it into a cultural theme.[40]

Tolerance did not spread consistently in Germany. For example, in 1712 the Count of Ysenburg and Büdingen issued a *Toleranzpatent,* or edict on tolerance.[41] This is an overlooked document at once typical and ahead of its time. This Protestant Count, Ernst Casimir, allowed at an unusually early date religious freedom beyond the Empire's three recognised confessions of Catholicism, Lutheranism, and Calvinism: "So wollen Wir Jedermann vollkommene Gewissens-Freyheit verstatten" [Thus we permit every one perfect freedom of conscience]. The edict reveals a mix of motives for granting this privilege: avoidance of the kind of terrible religious wars that had gone before, the promotion of piety, and not least the desire for economic growth. This *Toleranzpatent* stands for others that were issued in Germany and throws some of the attitudes of the time into relief.[42]

But five years later, in 1717, religious upheaval continued in other parts of Germany as the Moravians and Mennonites endured persecution because of their beliefs, and many in both groups fled abroad. In 1731 the Prince Archbishop of Salzburg, Leopold Firmian, banished from his territory over 20,000 Protestants who refused to be "recatholicised" as was his "constitutional right as a prince of the Holy Roman Empire."[43] Some refugees left for America, and others sought havens in European Protestant territories, such as was offered by the Prussian King, Friedrich Wilhelm I. Their plight and suffering became synonymous with infamy and were well-documented.[44] Gerhard Gottlieb Günther Göcking wrote the *Vollkommene Emigrationsgeschichte von denen aus dem Erzbistum Salzburg vertriebenen . . . Lutheranern* (Perfect Emigration History of the Lutherans Expelled from the Archbishopric of Salzburg, 1734), only six years before the new King of Prussia, Friedrich II, just three weeks into his reign on 22 June 1740, proclaimed: "Die Religionen müssen alle toleriert werden und muß der Fiskal nur ein Auge darauf haben, daß keine der anderen Abbruch tue, denn hier muß ein jeder nach seiner Façon selig werden" [All religions must be tolerated, and the government must only watch that none harms another, because here each must find salvation according to his fashion].[45] Göcking's work was a source for Goethe's popular story of the threatened idyll, *Hermann und Dorothea* (1797). Thomas Saine provides an important reminder, however, that "Frankfurt am Main and Hamburg were examples of territories where the dominant Lutherans had discriminated against both Calvinists and Catholics."[46]

Goethe himself reported that his great uncle, Johann Michael von Loen, involved himself in the religious controversies between the Church and State. Loen wrote, as Goethe recorded in his *Dichtung und Wahrheit:* "'Die einzige wahre Religion,' ein Buch, das die Absicht hatte, Toleranz, besonders zwischen Lutheranen und Calvinisten, zu befördern. Hierüber kam er mit den Theologen in Streit" [*The One True Religion* (1750), a book that had the intention to nurture tolerance, especially between the Lutherans and the Calvinists. On this point he came into conflict with the theologians]. The debate became so vitriolic and personal that Loen accepted a post offered to him by Friedrich II as an escape.[47]

Goethe also recalled his excitement as a young advocate in Frankfurt who worked for progressive legal change. He felt himself, at least retrospectively, to be a part of what scholars have called the "bureaucratic Enlightenment."[48] He wrote with enthusiasm that "ein Damm nach dem andern" [one dam after another] was broken through: opportunities to study increased for the lower classes, divorce between mismatched partners became more easily obtainable, prisons were improved, and tolerance between religions was practised and argued for in respect to Jews.[49] Emperor Joseph II, a Catholic ruler, issued his ground-breaking *Toleranzpatent* for all Hapsburg lands in 1781.[50] Joseph, like Ernst, issued the edict because he was "uiberzeugt eines Theils von der Schaedlichkeit alles Gewissenszwanges, und anderer Seits von dem grossen Nutzen, der fuer die Religion, und dem Staat, aus einer wahren christlichen Tolleranz entspringet" [convinced on one side of the harmfulness of all compulsion of conscience and on the other side of the great usefulness arising from a true Christian tolerance, both for religion and the State.][51] In a little-known piece, *Der Hausball: Eine deutsche Nationalgeschichte* (The House Ball: A German National History, 1781), with an optimistic introduction traced to Goethe, the reign of Emperor Joseph II is likened to the rising of the sun, a typical Enlightenment emblem.[52]

Yet progress was uncertain in the German lands. Friedrich Wilhelm II of Prussia enacted an edict, the so-called *Wöllnersches Religionsedikt* (Wöllner Edict on Religion, 1788), that was directed against Enlighteners,[53] favoured Lutheran orthodoxy,[54] blocked the advancement of Catholics, and yet guaranteed the freedom of conscience granted by Friedrich II to Jews, Mennonites, and Moravians.[55]

Napoleonic policy altered religious affairs in the Rhine territories. The German Imperial Recess of 1803 greatly weakened powerful episcopal principalities such as Mainz, Trier, and Cologne, as well as twenty-nine bishoprics that had previously been sovereign in political matters.[56] The reorganization and enlargement of Württemberg, Bavaria, and Baden necessitated a change in their religious policies, for with the expansion of their territory they gained citizens of different faiths. These changes culminated in increased tolerance with the 1806 Württemberg Edict on Religion.[57] Goethe tried to keep abreast of the emancipation of Jews, initiated by the 1808 Napoleonic Decree on Jewish Organisation, in the French-occupied Rhine area and Westphalia.[58]

The 1817 tercentenary of the Reformation motivated Goethe to reflect earnestly on the state of interfaith affairs in German society in an essay on the anticipated celebrations. And in 1817 Friedrich Wilhelm III issued a call to the Reformed and Lutheran Churches to merge into a single Evangelical Church. The policy was not altogether successful — interconfessional tolerance did not mean doctrinal and liturgical differences were abandoned — but other "Landeskirchen" [regional churches] were formed through similar unions in the Palatinate, Hesse, and Baden.[59]

The foregoing historical, socio-legal, and linguistic sketch shows that tolerance was a pressing issue during Goethe's lifetime. Enlightenment thinkers championed the idea of tolerance, and left an impressive intellectual legacy. John Locke's *A Letter Concerning Toleration*, first published in Latin in 1688 and translated into German in 1710, was among the first modern, systematic arguments in favour of tolerance, and attracted attention throughout Europe. Along with translations of other English thinkers like Richard Bentley and John Brown,[60] American statesmen Franklin and Jefferson,[61] and French philosophers Voltaire and Bayle,[62] German thinkers were contributing a growing number of texts to this *Aufklärung* [Enlightenment] discussion, including Basedow, Lessing, Dohm, and Mendelssohn, to name a few whose writings Goethe knew.[63]

Goethe admitted more than once that he was strongly influenced by the historian Justus Möser, who contributed "Über die allgemeine Toleranz: Briefe aus Virginien" (On Universal Tolerance: Letters from Virginia) to the journal *Berlinische Monatsschrift* (Berliner Monthly, 1787/1788).[64] Wieland, who penned "Gedanken von der Freyheit über Gegenstände des Glaubens zu philosophieren" (Thoughts on the Freedom to Philosophise on Objects of Belief, 1788), Goethe knew personally and referred to him as his "ächten Lehrer" [true teacher].[65] The journalist, poet, and musician, Schubart, published *Über die Vereinigung der christlichen Religionsparteien* (On the Union of Christian Religious Confessions, 1788) after ten years as a political prisoner, during which time he claimed that Goethe visited him once in 1779.[66]

Goethe's epistemology was at least partly influenced by Kant, as shown by the annotations in his copy of Kant's *Kritik der reinen Vernunft* (Critique of Pure Reason, 1781), most emphatically in the section "Vom Meynen, Wissen und Glauben" [On Opinions, Knowledge, and Belief]. He paid particular attention to Kant's arguments about the subjective nature of "doctrinalen Glauben" [doctrinal belief], a phrase he underlined.[67] When there is a striking parallel between images generated in Goethe's writings and those contained in Kant's definitive essay, *Was ist Aufklärung?* (What is Enlightenment?, 1784), I cite this in the footnotes, as it is in these images, among others, that the Enlightenment is embodied in metaphor by Goethe. The records do not indicate whether or not Goethe read this essay, although he was familiar enough with Kant's thought to write to Victor Cousin: "Die Methode Kants ist ein Princip der Humanität und Toleranz" [Kant's method is a principle of humanity and tolerance].[68] And certainly Kant stresses freedom of belief: "Ich habe den Hauptpunkt der Aufklärung, die des Ausganges der Menschen aus ihrer selbstverschuldeten Unmündigkeit, vorzüglich *in Religionssachen* gesetzt" [I have placed the main point of enlightenment, the emergence of people from their self-incurred tutelage, mainly *in matters of religion*]. And he praises strategically the Prussian King, Friedrich II, for his refusal to interfere in "Gewissensangelegenheiten" [matters of conscience].[69] John McCarthy analyses Kant's essay with acuity when he suggests that: "Freedom in matters of conscience is a first step toward civil liberties for Kant and the other Enlighteners."[70]

Another influence on Goethe's development of Enlightenment concerns can be traced to Johann Gottfried Herder. His first contact with Herder occurred in Strassburg in 1770; later Goethe helped to secure an ecclesiastical post for Herder in Weimar that he held until his death. Isaiah Berlin summarises his contribution: "Herder and his disciples believed in the peaceful coexistence of a rich multiplicity and variety of national forms of life, the more diverse the better."[71] Herder's influence was long-lasting. In an 1828 announcement in the journal *Ueber Kunst und Alterthum* (On Art and Antiquity), Goethe welcomed a new French translation of Herder's *Ideen zur Philosophie der Geschichte der Menschheit* (Ideas on the Philosophy of the History of Humanity,

1784–1791) with which he was familiar, and proclaimed that its influence on the education of the nation had been incredibly significant.[72] Goethe wrote similarly in his introduction to the English historian Thomas Carlyle's biography of Schiller, claiming that Herder's thoughts had been so far-reaching that his ideas were commonplace.[73]

While the scope of influence, even in well-documented cases, is difficult to define, Goethe found one of his theoretical hinges, the concept of "Eigenheit" [peculiarity or in some contexts individuality], if not first then most obviously in Herder's writings. Goethe's taking over of this concept, "that every human community had its own shape and pattern," is blended with Enlightenment universalism, the notion of a shared humanity, a "lowest common denominator which applies to all men at all times."[74] This way of understanding the world is the dialogical movement between "Generality and Particularity" or "Besonderes und Allgemeines."[75] Thus, in the following chapters I draw attention to the intersection of Herderian particularity and Enlightenment universalism and try to convey how Goethe's thought and writing to some degree resolves this tension. Tolerance is an epistemological concern and not only a socio-legal issue for Goethe. It involves accuracy of perception, where intolerance and prejudice make reasonable evaluations impossible. Therefore I also highlight at times Goethe's hermeneutics, for it betrays his intense anthropological interest in learning how to understand and relate to objects, individuals, and the world.

When a biographical detail appears particularly relevant I have cited it, but I have not ventured to arbitrate whether or to what extent Goethe may be classified as a Christian. It is fair to say that Goethe was sceptical of orthodoxy in a way not unlike Franklin whom he read, who compared a sectarian to "a Man travelling in foggy Weather: Those at some Distance before him on the Road he sees wrapt up in the Fog, as well as those behind him, and also the People in the Fields on each side; but neer him all appears clear — Tho' in truth he is as much in the Fog as any of them."[76]

I have also not aimed to discover whether or not Goethe was a particularly tolerant or intolerant man in his personal life. In later years he painted himself as tolerant, or as one who was perceived as such. On one occasion he compared literary production to natural seasons that bring forth both beautiful butterflies and irritating midges and proposes that people ought to cease wasting energy exterminating the gnats or in other words people should focus on the admirable: "Die Gesellschaft sah mich mit Verwunderung an, woher mir so viele Weisheit und so viele Toleranz käme?" [The society looked at me in amazement — where did so much wisdom and so much tolerance come from?][77] He was no less tolerant than most, and on certain issues more so than many of his time, precisely because of his commitment to Enlightenment ideals. On the other hand, he could not always sustain the optimism of Lessing's *Nathan der Weise* (Nathan the Wise, 1779). In fact, Goethe could be vituperative:

> Juden und Heiden hinaus! so duldet der christliche Schwärmer.
>   Christ und Heide verflucht! murmelt ein jüdischer Bart.
> Mit den Christen an Spieß und mit den Juden ins Feuer!
>   Singet ein türkisches Kind Christen und Juden zum Spott.
> Welcher ist der klügste? Entscheide! Aber sind diese
>   Narren in deinem Palast, Gottheit, so geh ich vorbei.[78]

[Jews and Pagans out! thus tolerates the Christian fanatic. Christian and Pagan be cursed, mutters a Jewish beard. The Christians on the spit and the Jews in the fire, sings a Turkish child, ridiculing Christians and Jews. Which is the wisest? Decide! But if these Fools are in your palace, Deity, I will go past.]

This book also represents an effort to balance the scales of scholarship to some degree, for there has been so much work on Lessing's idea of tolerance and his status as a representative of the *Aufklärung*[79] that the continuance of Enlightenment concerns among later German thinkers appears to be somewhat neglected.[80] Goethe saw himself as bearing the torch of tolerance that Lessing bore before him. In his autobiographical paralipomena he hinted that religious controversies exhausted Lessing: "Er wird müde . . . und stirbt. Was nach ihm eintritt?" [He becomes tired . . . and dies. What sets in after him?][81] Of course, Goethe had seized the literary baton long before he decided not to include those lines in *Dichtung und Wahrheit*. In *Über das deutsche Theater* (On the German Theatre, 1815) Goethe praises *Nathan der Weise* and Lessing's immense ethical achievement:

Möge doch die bekannte Erzählung, glücklich dargestellt, das deutsche Publicum auf ewige Zeiten erinnern, daß es nicht nur berufen wird, um zu schauen, sondern auch, um zu hören und zu vernehmen. Möge zugleich das darin ausgesprochene göttliche Duldungs- und Schonungsgefühl der Nation heilig und werth bleiben.[82]

[May this well-known story, happily presented, remind German audiences forever that it is not only called to look, but also to hear and perceive. At the same time may the pronounced heavenly feelings of tolerance and consideration expressed in it remain valued and holy to the nation.]

Haunting lines, given the subsequent course of German history.

The Enlightenment engaged Goethe for most of his life, so it is important to explore works that span his lifetime, an inquiry that can be attempted in a selective sampling only. The theme of tolerance inhabits all of the main genres in his oeuvre: prose, poetry, and drama.[83] Although tolerance cannot be claimed as an overriding interest in all of the pieces here studied — and certainly focusing narrowly on any aspect of Goethe's writings flattens them somewhat — yet an examination of its role also reveals new dimensions in them.

I have selected two of Goethe's major dramas, *Iphigenie auf Tauris* (Iphigenie on Tauris, 1779) and *Egmont* (1787) and two major works of fictional prose, *Die Leiden des jungen Werthers* (The Sufferings of Young Werther, 1773) and *Wilhelm Meisters Wanderjahre oder Die Entsagenden* (Wilhelm Meister's Journeyman Years or the Renunciants, 1829) to ensure generic distribution, but above all because these works clearly illustrate facets of Enlightenment thought. I have also employed this thematic approach in examinations of lesser-known, even overlooked texts such as *Brief des Pastors zu *** an den neuen Pastor zu **** (Letter of the Pastor at *** to the new Pastor at ***, 1773) and the *Sankt-Rochus-Fest zu Bingen* (Saint Roch Festival at Bingen, 1817), as well as several essays.

Goethe's Enlightenment concerns can be documented as early as the 1770s when he probed social tolerance in the best-selling novel *Werther,* as well as a fragment of the *Faust* drama, and in his notebook *Ephemerides* (Ephemeral Writings). In *Brief des Pastors* Goethe addressed religious toleration directly. I also cite, selectively, the earlier prose edition of *Iphigenie,* an important choice as it proves that Goethe had formulated thoughts on intercultural tolerance at an early date. The drama revolves around real, abstract, and potential relationships that in turn converge on Iphigenie: father-daughter, husband-wife, brother-sister, priestess-king, male-female, Greek-Barbarian. These roles regulate her allegiances and she must negotiate them.

It is perhaps unsurprising, given the desire of Enlightenment thinkers to address rulers directly, that *Egmont* so clearly showcases perspectives on tolerance. Moreover, Goethe selected a chapter of history, the Dutch Revolt, which allowed him to merge the several overt dialogues on tolerance seamlessly with the action of the play. And religious toleration is itself blended with, or perhaps even gives way to, the question of intercultural tolerance: will the Spanish Inquisition and its armies overwhelm Dutch cultural particularity? Following the Napoleonic wars, Goethe refused to follow the nationalistic lead of some of his countrymen, and instead renewed the Enlightenment theme of universal brotherhood. The remarkable (and neglected) *Sankt Rochus-Fest zu Bingen* is a humane answer to the vexing and recurring question of how to rebuild war-torn communities and put aside animosities, while the architects of the European community in Vienna were failing to do just that. On one side of the Rhine live Protestants, on the other side Catholics. The region had been further divided during the war as the French occupied the left bank, the Catholic side. With the enemy forces ousted, the two economically interdependent German communities try to find their way to each other by co-operating in a spirit of good will to restore a ruined Catholic chapel that rests on a hill overlooking the Rhine Gorge. Goethe, an eyewitness, documents the festival with warmth, wit, and respect.

In his 1816 *Morgenblatt* essay on *Die Geheimnisse* (The Mysteries), Goethe purposely revisits an eighteenth-century fragment and takes pleasure in sketching how his grandly conceived epic about twelve distinct faiths would have ended in a kind of utopian and enlightened parliament of world religions. The intriguing essay *Zum Reformationsfest* (For The Reformation Festival, 1816) displays Goethe's sensitivity when contemplating the intertwined worlds of politics and religion as he outlines his vision for a commemoration of Luther's achievement that would overcome the divisions between Christians, Muslims, Jews, and heathens.

Muslims were on Goethe's mind at the time, for he had just announced his *West-östlicher Divan* (West-Eastern Divan, 1819). The books of poetry that comprise the *Divan* with its lengthy final book of commentary, *Besserem Verständniss* (For Better Understanding) is a *tour de force* of Goethe's intercultural interests on a scale beyond anything he had before written. In this collection of poetry, proverbs, and prose Goethe explicates his thoughts on international, interreligious, and intercultural relations, and lays the theoretical groundwork for the practical development of *Weltliteratur* [world literature], an idea that he promoted with vigour in the following decade.

The second version of *Wilhelm Meisters Wanderjahre* (1829) opens up various plans for creating new communities. As the nineteenth century moves onward, and some of its challenges are depicted, the novel reminds readers that the ideas of the eighteenth century are portable. There is a veritable parade of Enlightenment thinkers brought into view as Goethe establishes an intellectual genealogy and alerts readers to the fact that many present freedoms are a result of the efforts of courageous thinkers who fought injustice and intolerance. The quintessential Enlightenment clarion call — religious freedom — is stressed throughout the novel.

In the following chapter, an excursus, I consider the case of Jews within the matrix of Goethe's thoughts on religious liberty. The concluding chapter explores Goethe's attempts to mediate the tensions between cultural peculiarities and the universal humane as formulated in a few of his final essays.

Goethe assimilated key philosophical points of the Enlightenment tolerance discourse and also contributed to it by drawing creative inspiration from historical figures and contexts and then reworking them for his own time and circumstances. For example, his use of the Dutch Revolt in *Egmont* to highlight aspects of intercultural relations is a fruitful anachronism, and says more about eighteenth-century than about sixteenth-century ideas on tolerance.[84] Similarly, when William Penn (1644–1718) is celebrated in *Wilhelm Meisters Wanderjahre,* echoes of the Englishman's "holy experiment"[85] in Pennsylvania resonate in the novel's nineteenth-century communities. Throughout his writing Goethe coins new concepts, like *Weltfest* [world festival] or galvanises his favourite ones, like *gelten lassen* [to accept], in order to create fresh ways to speak about Enlightenment ideas. Near the end of his life in 1829, he formulated this compelling dictum: "Toleranz sollte nur eine vorübergehende Gesinnung sein: sie muß zur Anerkennung führen. Dulden heißt beleidigen," and he added, "Die wahre Liberalität ist Anerkennung" [Tolerance should only be a passing conviction: it must lead to recognition. To tolerate is offensive. True liberality is recognition].[86] This book aspires to contribute to the intellectual history of how one of Germany's greatest thinkers and authors attempted to weave Enlightenment ideas into the cultural fabric of his nation.

Notes

[1] *Goethe und unsere Zeit* (Frankfurt am Main: Suhrkamp, 1999), 39.

[2] Ernst Cassirer, *Die Philosophie der Aufklärung* (Tübingen: Mohr, 1932); Peter Gay, *The Enlightenment: An Interpretation,* 2 vols. (New York: Norton, 1995–1996); Peter Pütz, *Die deutsche Aufklärung,* Erträge der Forschung 81

(Darmstadt: Wissenschaftliche Buchgesellschaft, 1978); Ulrich Im Hof, *Das Europa der Aufklärung*, 2nd ed. (Munich: Beck, 1995).

[3] Dorinda Outram, *The Enlightenment*, New Approaches to European History 7 (Cambridge: Cambridge UP, 1997), 8; Werner Schneiders, *Die wahre Aufklärung: Zur Aufklärung der deutschen Aufklärung* (Munich: Karl Alber, 1974), 195–200.

[4] See Thomas Munck, *The Enlightenment: A Comparative Social History 1721–1794* (London: Arnold, 2000); *Geography and Enlightenment*, ed. by David N. Livingstone and Charles W. J. Withers (London: U of Chicago P, 1999); Ursula Stephan-Kopitzsh, *Die Toleranzdiskussion im Spiegel überregionaler Aufklärungszeitschriften*, Europäische Hochschulschriften, Reihe 3, Geschichte und ihre Hilfswisssenschaften, 382 (Frankfurt am Main: Lang, 1989).

[5] Norman Hampson, *The Enlightenment: An Evaluation of its Assumptions, Attitudes and Values* (London: Penguin, 1990), 146.

[6] Outram, *Enlightenment*, 2 and 12. See also Thomas P. Saine, *Von der Kopernikanischen bis zur Französischen Revolution: Die Auseinandersetzung der deutschen Frühaufklärung mit der neuen Zeit* (Berlin: Schmidt, 1987).

[7] Im Hof, *Aufklärung*, 11–16. Im Hof explains briefly the history of the European designations: "Enlightenment," "Lumières," "Aufklärung," "Illuminismo," and "Illustración." Pütz analyses the semantic development of the word *Aufklärung* (*Die deutsche Aufklärung*, 10–25).

[8] Hans Kohn, *The Mind of Germany: The Education of a Nation* (New York: Harper & Row; 1965), 22 (see also 23–42).

[9] Terence James Reed, "Die Geburt der Klassik aus dem Geist der Mündigkeit," *Jahrbuch der deutschen Schiller-Gesellschaft* 32 (1988), 367–74. Gottfried Willems argues that Goethe's writing is rooted in the eighteenth-century Enlightenment in his "Goethe — ein 'Überwinder der Aufklärung'? Thesen zur Revision des Klassik-Bildes," *Germanisch-romanische Monatsschrift*, 40 (1990): 22–40, (31). For a different view: Dieter Borchmeyer, "Wie aufgeklärt ist die Weimarer Klassik? Eine Replik auf Beiträge von John A. McCarthy und Gottfried Willems," *Jahrbuch der deutschen Schiller-Gesellschaft* 36 (1992): 433–40, (437).

[10] Cf. Gerhard Sauder, "Aufklärung des Vorurteils — Vorurteile der Aufklärung," *Deutsche Vierteljahresschrift* 57 (1983) 259–77. Cf. Gerhard Sauder, "'Verhältnismässige Aufklärung': Zur bürgerlichen Ideologie am Ende des 18. Jahrhunderts," *Jahrbuch der Jean-Paul-Gesellschaft* 9 (1974): 103–26.

[11] For a discussion on "toleration" versus "tolerance," see: Preston King, *Toleration* (London: Allen & Unwin, 1976), 12–13. Cf. A penetrating analysis of

Toleranz in: Alois Wierlacher, "Was ist Toleranz? Zur Rehabilitation eines umstrittenen Begriffs," *Jahrbuch Deutsch als Fremdsprache* 20 (1994): 115–37.

[12] Cf. Gustav Mensching, *Toleranz und Wahrheit in der Religion* (Heidelberg: Quelle & Meyer, 1955). See also: Rudolf Schottlaender, "Der Gedanke der Toleranz und seine Geschichte," *Studium Generale* 6 (1949): 307–14.

[13] Panajotis Kondylis, *Die Aufklärung im Rahmen des neuzeitlichen Rationalismus* (Munich: Deutscher Taschenbuch Verlag, 1986), 117.

[14] Cf. Ricarda Huch, *Das Zeitalter der Glaubenspaltung* (Frankfurt am Main: Weisbecker, 1954; Zurich: Atlantis, 1937). See also Henry Arthur Francis Kamen, *The Rise of Toleration* (London: Weidenfeld and Nicholson, 1967).

[15] Cf. Helmut Kiesel, "Problem und Begründung der Toleranz im 18. Jahrhundert," in *Festgabe für Ernst Walter Zeeden,* ed. by Horst Rabe et al. (Münster: Aschendorf, 1976), 370–85.

[16] Moses Mendelssohn, *Jerusalem: Oder ueber die religiöse Macht und Judentum* (Berlin: Friedrich Maurer, 1783), 139–41.

[17] Eda Sagarra, *A Social History of Germany 1648–1914* (London: Methuen, 1977), 205.

[18] Klaus Schreiner gives a brief etymology of *Toleranz*. He relates the Latin *tolerantia* to the Old High German *fartraganii,* and the Latin *patientia* to the Old High German *kedult* and shows that Luther translates *tolerantia* as *toleranz. Geschichtliche Grundbegriffe: Historisches Lexikon zur politisch-sozialen Sprache in Deutschland,* ed. by Otto Brunner et al., 8 vols. (Stuttgart: Klett-Cotta, 1972–1997), vol. 6 (1990), 448.

[19] Johann Heinrich Zedler, *Grosses Vollstaendiges Universal Lexikon Aller Wissenschaften und Kuenste welche bisher durch menschlichen Verstand und Witz erfunden worden,* 64 vols [in 32] (Leipzig and Halle: Johann Heinrich Zedler, 1737–1750), vol. 43: entry "Toleranz" (1745), column 1115. Cf. Gerd Quedenbaum, *Der Verleger und Buchhändler Johann Heinrich Zedler 1706–1751: Ein Buchunternehmer in den zwängen seiner Zeit* (Hildesheim: Olms, 1977).

[20] See Michael Maurer, *Aufklärung und Anglophilie in Deutschland* (Göttingen: Vandenhoeck & Ruprecht, 1987), 67–70, on England as a land of sects. Cf. Ursula Ruth Quixano Henriques, *Religious Toleration in England, 1787–1833* (London: Routledge and Paul, 1961). Cf. Wilbur Kitchener Jordan, *The Development of Religious Toleration in England,* 4 vols. (London: Unwin, 1932). Cf. the section on *Anglomanie* in Goethe's *Farbenlehre* (Theory of Colours, 1810): FA 23/1, 874.

[21] Zedler, *Universal Lexikon,* columns 1115–116.

[22] Johann Christoph Adelung, *Versuch eines vollstaendigen grammatisch-kritischen Woerterbuches der Hochdeutschen Mundart mit bestaendiger Vergleichung der uebrigen Mundarten,* 5 vols. (Leipzig: Bernhard Christoph Breitkopf und Sohn, 1774–1786), vol. 1: entry "Duldung," (1774), column 1434. Cf. Margrit Strohbach, *Johann Christoph Adelung: Ein Beitrag zu seinem germanistischen Schaffen mit einer Bibliographie seines Gesamtwerkes* (Berlin: Walter de Gruyter, 1984).

[23] Adelung, *Versuch eines vollstaendigen grammatisch-kritischen Woerterbuches,* vol. 1, column 1433. For an etymology of *dulden* see *Etymologisches Wörterbuch des Deutschen,* ed. by Wolfgang Pfeifer (Berlin: Akademie-Verlag, 1989), 316.

[24] Zedler, *Universal Lexikon,* vol. 45, column 1116.

[25] *Realwörterbuch für Kameralisten und Oekonomen.* This definition and those following are taken from Gerhard Besier's collection in "Toleranz." *Geschichtliche Grundbegriffe: Historisches Lexikon zur politisch-sozialen Sprache in Deutschland.* Edited by Otto Brunner et al. 8 vols. Stuttgart: Klett-Cotta, 1972–1997. Vol. 6 (1990), (510–11).

[26] *Beantwortung der Frage: Was ist Aufklärung?,* in Immanuel Kant, *Werke,* ed. by Wilhelm Weischedel, 6 vols. (Frankfurt am Main: Insel, 1960–1964), vol. 6: *Schriften zur Anthropologie, Geschichtsphilosophie, Politik, und Pädagogik,* 53–61, (60).

[27] Terence James Reed, *The Classical Centre: Goethe and Weimar 1775–1832* (Oxford: Oxford UP, 1986), 93.

[28] Cf. Julius Ebbinghaus, "Über die Idee der Toleranz: Eine staatsrechtliche und religionsphilosophische Untersuchung," *Archiv für Philosophie* 4 (1950): 1–34.

[29] Cf. Alexander Altmann, *Die trostvolle Aufklärung: Studien zur Metaphysik und politischen Theorie Moses Mendelssohns* (Frommann-Holzboog, 1982), 244–75.

[30] Cf. Martin Brecht, "'Ob ein weltlich Oberkait Recht habe, in des Glaubens Sachen mit dem Schwert zu handeln': Ein unbekanntes Nürnberger Gutachten zur Frage der Toleranz aus dem Jahre 1530," *Archiv für Reformationsgeschichte* 60 (1969): 65–75. Cf. Robert A. Kann, *A History of the Habsburg Empire 1526–1918* (Berkeley: U of California P, 1980), 45–53.

[31] A modern definition of *Toleranz* in: *Philosophisches Wörterbuch,* ed. by Georg Klaus and Manfred Buhr, 2 vols. (Leipzig: VEB Bibliographisches Institut Leipzig, 1976), 2: 1226.

[32] Schreiner, *Geschichtliche Grundbegriffe,* 447.

[33] Ole Peter Grell, "Introduction," in *Tolerance and Intolerance in the European Reformation*, ed. by Ole Peter Grell and Bob Scribner (Cambridge: Cambridge UP, 1996), 7.

[34] *Monatschrift der Gesellschaft des vaterländischen Museums in Böhmen* (1830): FA 22, 846.

[35] I. Gampl, "Toleranz(-patent)," *Handwörterbuch zur deutschen Rechtsgeschichte*, edited by Adalbert Erler et al. 5 vols. (Berlin: Erich Schmidt, 1971–1998): Vol. 5 (1998), 270–73. For an overview of the religious laws of the Empire, see: Karl Schwarz, "Die Toleranz im Religionsrecht des Heiligen Römischen Reiches Deutscher Nation, in Brandenburg-Preussen und in Österreich," *Österreichisches Archiv für Kirchenrecht* 3 (1985): 258–81.

[36] *Church and State through the Centuries: A Collection of Illustrative Documents*, ed. and translated Sidney Z. Ehler and John B. Morrall (London: Burns and Oates, 1954), 193–98.

[37] Sagarra, *A Social History of Germany 1648–1914*, 108.

[38] *Dichtung und Wahrheit* (Poetry and Truth, 1811–1833; hereafter DuW) IV/16: FA 14, 728. Goethe was particularly interested in the article on Spinoza. Cf. Joseph S. J. Lecler, *Histoire de la tolérance au siècle de la Réforme*, 2 vols., Théologie 31(Paris: Aubier, 1955).

[39] Cassirer, *Die Philosophie der Aufklärung*, 222–23. Cf. Luisa Simonutti, "Between Political Loyalty and Religious Liberty: Political Theory and Toleration in Huguenot Thought in the Epoch of Bayle," *History of Political Thought* 17 (1996): 523–54.

[40] Erich Haase, "Das literarhistorische Interesse an den Toleranzkontroversen am Ende des Grand Siècle," *Germanisch-romanische Monatsschrift* 35 (1954): 138–49.

[41] Matthias Benad, *Toleranz als Gebot christlicher Obrigkait: Das Büdinger Patent von 1712*, Studia Irenica 27 (Hildesheim: Gerstenberg, 1983). Cf. Franz Reischer, *Die Toleranzgemeinden Kärntens nach einem Visitationsbericht vom Jahre 1786*, Series Archiv für vaterländische Geschichte und Topographie 60 (Klagenfurt: Verlag des Geschichtsvereines für Kärnten, 1965). Cf. Joachim Whaley, *Religious Toleration and Social Change in Hamburg, 1529–1819* (Cambridge: Cambridge UP, 1985).

[42] Benad, *Toleranz als Gebot christlicher Obrigkeit*, 46. Squabbling among the religious confessions broke out not long after the *Toleranzpatent* was issued.

[43] Peter Morgan, *The Critical Idyll. Traditional Values and the French Revolution in Goethe's Hermann und Dorothea*, Studies in German Literature, Linguistics, and Culture 54 (Columbia, SC: Camden House, 1990), 100 (see

entire chapter). Cf. *Handwörterbuch zur deutschen Rechtsgeschichte,* 1290. The expulsions had already started to a lesser degree in 1684 and 1686.

[44] Cf. Mack Walker, *The Salzburg Transaction: Expulsion and Redemption in Eighteenth-Century Germany* (Ithaca: Cornell: UP, 1992).

[45] As quoted in Hans Joachim Schoeps, "Über Toleranz," *Tradition und Leben* 14 (1962): 13–15, (14). Cf. Hermann Hoffmann, *Friedrich II. von Preussen und die Aufhebung der Gesellschaft Jesu,* Bibliotheca Instituti Histoirici, S. I., 30 (Rome: Institutum Historicum, S. I., 1969).

[46] Thomas P. Saine, *Black Bread — White Bread: German Intellectuals and the French Revolution,* Studies in German Literature, Linguistics, and Culture 36 (Columbia, SC: Camden House, 1988), 15–16.

[47] DuW I/2: FA 14, 84–88.

[48] Cf. Ritchie Robertson, "Joseph Rohrer and the Bureaucratic Enlightenment," *Austrian Studies* 2 (1990): 23–42.

[49] DuW III/13: FA 14, 615–16.

[50] Cf. Josef Karniel, *Die Toleranzpolitik Kaiser Joseph II.,* translated from the Hebrew by Leo Koppel, Schriftenreihe des Instituts für Deutsche Geschichte, Universität Tel Aviv 9 (Gerlingen: Bleicher, 1986).

[51] Karniel, *Die Toleranzpolitik Kaiser Joseph II.,* 554 (an excerpt from: *Das Toleranzpatent für die christliche Minderheiten: das vollständige Rundschreiben für Oberösterreich, Linz,* 1781). Cf. Charles H. O'Brien, "The Ideas of Religious Toleration at the Time of Joseph II: A Study of the Enlightenment among Catholics in Austria," *Transactions of the American Philosophical Society* 59 (1969): 1–77.

[52] FA 8, 572.

[53] *Church and State in the Modern Age: A Documentary History,* ed. by J. F. Maclear (New York: Oxford UP, 1995), 33.

[54] Saine argues this point strongly, but with balance, in *Black Bread — White Bread,* 12–14.

[55] *Handwörterbuch zur deutschen Rechtsgeschichte,* see entry: "Wöllnersches Religionsedikt," 1517.

[56] Maclear, *Church and State,* 105.

[57] Maclear, *Church and State,* 109.

[58] Maclear, *Church and State,* 111. Cf. Letters to Bettine Brentano 24 February 1808 (WA IV/20, 21–22) and 3 April 1808 (WA IV/20, 42). See also: Peter R. Ersparnen, *The Elusiveness of Tolerance: The "Jewish Question" from Lessing to the Napoleonic Wars,* University of North Carolina Studies in the

Germanic Languages and Literatures 117 (Chapel Hill: U of North Carolina P, 1997).

[59] Maclear, *Church and State*, 185. Cf. *Toleranz am Mittelrhein: Referate der 35. Jahrestagung der Gesellschaft für mittelrheinische Kirchengeschichte vom 12. und 13. April 1983 in Worms*, ed. by Isnard Wilhelm Frank, Quellen und Abhandlungen zur mittelrheinischen Kirchengeschichte 50 (Mainz: Selbstverlag der Gesellschaft für mittelrheinische Kirchengeschichte, 1984).

[60] Bentley, *Remarks upon a late Discourse of freethinking: in a letter to —* (1743; German, 1745). Brown: *Thoughts on civil liberty, on licentiousness, and faction* (1765; German, 1771).

[61] Benjamin Franklin, *Autobiography* (published after Franklin's death in 1790; incomplete German translation *Jugendjahre*, 1792; *Kleine Schriften*, 1794). Goethe read in Franklin's *Autobiography* several times through the years 1794–1829. Thomas Jefferson, *Notes on the State of Virginia* (1784; German 1789). Goethe read excerpts from Jefferson's *Notes* in Duke Bernhard's *Reisebericht* and he also read Jefferson's *Memoir, Correspondence and private papers* (London 1829). Victor Lange, "Goethes Amerikabild: Wirklichkeit und Vision," in *Amerika in der deutschen Literatur: Neue Welt – Nordamerika – USA*, ed. by Sigrid Bauschinger et al. (Stuttgart: Reclam, 1975), 63–74, (65).

[62] Voltaire: *Traité sur la tolerance* (1763; German 1764). Cf. Goethe's entry on *Voltaire* in the *Farbenlehre*: FA 23/1: 869–72. He translated Voltaire's drama *Mahomet* in 1799; first staged in Weimar in 1800. Pierre Bayle: *Pensées diverses écrites à un docteur de Sorbonne à l'occasion de la comète qui parut au mois de décembre* (1680; German 1741). Cf. H. B. Nisbet, "Lessing and Pierre Bayle," in *Tradition and Creation: Essays in Honour of Elizabeth Mary Wilkinson*, ed. by C. P. Magill et al. (Leeds: Maney & Sons, 1978), 13–29.

[63] Johann Bernhard Basedow: *Betrachtung über die wahre Rechtgläubigkeit und die im Staate und in der Kirche nothwendige Toleranz* (1766); Gotthold Ephraim Lessing: *Gedanken über die Herrnhuter* (1750) and *Nathan der Weise* (1779); Christian Wilhelm von Dohm: *Über die bürgerliche Verbesserung der Juden* (1781); Moses Mendelssohn: *Jerusalem: Oder ueber die religiöse Macht und Judentum* (1783). Cf. Ursula Bohn, "Moses Mendelssohn und die Toleranz," in *Toleranz heute: 250 Jahre nach Mendelssohn und Lessing*, ed. by Peter von der Osten-Sacken (Berlin: Institut Kirche und Judentum, 1979), 26–36.

[64] Goethe knew especially Möser's *Osnabrückische Geschichte* (1768) and *Patriotische Phantasien* (1774). Goethe wrote an article about Möser in *Ueber Kunst und Alterthum*: IV/2, 1823. Cf. DuW III/13: FA 14, 647–48. Cf.: Winfried Woesler, "Möser und Goethe," *Goethe Jahrbuch* 114 (1997): 23–36.

[65] Letter to Reich, 20 February 1770: WA IV/1, 230. Wieland's piece was first published in the *Teutscher Merkur* (German Mercury). Cf. Goethe's *Rede zu Wielands Andenken* (Speech in Memory of Wieland, 1813): FA 17, 426–48.

[66] This claim remains one-sided. Cf. R. Krauss, "Schubart und Goethe," *Goethe-Jahrbuch* 23 (1902): 118–29.

[67] Géza von Molnár, *Goethes Kantstudien*, Schriften der Goethe-Gesellschaft 64 (Weimar: Böhlau, 1994), 851–59. He reproduces the marked pages of Goethe's copy of *Kritik der reinen Vernunft*.

[68] 18 October 1817 (as quoted by Harald Fricke in FA 13, 817). Cf. *Wanderjahre*, II/"Betrachtungen": FA 10, 561. Cf. Goethe's thoughts: "Kurze Vorstellung der kantischen Philosophie von D. F. V. R." [Brief Introduction of the Kantian Philosophy of D. F. V. R.]: FA 20, 605.

[69] *Was ist Aufklärung?*, 60.

[70] John A. McCarthy, "Politics and Morality in Eighteenth-Century Germany," *Deutsche Vierteljahresschrift* 68 (1994): 77–98, (85). Cf. *"Was ist Aufklärung?": Thesen und Definitionen*, ed. by Ehrhard Bahr (Stuttgart: Reclam, 1989). See also: *"What is Enlightenment?": Eighteenth-Century Answers and Twentieth-Century Questions*, ed. by James Schmidt, Philosophical Traditions 7 (Berkeley: U of California P, 1996).

[71] Isaiah Berlin, *The Crooked Timber of Humanity: Chapters in the History of Ideas* (London: Fontana, 1991), 245.

[72] *Idées sur la Philosophie de l'Histoire de l'Humanité* in *Ueber Kunst und Alterthum* VI/2: FA 22, 489. Cf. Hans Dietrich Irmscher, "Goethe und Herder im Wechselspiel von Attraktion und Repulsion," *Goethe Jahrbuch* 106 (1989): 22–52. Hugh Barr Nisbet, "Goethes und Herders Geschichtsdenken, *Goethe Jahrbuch* 110 (1993):115–33.

[73] Goethe's 1830 foreword to the German edition of Carlyle's *Life of Schiller*: FA 22, 871. Cf. Bernd Fischer, *Das Eigene und das Eigentliche: Klopstock, Herder, Fichte, Kleist. Episoden aus der Konstruktionsgeschichte nationaler Intentionalitäten*, Philologische Studien und Quellen 135 (Berlin: Schmidt, 1995).

[74] Berlin, *The Crooked Timber of Humanity*, 244–45.

[75] Leo Damrosch, "Generality and Particularity," in *The Cambridge History of Literary Criticism*, ed. by Hugh Barr Nisbet and Claude Rawson, 8 vols. (Cambridge: Cambridge UP, 1989–), vol. 4: *The Eighteenth Century*, ed. by Hugh Barr Nisbet and Claude Rawson (1997), 381–93, (381). And: Willems, "Goethe — ein 'Überwinder der Aufklärung'?," 32.

[76] Benjamin Franklin, *Autobiography and Other Writings*, ed. by Ormond Seavey (Oxford: Oxford UP, 1993), 120. Cf. Blanka Horacek, "Goethe und das Christentum," *Jahrbuch des Wiener Goethe-Vereins* 77 (1973): 88–104. Gerhard Möbus, *Die Christus-Frage in Goethes Leben und Werk* (Osnabrück: Fromm, 1964).

[77] DuW III/12: FA 14, 597.

[78] *Nachlass — Venezianische Epigramme:* FA 1, 467. Goethe may be making an allusion to the famous parable of the ring in *Nathan the Wise* and the judge's accusation that none of the three religions have proven themselves, through their actions, to be true (III, 7, lines 501–510). *Gotthold Ephraim Lessing Werke und Briefe*, 12 vols. (Frankfurt am Main: Deutscher Klassiker Verlag, 1985–), vol. 9, ed. by Klaus Bohnen and Arno Schilson (1993), 559.

[79] Cf. *Lessing und die Toleranz: Beiträge der vierten internationalen Konferenz der Lessing Society in Hamburg vom 27. bis 29. Juni 1985*, Sonderband zum Lessing Yearbook, ed. by Peter Freimark, Franklin Kopitzsch and Helga Slessarev (Munich: edition text + kritik; Detroit: Wayne State UP, 1986); Walter Jens, "'Nathans Gesinnung ist von jeher die meinige gewesen,'" in Walter Jens and Hans Küng, *Dichtung und Religion* (Munich: Kindler, 1985), 102–18; Franklin Kopitzsch, "Lessing und seine Zeitgenossen im Spannungsfeld von Toleranz und Intoleranz," *Jahrbuch des Instituts für Deutsche Geschichte* 3 (1980): 29–85; Harald Schultze, *Lessings Toleranzbegriff: Eine theologische Studie* (Göttingen: Vandenhoeck & Ruprecht, 1969).

[80] There are initial studies completed on both Herder and Wieland. Cf. Wulf Köpke, "Johann Gottfried Herder: Der Ruf nach Vernunft und Billigkeit," *Jahrbuch Deutsch als Fremdsprache* 20 (1994): 237–55; Alfred E. Ratz, "C. M. Wieland: Toleranz, Kompromiß und Inkonsequenz. Eine kritische Betrachtung," *Deutsche Vierteljahresschrift* 42 (1968): 493–514; Gottfried Willems, "Von der ewigen Wahrheit zum ewigen Frieden: 'Aufklärung' in der Literatur des 18. Jahrhunderts, insbesondere in Lessings 'Nathan' und Wielands 'Musarion,'" *Wieland-Studien* 3 (1996): 10–46.

[81] WA I/53, 379. Cf. J. A. Leisewitz's 14 August 1780 journal note that Goethe spoke with greatest respect about Lessing and *Nathan der Weise* (*Goethes Gespräche*, 1, 301). Cf. *Gespräche mit Goethe in den letzten Jahren seines Lebens 1823–1832 von Johann Peter Eckermann* [Conversations with Goethe in the last years of his life 1823–1832 by Johann Peter Eckermann], 7 February 1827: FA 39, 235.

[82] FA 19, 682.

[83] Cf. Carl Riemann, "Goethes Gedanken über Toleranz," *Jahrbuch der Goethe-Gesellschaft* 21 (1959): 230–54.

[84] The Dutch Revolt was itself, of course, a key moment in the history of tolerance. Cf. Hans R. Guggisberg, "Wandel der Argumente für religiöse Toleranz und Glaubensfreiheit im 16. und 17. Jahrhundert," in *Zur Geschichte der Toleranz und Religionsfreiheit,* ed. by Heinrich Lutz, Wege der Forschung 246 (Darmstadt: Wissenschaftliche Buchhandlung, 1977), 455–81.

[85] Penn's 25 August 1681 letter to James Harrison William in *The Papers of William Penn, 1680–1684,* ed. by Richard S. Dunn and Mary Maples Dunn, 5 vols. (Philadelphia: U of Pennsylvania P, 1981–1987), vol. 2: *1680–1684* (1982), 108.

[86] *Sprüche* (Aphorisms): FA 13, 249. Schlüter sees in this dictum the teleology of tolerance from 1685–1787. Gisela Schlüter, *Die französische Toleranzdebatte im Zeitalter der Aufklärung: Materiale und formale Aspekte,* Untersuchungen zu den romanischen Literaturen der Neuzeit 15 (Tübingen: Niemeyer, 1992), 23.

1: The Emergence of Enlightenment Concerns

GOETHE, RAISED A PROTESTANT, was aware that his native Frankfurt was home to Separatists, Pietists, Herrnhuters, and other religious groups that distanced themselves from the recognised churches.[1] In 1677 William Penn sought recruits in the imperial city to join his Quakers in America, and in the 1730s Count Zinzendorf founded a branch of the Herrnhuters in Frankfurt. By the late eighteenth century Frankfurt had a reputation for being home to all manner of sects.[2] Goethe's mother had Pietistic tendencies whereas his father assembled a large library (over 2,000 volumes) of legal, humanistic, and Enlightenment works.[3] Goethe also had firsthand knowledge of Jews in his home city.[4]

In the *Labores juveniles* (1757), Goethe's school notebooks filled with lessons in German, Latin, and Greek, are an assortment of exercises on history and religion.[5] From 1762–1765 he considered writing poetic works about biblical themes, including "Joseph," and in fact began "Belsazar." In 1765, prior to his departure for university studies, he jotted the poem "Das ist mein Leib" (This is My Body) in one of his mother's books:

> Das ist mein Leib, nehmt hin und esset.
> Das ist mein Blut, nehmt hin und trinckt.
> Auf daß ihr, meiner nicht vergesset,
> Auf daß nicht euer Glaube sinckt.
> Bey diesem Wein, bey diesem Brod,
> Erinnert euch an meinen Tod.[6]

[This is my body, take and eat; this is my blood, take and drink: that you forget me not, that your faith may not sink. With this wine, with this bread, remind yourselves of my death.]

The final stanza in "Poetische Gedanken über die Höllenfahrt Jesu Christi" (Poetic Thoughts on the Descent of Christ into Hell, 1766), illustrates how effectively Goethe could imitate the voice of the Church Triumphant:

Der Gott-Mensch schließt der Höllen Pforten,
Er schwingt Sich aus den dunklen Orten,
  In Seine Herrlichkeit zurück.
Er sitzet an des Vaters Seiten,
Er will noch immer für Uns streiten.
  Er wills! O, Freunde! Welches Glück?
Der Engel feierliche Chöre,
  Die jauchzen vor dem großen Gott,
Daß es die gantze Schöpfung höre:
  Gros ist der Herr Gott Zebaoth![7]

[The God-Man shuts Hell's gates; He soars out of darkened places, back into His glory. He sits on His Father's side; He will ever for us fight. He will! O, friends! What bliss? The choir of the heavenly hosts, they rejoice before the great God, so that all creation hears: *Great is the Lord God of Sabaoth!*]

His university years at Leipzig from 1765 to 1768 exposed Goethe to rationalist thought and European theatre, but a serious illness and emotional crisis forced his return to Frankfurt. Recuperating, he gravitated towards Pietism through the devoted ministrations of a family friend, Susanne Catharina von Klettenberg (1723–1744), and attended meetings of the *Brüdergemeinde* (Moravian Brethren) until he resumed university studies at Strassburg in 1770. He was deeply influenced by Gottfried Arnold's *Unparteyische Kirchen- und Ketzer-Historie* (Impartial History of Churches and Heretics, 1699) an "uncompromisingly individualist history of heretics of every denomination, united only by their opposition to the ecclesiastical establishment."[8] Arnold, a Pietist, wrote to help overcome "dispüten und kriege unter bruedern" [disputes and wars among brethren].[9] He tactfully acknowledged Friedrich III for "ungekraenckter Gewissens-Freyheit" [unhindered freedom of conscience], and implied that its lack was the cause of the "blutigsten Kriege, inquisitiones und verfolgungen" [bloodiest wars, inquisitions, and persecutions]. Furthermore, he recommended "billichkeit" [fairness], a concept that arises again in *Iphigenie*.[10]

The early 1770s were a literary watershed for Goethe, and a period of renewed religious reflection. He studied the Qur'an (and translated Suras from the Latin), the Bible (he translated the Song of Solomon from the Latin), the writings of Emanuel Swedenborg (1688–1772), and of course became acquainted with the pastors Herder and Lavater. During these years the contours of his Enlightenment interests begin to manifest themselves. His intellectual journal, *Ephemerides* (1770–1771)

— itself a typical Enlightenment genre — contains notations on and quotations from his learning stretching into his Strassburg days. While alchemical notes tend to dominate, one critic perceives a Humanist-Enlightenment ethos in the notebook.[11] Sauder sees in *Ephemerides* themes that would emerge in the *Urfaust* and in the earliest version of *Götz von Berlichingen* or, as it was called in 1771, *Geschichte Gottfriedens von Berlichingen mit der eisernen Hand*.[12] One of the lengthiest excursions is a note on Moses Mendelssohn's *Phädon* (Phaedon). Goethe is interested in the suicide of Socrates, particularly its description as an act of a wise man.[13] The snippet could be construed as an attempt to redefine suicide as an ethically positive act.

The subject of suicide was so sensitive that even David Hume (1711–1776), an Enlightener not known for his timidity, decided against publishing an essay he had written on it.[14] A text in the *Labores juveniles* castigates the 1757 suicide of Johann Georg Junker, proving that Goethe had read about suicide since his early youth.[15] It is well known that Goethe was shocked by the 1772 suicide of Karl Wilhelm Jerusalem in Wetzlar and that he familiarised himself with the case as he conceived *Die Leiden des jungen Werthers*.[16]

The closing words of this famous epistolary novel contain an image of the social rejection of a suicide in the eighteenth century: "Kein Geistlicher hat ihn begleitet" [No clergyman accompanied him].[17] As Werther plans his suicide and writes his final words to Lotte, he worries for he knows he will not have a Christian burial. His words have a sad and sarcastic tone as he supposes that "righteous" individuals would not want to be buried near him.[18]

That Werther eventually commits suicide does not surprise, as it is unremittingly foreshadowed throughout the novel.[19] What strikes the modern reader — and it was this that caused the theological faculty at Leipzig to denounce the book, thus hindering its publication there — is the presentation of a potentially sympathetic view of a person who commits suicide. In this narrow sense, J. August Ernesti's letter to the book commission on behalf of the Leipzig theological faculty assesses *Werther* with some acuity, for it warns that the book is not only an apology for suicide, but also that it is well written, even gripping.[20] Certainly *Werther* is not a recommendation to commit suicide. In *Dichtung und Wahrheit* Goethe describes in morbid detail how he at one low point in his life struggled with thoughts about it.[21] Yet interpreting *Werther* as an apology for one who commits suicide may not be an unfair assessment. Indeed, Goethe's wrestling with such thoughts, combined with the impressions left by Jerusalem's suicide, converged so powerfully in him that he claims to have written the novel in a mere four weeks.[22]

The greater part of the novel is written in the first person, a rhetorical strategy that allows the reader to view Werther through his own eyes. This perspectival shift to interiority within a seamlessly factual exterior frame (the work is presented as if an editor has pieced together Werther's letters) and the penetration of a secularised Pietist discourse into a novel broke new ground in German literature. Goethe had created a work that compelled the reader to at least attempt to understand so irreversible and serious an act as suicide.

Similarly, the letter of the Leipzig commissioner of books, Carl Andreas Bel, to the city council expressed his concern that the novel's imaginative and fine language, its ability to captivate readers, may be dangerous for young people (Ernesti expressed particular concern for female readers). Especially, he continues, because the author writes too indeterminately about suicide.[23] Bel's anxiety centres on the maturity of a reader. The issue of maturity is important in *Werther*. In the 1775 publication of the work, Goethe prefaced part 2 of the novel with a motto poem directed at young male readers that concluded: "*Sei ein Mann, und folge mir nicht nach*" [Be a man, and do not follow me].[24]

In the letter of 13 May Werther proclaims his self-reliance to Wilhelm and declares that he refuses to be led any longer.[25] Nevertheless, his shoulder-squaring resolution does not remain unambiguous, as a letter of 22 May suggests that adults are like children, impulsive and ruled by inconsequential desires.[26] The novel plays upon a paradox of Christian teachings, namely, that one ought to become as a little child.[27]

This raises the question of what it means to be an adult. Werther concludes that an adult recognises that within his reach is the freedom to exit the prison of existence when he wishes.[28] This attitude implies that ending one's life is a right, that the ability to do so may meet a human need that may arise at any time, and that such an act may even be heroic.[29] Martin Swales reminds us that when Werther does take his own life, Lessing's *Emilia Galotti* (1772) is on the table — "a play that pits against the scandal of princely absolutism the moral seriousness and dignity of bourgeois life."[30] In Werther's case his action is set against the religious and societal norms of the time.

The fictive editor splices Werther's final letters and notes, as well as the testimonies of Lotte, Albert, and others in order to recreate his final days. The editor's depiction of events is important, for it emerges that Werther had decided carefully to take his own life.[31] Reinforcing the point, he stresses that Werther's suicide was not an unavoidable event, but "a considered resolution, a conscious act of will."[32] A sober maturity is expressly claimed in the 21 December letter in which Werther tells Lotte that he has no exaggerated romantic notions about his desire to die.[33]

However, the editor also presents a different account of Werther's suicide, one in which he is less in control of himself. Werther is no longer the convinced rationalist choosing calmly to die by his own hand. He is at times portrayed as a victim of circumstance, one who is driven to the deed.[34] In the same letter of 21 December he presents himself as an offering to Lotte, and attempts to lend his self-sacrifice the aura of necessity by adding that he had thought often about murdering her husband Albert.[35] The implication is that by taking his own life he would be preventing murder.

Yet another cause for Werther's suicide is given: "Krankheit" [illness]. This theme recurs throughout the novel. In the 28 August letter Werther implies that his is not a physical, but an emotional or psychological sickness.[36] Some critics refer to his illness as a "complex pathological condition."[37] Werther believes he is melancholic, and refers to himself, in an overlap of motifs, as a sick child.[38] In recounting to Albert the story of a young woman who committed suicide, Werther speculates that an emotional illness may have been the underlying cause. He asserts that in some cases death is a necessity that has nothing to do with choice or morals.[39] He likens this circumstance to a fever that either passes or does not, thus making it impossible for one to predict recovery.[40] The illness must run its course, and if it ends in suicide, it is no less natural than if it had ended in healing — and just as little a matter of moral responsibility.

Regardless of what explanatory theme one traces, and the brief sketches provided here by no means exhaust them, the novel presents several reasons for Werther's suicide. During the same 12 August conversation with Werther, Albert confesses that he is bewildered by suicide. Werther's response, read as a defence of his future actions, proffers a new morality that considers the psychological state of a person who commits any act.[41]

Establishing a causal criterion for human actions, according to Werther, ought to moderate moral judgement. And this moderation is a form of social tolerance. Albert functions as the substantive spokesman for the conventional morals of his time and still wishes to call certain actions immoral in and of themselves. Werther agrees in general, but cites exceptions that in his opinion ought to compel compassion rather than harsh societal punishments. His reservations, which read like an Enlightenment agenda, include theft due to hunger; crimes of passion; and immoral conduct, specifically sexual relations outside of marriage. He castigates those who would condemn a suicide without seeking to understand its causes. Nevertheless, he knows that Albert has not understood him, and his final comment suggests the difficulty of interpersonal communication in general and, in the context of the discussion, the challenge of putting oneself in the place of another who holds views that arouse aversion.[42] It is this desire to communicate and to understand that forms the hermeneutic circle in the narrative, for communication is achieved as the reader "can identify with him [Werther], understand himself through him, and in so doing, acquire a new sense of dignity and self-worth."[43] This self-identification broadens the reader's sympathies.

While the evaluation of a suicide, rather than its outright condemnation, is in line with Enlightenment thought, Swales highlights a key point of convergence between Enlightenment and "Empfindsamkeit" [Sentimentality], despite their differences, for "both assert the individual's freedom from established doctrine or received wisdom; both assert that any proposition or tenet or value is true in so far as the individual heart or mind recognizes it as true — no external authority can or should usurp the validating role of individual experience."[44]

Infanticide, like suicide, caught Goethe's interest: "the sensational tale of Catharina Maria Flindt . . . reached the Leipzig press during his student days: sentenced to death for the murder of her illegitimate child, she had been rescued from prison by her lover, but overwhelmed by her conscience had freely returned to execution."[45] And the execution of Susanna Margarete Brandt for infanticide in Frankfurt on 14 January 1772 was something that Goethe would have known more than most about.[46] Infanticide and its punishment were frequently discussed topics in the eighteenth century. In 1746 Friedrich II reformed the penal code, ending all ecclesiastical punishments for *delicta carnis* [crimes of the flesh] and writing a treatise on the subject. Since the publication of Rousseau's *Émile* (1762), infanticide had become a general literary topic, and in 1764 a noted legal reformer and Enlightener, Cesare Beccaria, published a treatise, *Dei delitti e delle pene* (On Crimes and Punishment, 1764) against, among other things, capital punishment for infanticide. Heinrich Leopold Wagner's *Kindermörderin* (Child Murderess, 1776) and Johann Heinrich Pestalozzi's *Über Gesetzgebung und Kindsmord* (On Lawgiving and Child Murder, 1780) were catalysts to discussion amongst the German-reading public. In

1780 a Mannheim essay contest was initiated on the best ways to decrease child murder without encouraging sexual offences.[47]

Infanticide is an issue that arises in an early version of *Faust*, probably written about 1774.[48] Gretchen, a young woman, conceives a child by Faust out of wedlock. After killing her brother in a street fight, Faust flees, and she, who has unwittingly caused the death of her mother, eventually drowns their child. Gretchen is imprisoned and awaits her execution. Faust attempts to free Gretchen, who is half-mad with guilt, from jail; rather than escape with Faust and Mephistopheles, she chooses to await her execution and face the judgement of God.

Goethe's academic interest in infanticide is exemplified in Thesis 55 of his *Positiones Juris* (1771), one of fifty-six disputation points deriving from material culled in part from his Strassburg dissertation. It reads: "An fœmina partum recenter editum trucidans capite plectenda sit? quæstio est inter Doctores controversa" [Whether a woman who murders her newborn child is subject to capital punishment is a disputed question among doctors].[49] In October 1783 Goethe was asked to give his thoughts on the punishment of infanticide in a Weimar case, and he wrote an essay on the subject. The essay is lost, but its thesis is suggested in a comment Goethe made regarding it in November 1783, in which he suggests retaining capital punishment.[50]

Ephemerides, Werther, and *Urfaust* illustrate Enlightenment concerns in Goethe's thought and writing in the 1770s. Goethe, like other Enlighteners, attempted to overcome the strife caused by religious matters. His lost Strassburg dissertation sprang from his deep and life-long interest in church history. In it Goethe examines the strained relationship between the church and state, calling it an eternal quarrel.[51] This constellation of conflict would manifest itself again most clearly in *Egmont* (1787). And almost a decade after his dissertation, in a political rather than an academic setting, his Enlightenment views would show through as he delineated the domains of civil and ecclesiastical power in his essay, *Über die Abschaffung der Kirchenbuße* (On the Abolition of Church Penance, 1780). Gordon Craig writes that during the "controversy over the question of the church's right to maintain obligatory public penance for sins of the flesh, perjury, blasphemy, and immoral conduct . . . [Goethe] believed it should be reduced to a private encouragement to repentance and improvement."[52]

Nicholas Boyle detects another Enlightenment strain in connection with Goethe's reading of Arnold's "powerful solvent of all ecclesiologies," the *Unparteyische Kirchen- und Ketzer-Historie*: "It is but a step from the impartial history of heresies to Voltaire's dismissal, quoted at length [in the *Ephemerides*], of religious dogmas as 'd'absurdes chimères,' among which other notes suggest Goethe would have included theories about an original sin, and the fate of unbaptized infants."[53] Yet, the Voltaire excerpt could also be considered a constructive piece of religious thinking, and not merely religious scoffing. Voltaire seeks an end to religious strife by employing a typical Enlightenment rationale — to remind the disputants that they are by their own theology children of God and therefore brothers.[54] Goethe's exposure to Arnold's work helped him to understand that so-called heretics were human beings who sought after truth in their own way, much as Goethe himself did.[55]

The need for fraternity would be woven into an important work that situates Goethe as a direct intellectual descendant of the Enlightenment, namely, *Brief des Pastors zu *** an den neuen Pastor zu ***. Aus dem Französischen.* Published in 1773, it was reprinted later that year and again in 1775.[56] Goethe dons the mask of a Protestant pastor in order to express the importance of *Toleranz,* which he called the chief concern of the piece and a much discussed issue — at least, he recorded wryly, among the better intellects.[57]

In this fictitious epistle an established pastor mentors a newly installed one from a neighbouring area. He addresses his junior co-religionist throughout the letter as "Amtsbruder" [brother in office], "Bruder" [brother], and *confrater.* This rhetorical strategy not only underscores the fraternity of the two pastors, but the brotherhood of man, a theme that arises more than once in the letter. Indeed, the first doctrinal point the pastor discusses is that the damnation of the heathen is not congruent with the ways of the God of Love. He points out the irony of a Christian congregation that takes pleasure in hoping that the heathen will be tortured eternally.[58] The pastor counsels his young colleague that tolerance is compatible with a commitment to truth and does not lead to indifference. Rather his faith in the eternal love of God leads him to envision more than one path to heaven.[59] Indifference is the common derogatory term for the tolerant, used by those who disapprove of tolerance.[60]

The pastor holds that his office does not extend beyond the grave, and that a clergyman has so many temporal matters to attend to that he is happy to leave the eternal matters to God, especially obscure doctrines that he believes nobody understands anyway.[61] There is an extra philosophical force behind this thought: it suggests that there are things about which knowledge is not possible — a point that would be central to Kant's argument against metaphysics in his *Kritik der reinen Vernunft*.

The pastor addresses a conflict that confronted one of his colleagues in another parish, namely, the question of one's view of and attitude toward philosophers. Goethe would well know the at times strained relationship between pastors and philosophers, so the letter is particularly intriguing at this point. The pastor cites the lack of tolerance on the part of certain philosophers who talk of tolerance constantly and yet are themselves prejudiced.[62] This remark, aimed at the narrow-minded, suggests that reason and tolerance are principles that cut both ways, and that prejudice may be found in many places, and not only among those preaching the gospel but also among those professing philosophy. In his *Teutsche Chronik* [German Chronicle] review of *Brief des Pastors* Schubart argues that it is aimed at intolerant clergy and theologians.[63] As Koopmann puts it, tolerance is an allowance of subjectivity and the right to follow one's own "Erlebnisse und Empfindungen" [experiences and sensory perceptions], which is for Goethe essentially the freedom of belief.[64]

Goethe's pastor cites the fact that Jesus did not force others to believe, and reminds his colleague that the Lord wanted to knock on doors, not smash them in.[65] And he outlines his hope for universal brotherhood: "Welche Wonne ist es zu denken, daß der Türke der mich für einen Hund, und der Jude der mich für ein Schwein hält, sich einst freuen werden meine Brüder zu sein" [What joy it is to think that the Turk who holds me for a dog and the Jew for a swine, will one day rejoice to be my brethren].[66] Throughout the letter the pastor never loses sight of this Lessing-like vision: the peaceful co-existence of all religions. Looking again to the less than ideal realities, he points to the difficulties of achieving even a brotherhood of Christians, whom he accuses of being intolerant of each other, let alone of others who are not Christian. Not that he wishes to impose a union of confessions.[67] The diversity of Christian denominations, the pastor reasons, is not something to be artificially erased, yet shared central features can be highlighted, a typical Enlightenment postulate. Both denominational and cultural differences warrant tolerance, and neither is seen as changing the essence of being a "Mensch" [human].[68]

Goethe's pastor anticipates Friedrich Schleiermacher, another Protestant pastor, by claiming that the veracity of religious experience is based on feelings. He presses this claim in order to buttress his commitment to tolerance, pointing out how foolish and tyrannical it is to force opinions on others and demand that people feel what they cannot.[69] Arguing along Lutheran theological lines, he posits that since faith is a gift of God and man can avail nothing of himself, how can one then condemn another for lacking it?[70] Goethe's humorous "Katechisation" [Catechism], published in the same year as *Brief des Pastors*, impugns the practice of positing religious truths inductively:

LEHRER: Bedenk o Kind woher sind diese Gaben
          Du kannst nichts von dir selber haben.

KIND: Ei alles hab ich vom Papa!

LEHRER: Und der, woher hats der?

KIND: Vom Großpapa!

LEHRER: Nicht doch! Woher hats denn der Großpapa bekommen.

KIND: Der hats genommen.[71]

[Teacher: Consider o child where these gifts are from. You can have nothing of yourself. / Child: Oh all I have is from Papa! / Teacher: And from where did he receive them? / Child: From Granpa! / Teacher: No, no! From where did your Granpa get them. / Child: He took them.]

The pastor concludes his letter by exhorting his colleague to accept the truth wherever he may find it, and to rejoice should he find it in an unexpected place. He paraphrases James 1:5 in order to remind his *confrater* that all may ask God for wisdom, including enthusiasts, and warns him not to discount the workings of the Spirit.[72] Finally, he appeals to his colleague to preach love from the pulpit.

When it came to pastors, Goethe had a powerful literary model close to hand, namely, Oliver Goldsmith's *The Vicar of Wakefield* (1766). In 1771 Goethe's friend Johann Gottfried Herder introduced him to the novel, and he was immediately impressed. In 1773, the year *Brief des Pastors* was published, Goethe translated Goldsmith's haunting poem "The Deserted Village." And in *Werther* the reader learns that Werther and Lotte have both read *The Vicar of Wakefield*. Years later, in his autobiography, Goethe describes the Vicar in words that also identify the registers of spirituality he feels are necessary to lead a religious community, and the final quality he lists is a "lächelnde Duldung" [smiling tolerance].[73] Goethe would read the *Vicar of Wakefield* again in the closing years of his life, and in an 1829 Christmas day letter to Zelter, he ponders on the impact that the work had had on him and his attitudes in the 1770s, and concludes that he was impressed by the Vicar's "Billigkeit" [fairness].[74]

In a letter to Goethe dated 23 December 1773 Johann Caspar Lavater, the famous propagator of physiognomic studies, and a dedicated Swiss pastor, exclaims how taken he is by *Brief des Pastors*. For over a decade thereafter, Lavater attempted to convert Goethe to his version of Christianity. On one occasion Goethe rebuked Lavater, who had overstepped the mark, and wrote with polemical curtness that he was a "*dezidirter Nichtkrist*" [decided non-Christian]. Goethe also wrote that he was neither a "Widerkrist" [anti-Christian] nor an "Unkrist" [un-Christian].[75]

Goethe soon sent a more or less conciliatory letter to Lavater, but he did not budge from his position that God had been merciful to other men, not only the writers of the Gospel, and that these had produced thousands of written pages that were for humankind equally glorious and indispensable.[76] What irked him most was not the earnestness with which Lavater held his religious beliefs, but rather his "Intoleranz." Goethe's stance is illustrated charmingly in a poem he wrote in 1774, "Zwischen Lavater und Basedow" (Between Lavater and Basedow). He describes a pleasant journey down the Rhine during which he is enjoying a meal, and his two companions, Lavater and Basedow, are busy enthusiastically explicating theological problems to fellow passengers who do not appear too interested. In 1815 Goethe added the following conclusion, and the poems were published together as "Diné zu Koblenz im Sommer 1774" (Dinner at Coblenz in the Summer of 1774):

> Und wie nach Emmaus, weiter ging's
> Mit Sturm und Feuerschritten:
> Prophete rechts, Prophete links,
> Das Weltkind in der Mitten.[77]

[And as to Emmaus, we went along, with storm and steps of fire. Prophet left and prophet right, the child of the world in the middle.]

The 1770s mark a clear emergence of Enlightenment concerns in Goethe's writings for they advocate social, religious, and intercultural tolerance. During these years tolerance is for Goethe a kind of litmus test that determines whether or not an individual is humane, civilised, and modern — regardless of religious or cultural background. In 1779 the *Brief des Pastors* was included in a Leipzig publication celebrating the best prose pieces in Germany.[78] In this year *Iphigenie auf Tauris* was first performed, a drama that can be interpreted as the culmination of Goethe's thinking on tolerance during this decade.

Notes

[1] DuW I/1: FA 14, 50. Cf. Gerhard Sauder, "Der junge Goethe und das religiöse Denken des 18. Jahrhunderts," *Goethe Jahrbuch* 112 (1995): 97–110; Franz Blanckmeister, *Goethe und die Kirche seiner Zeit* (Dresden: Sturm, 1923); Heinrich Hoffmann, *Die Religion des Goetheschen Zeitalters* (Tübingen: Mohr, 1917); Hermann Henkel, *Goethe und die Bibel* (Leipzig: Biedermann, 1890).

[2] Heinrich Voelcker, "Kirche und Religiöses Leben in Frankfurt am Main," in Die Stadt Goethes: Frankfurt am Main im XVIII. Jahrhundert, ed. by H. Voelcker (Frankfurt am Main: Werner u. Winter Universitätsdrückerei, 1932), 135–36. Cf. J. Taylor Hamilton and Kenneth G. Hamilton, *History of the Moravian Church: The Renewed Unitas Fratrum 1722–1957*, 2nd ed. (Bethlehem, PA: Moravian Church in America, 1983).

[3] Franz Götting, *Die Bibliothek von Goethes Vater*, Nassauische Annalen 64 (Wiesbaden: Verlag des Vereins für Nassauische Altertumskunde und Geschichtsforschung, 1953).

[4] DuW I/1: FA 14, 165.

[5] MA 1.1, 30–58.

[6] FA 1, 23 (first published in 1886).

[7] Lines 151–60: FA 1, 21.

[8] Nicholas Boyle, *Goethe: The Poet and the Age*, rev. ed. (Oxford: Oxford UP, 1992), vol.1: *The Poetry of Desire 1749–1790*, (1992), 76.

[9] Gottfried Arnold, *Gottfrid Arnolds Unparteyische Kirchen- und Ketzer-Historie, von Anfang des Neuen Testaments biß auff das Jahr Christi 1688*, 2 vols. (Frankfurt am Main: Thomas Fritsch, 1699–1700), 1: "Vorrede," paragraph 39.

[10] Arnold, *Kirchen- und Ketzer-Historie,* dedication to Friedrich III (following title page).

[11] Heinz Nicolai in HA 14, 390–91.

[12] MA 1.2, 876.

[13] MA 1.2, 532–33.

[14] David Hume, "Of Suicide," in *Essays: Moral, Political and Literary*, ed. by Eugene F. Miller, rev. ed. (Indianapolis, IN: Liberty Fund, 1985), 577–89.

[15] MA 1.1, 33–34.

[16] DuW III/13: FA 14, 638–39. Goethe's interest in writing this kind of novel predates 1772. Cf. Hans Rudolf Vaget, "Die Leiden des jungen

Werthers," in *Goethes Erzählwerk: Interpretationen,* ed. by Paul Michael Lützeler and James E. McLeod (Stuttgart: Reclam, 1985), 37–72, (62).

[17] FA 8, 266.

[18] FA 8, 262.

[19] See Werther's letters of 22 May, 16 July, 12 and 30 August, 10 September,
20 February, 15–16 March, 27 October as well as 3, 21, 30 November and
17 December.

[20] Letter in MA 1.2, 786.

[21] DuW III/13: FA 14, 636.

[22] DuW III/13: FA 14, 639.

[23] Letter in MA 1.2, 786.

[24] Brecht: FA 8, 917.

[25] FA 8, 16.

[26] FA 8, 22–24.

[27] 29 June: FA 8, 60. Cf. Matthew 18:3–4.

[28] 22 May: FA 8, 24. Cf. Stefan Blessin, *Goethes Romane: Aufbruch in die Moderne* (Paderborn: Schöningh, 1996), 80.

[29] 12 August: FA 8, 96.

[30] Martin Swales, *Goethe: The Sorrows of Young Werther* (Cambridge: Cambridge UP, 1987), 4.

[31] FA 8, 210; 256–62.

[32] Eric A. Blackall, *Goethe and the Novel* (Ithaca: Cornell UP, 1976), 38. Cf.
Hans Reiss, *Goethes Romane* (Bern: Francke, 1963), 18.

[33] FA 8, 222.

[34] Cf. the tale Werther's Grandmother told him about the "magnet mountain" that would pull all the iron out of passing ships thus sinking them (26
July: FA 8, 84).

[35] FA 8, 224.

[36] FA 8, 110.

[37] Pamela Currie, *Literature as Social Action: Modernist and Traditionalist
Narratives in Germany in the Seventeenth and Eighteenth Centuries* (Columbia, SC: Camden House, 1995), 198. Cf. Gert Mattenklott, "Die Leiden des
jungen Werthers," in *Goethe-Handbuch,* ed. by Bernd Witte and others, 4
vols. (Stuttgart: Metzler, 1996–1998), 3: *Prosaschriften,* ed. by Bernd Witte
and others (1997), 51–101, (91–94).

[38] 13 May: FA 8, 16.

[39] 12 August: MA 1.2, 235–36.

[40] 12 August: FA 8, 94–96.

[41] 12 August: FA 8, 94.

[42] FA 8, 94–96.

[43] Currie, *Literature as Social Action*, 207.

[44] Swales, *Goethe: The Sorrows of Young Werther*, 6.

[45] Boyle, *Goethe: The Poet and the Age*, vol. 1, *The Poetry of Desire (1749–1790)*, 88.

[46] Cf. MA 1.2, 744.

[47] Hannelore Schlaffer provides a more detailed historical sketch in MA 2.2, 942–43.

[48] This version, called the *Urfaust*, was discovered posthumously and published in 1887.

[49] MA 1.2, 556.

[50] MA 1.2, 671–72.

[51] DuW III/11: FA 14, 516–17.

[52] Gordon Craig, *The Politics of the Unpolitical: German Writers and the Problem of Power* (New York: Oxford UP, 1995), 10.

[53] Boyle, *Goethe: The Poet and the Age*, vol. 1, *The Poetry of Desire (1749–1790)*, 76.

[54] MA 1.2, 521.

[55] DuW II/8: FA 14, 382.

[56] Helmut Koopmann, "Brief des Pastors zu *** an den neuen Pastor zu ***. Aus dem Französischen" in *Goethe-Handbuch*, ed. by Bernd Witte et al., 4 vols. (Stuttgart: Metzler, 1996–1998), vol. 3: *Prosaschriften* (1987), 526–32 (526).

[57] DuW III/12: FA 14, 557.

[58] FA 18, 119.

[59] FA 18, 121.

[60] Ernst Cassirer contends that indifference was not the primary motivation for the defence of tolerance by Enlightenment thinkers. He argues that freedom of conscience was rather an empowerment of religious belief (*Die Philosophie der Aufklärung*, 219).

[61] FA 18, 122.

[62] FA 18, 122. Thomas Saine argues that some Protestant Enlighteners were intolerant of Catholicism: Thomas Saine, "'Was ist Aufklärung?': Kulturgeschichtliche Überlegungen zu neuer Beschäftigung mit der deutschen Aufklärung," *Zeitschrift für deutsche Philologie* 93 (1974): 522–45 (538).

[63] MA 1.2, 846.

[64] Koopmann, "Brief des Pastors," 529.

[65] FA 18, 126. Cf. Revelation 3:20.

[66] FA 18, 123.

[67] FA 18, 123 and 126.

[68] FA 18, 124.

[69] FA 18, 127.

[70] FA 18, 120–21.

[71] FA 1, 216–17.

[72] FA 18, 128. For a less sympathetic portrayal of enthusiasts, see Goethe's play, *Satyros*, also written in 1773. Cf. Katharina Mommsen, *Goethe — Warum? Eine repräsentative Auslese aus Werken, Briefen und Dokumenten*, Insel Taschenbuch 759 (Frankfurt am Main: Insel, 1984), 345.

[73] FA 14, 465.

[74] Letter to Zelter, 25 December 1829: WA IV/46, 192–94. For an account of Goldsmith's influence on Goethe, see: Lawrence Marsden Price, *The Reception of English Literature in Germany* (Berkeley: U of California P, 1932), 248–56.

[75] 29 July 1782: WA IV/6, 20.

[76] 9 August 1782: WA IV/6, 36.

[77] FA 1, 163–64.

[78] Koopmann, "Brief des Pastors," 526.

2: Adoption, Adaptation, and Assimilation in *Iphigenie auf Tauris*

*I*PHIGENIE AUF TAURIS, first performed in Weimar in 1779 (and published in verse form in 1787) has since its initial reception by Wieland, Schiller, and Hegel been canonised as a celebration of humanity.[1] The drama is regarded increasingly as representative of the German late Enlightenment,[2] and Alois Wierlacher locates the drama within the eighteenth-century discussion of human rights, natural law, and international relations.[3] Francis Lamport argues that *Iphigenie*, Lessing's *Nathan der Weise,* and Schiller's *Don Carlos* are all "domestic dramas, their plots turning on family relationships." Lessing's and Goethe's plays are seen to achieve literal and symbolic family reunions "under the patronage of an enlightened secular authority."[4] Notions of family are important in *Iphigenie*, but not only as motifs of unity. Metaphorical family relationships can also define distance as when Iphigenie views Thoas as a second father, thus distancing him as a potential suitor.

In the later version of the play Iphigenie asks a crucial question: "Kann uns zum Vaterland' die Fremde werden?" [Can a foreign land ever become for us the fatherland?][5] This alters the original reading: "Die süße Fremde ist nicht Vaterland" [The sweetest foreign land is not the fatherland], for the verse version leaves open the possibility of cultural adoption.[6] Questions of cultural adoption, adaptation, and assimilation reassert themselves in various forms in the play. Although the 1787 *Iphigenie* is a more stylistically perfected work than the 1779 prose version, I draw liberally from the earlier text to document that Goethe's attention was drawn to intercultural understanding nearly a decade earlier.

In her opening monologue Iphigenie considers her woeful situation, that of being a foreigner and being held in a kind of noble servitude. Separated from her family, she is filled with yearning for Greece and her father's home. Her prayer to Diana, her goddess and rescuer, as an outcast daughter, is a supplication to another daughter, the daughter of Jove, and a petition that she be reunited with her family.[7] When she speaks with Arkas, servant of and counsellor to King Thoas, she compares herself to the orphaned and the expelled, signifying both her separation from her parents and her status as an exile.[8] Arkas describes perceptively Iphigenie's double bind, commenting that her "fatherland" is now more foreign to her than the foreign land where she lives, an assessment that heightens the reader's curiosity about her predicament.[9] Iphigenie compares family ties to the relationship of branches to a tree.[10] She has, in essence, been severed physically from the tree and transplanted elsewhere and this is an overarching concern of the play: does the transplantation work? The plot thickens when Arkas informs Iphigenie that King Thoas wants to marry her.

He emphasises that Thoas has extended his special friendship to Iphigenie and treated her with respect.[11] In the verse version "Neigung" [inclination] replaces "Freundschaft" [friendship], thus increasing the tension of Iphigenie's plight — how to decline the marriage proposal of a king who, by sparing her life, broke with the Taurian tradition of sacrificing foreigners washed up on its shores. In either case the king's warmth is stressed.[12] Arkas reminds her that she has been well received into the Taurian polity.[13] Interestingly, the 1779 construction suggests that the Scythians were friendly toward Iphigenie, while the 1787 construction hints at her growing fondness for them.[14]

Iphigenie, herself an exile and near-sacrifice, became the advocate for other foreigners who would normally have been offered up at Diana's altar, something that Arkas reminds her of: her marriage to the king can secure mercy for these other foreigners. Wierlacher believes Iphigenie is a kind of divinely commissioned missionary who has been sent to atone for and convert the people.[15] Using a religious metaphor,[16] it seems that Iphigenie is something of a secular saint (she is after all a priestess) who intervenes as best she can for those unfortunate foreigners shipwrecked on the shores of Tauris.

Iphigenie's plight is a serious one, for the king has his own difficulties: since his son's death he has become mistrusting of those around him, and faces a dynastic impasse. Therefore, Iphigenie's consent to marriage would stabilise the kingdom. Yet she views the proposal as a threat, since she is a virginal priestess to Diana.[17] It also seems that she longs ultimately for a return to Greece and may be using her religious office as a justification for declining his proposal.[18] There is yet another reason that Iphigenie cannot marry Thoas.

Marriage would be one way to answer positively Iphigenie's previously cited question about making the foreign her own. She would share the king's life and goods as well as his home.[19] Iphigenie, however, views Thoas as a father figure. Later in the play when she is

tempted by her brother Orest and his friend Pylades to lie to the king
so that they may steal the Diana idol and escape from Tauris, she refuses on the grounds that he has been a second father.[20]

And in another way, Thoas has become her only father after she
learns through Pylades[21] and Orest[22] that her biological father, Aga-
memnon, has been ambushed and murdered by her mother,
Clytemnestra and her lover, Aegisth. Later, as Orest faces Thoas with
drawn sword wanting to fight his way back to the Greek ship, Iphigenie
chastises him and refers to the king as "meinen väterlichen Beschützer"
[my fatherly protector].[23] In Iphigenie's final words in the play, an appeal to Thoas for his blessing before returning to her people — not unlike that which a daughter or son receives from a parent — she tells the
king plainly that she treasures him as much as anyone can a second father, and will continue so to do.[24]

A metaphorical incest taboo is implied by the tension of Thoas as
both a father figure and potential suitor. Such a marriage could therefore be seen as a symbolic transgression and therefore continue the
curse upon Iphigenie's family. Even Thoas recognises the ambiguity of
their relationship when he, hurt because of Iphigenie's rejection, lashes
out bitterly that women are ungrateful to both father and husband.[25]
Yet, Iphigenie appears to wish sincerely to draw Thoas into the "Fami-
liennexus" [nexus of the family] — she and her brother are indeed fa-
therless — and she extends this possibility to the king at the end of the
play.[26]

This is difficult for Thoas, as he has thought that kindness would
lead to marriage.[27] In the verse version the king chastises himself because of his "Nachsicht" [forbearance] and "Güte" [kindness] toward
Iphigenie, and he speaks disparagingly of her obstinacy, which moral
agency Theodor Adorno has called her "Kantisches Recht" [Kantian
right].[28] Thoas desperately wants things to go his way, but Iphigenie
will choose, in Enlightenment manner, what is best for herself. His is a
similar situation to the one that Margarete of Parma, Catholic Regent
of the Netherlands, finds herself in with the Protestants in *Egmont*. She
too has attempted through "meine Güte, meine Nachsicht" [my kindness, my forbearance] to be a conscientious ruler, but this does not
mean that the Dutch will fall into line with Madrid's dictates or with
Catholicism.[29] But what also appears to be frustrating Thoas is that he
feels unthanked, and that his more civilised behaviour is being taken for
granted, not unlike Margarete's situation.[30] Here again is the problem
of preserving a balance between learning from another culture, changing attitudes, and trying to keep what is one's own. What complicates

Thoas's situation psychologically is precisely the fact that the finer values Iphigenie allegedly takes for granted are the ones that she has had to inculcate in him. The drama poses the question about how deeply that process went.

A further complication is the issue over the ownership of the idol, for it appears that the Greeks, including Iphigenie, who hold to supposedly civilised values, are plotting to deceive and rob the king. They too have a desire to make what is foreign their own — through theft. And Thoas declares that this is not the first time that the Greeks have appropriated the foreign through force and deception, as he lists other occasions on which they have thieved from supposedly barbaric cultures.[31]

The limits of intercultural understanding are here drawn in two directions: tolerance does not imply that closer personal relations need necessarily follow (Iphigenie rejects Thoas); nor does it mean tolerating everything (Thoas will fight for the idol). Indeed, theft and violence are not even candidates for tolerance. Thus, while the means of obtaining the idol are impugned, at heart is a question of opposing and strongly held religious views. The king maintains that the idol belongs to Tauris, for he believes it has helped his people to victories on the battlefield.[32] Nevertheless, the Greeks too feel that they have divine confirmation from an oracle that the idol belongs to them. It is not only a matter of religious differences, however, but cultural prejudices that cause conflict. This reading is borne out by the condescending attitudes of the Greek characters toward Thoas and the Taurians, who are seen as primitives.[33]

Thoas, who measures foreigners with mistrust, recognises that the Greeks look down on him as a savage and a coarse barbarian.[34] When Iphigenie begins to have second thoughts about deceiving Thoas and allowing Pylades and Orest to steal the idol, Pylades tries to convince her by stating that they are purloining the treasure from a "rauh unwürd'gen Volk" [rough unworthy people].[35] This goes much further than having Thoas's kindness taken for granted. The Greeks seem to have a fixed view of barbarians (and to act nobly is a crucial part of Thoas's challenge). The stereotype of an "unworthy people" is contrasted with another, also spoken by Pylades, of Greece as civilised.[36] Pylades gives voice to the Greek perception of Tauris and its inhabitants when he matches the roughness of their shore to the coarseness of their character.[37] Goethe worked precisely against the kind of prejudice that utilised geography as the sole index of civilisation. Orest considers the king to be incalculable and wild,[38] and there is an irony in his recounting the great deeds of his forefathers when they hunted robbers. He does not appear to see himself as a thief, although he and his friend are planning to plunder the Taurian temple.

During the first conversation between Orest and Thoas, Orest insists upon his cultural preference that each side choose a representative hero to fight it out, insinuating that this is a universal practice. Even when Thoas tells him Taurian custom does not grant this right to foreigners, Orest attempts to seize the moral high ground by calling it a noble custom, a move that could make Taurian tradition appear cowardly. It is, of course, a convenient time for Orest to challenge the honour of the old king since Arkas has just reported that the Greeks are on the verge of being routed: "Ihr Schiff ist unser und ein Wort von dir so stehts in Flammen" [Their ship is ours and one word from you and it stands in flames].[39] In Goethe's implicit moral defence of Thoas, there is a resonance of Herder who, as Robert Clark has written, "attacked the complacency and self-glorification of the 'Aufklärer,' because he was not at all convinced that the savage needed civilizing as much as the so-called civilized man needed it. . . . His tolerance demanded that the uncivilized races be left alone to develop toward their own respective destinies."[40]

The Greek ship does not suffer a fiery fate: Thoas offers a conciliatory farewell after Iphigenie promises to honour his people, even as she suddenly praises his "Milde" [mildness], a near antonym of "rauh" [rough], and Orest now calls Thoas noble.[41] A significant excision occurs as Orest's apology, a sign of humility in the prose text, is removed from the later verse version: "Vergib' uns unsern Anschlag unsre Künste" [Forgive us our attempt on your life, and our tricks].[42] Whilst the play's ending may appear somewhat contrived, it is less so than Lessing's *Nathan der Weise,* in which the main characters discover they are related one to another. Thoas's reaction to the Greek plot is by no means a given, and the suspense is maintained until the conclusion of the drama. The truce that is arrived at is delicate, reflecting the real-life fragility of international peace.

Iphigenie's question, "Can a foreign land ever become for us the fatherland?" is answered ambivalently. She departs for Greece and the king's terse farewell could appear to be rhetorically extracted rather than given as a true sign of his blessing. What one is left with, however, is the possibility of future understanding in what Wierlacher calls an "ent-fremdete Fremde" [a de-foreignised foreign land]. Given the deep-rooted prejudices of the Greeks and Thoas, how is it possible to have come even this far?

Orest averts disaster by interpreting the Delphic oracle differently than he had at first, or in a more civilised manner: he is to bring *his* sister (Iphigenie) home, not Apollo's sister, represented by the Diana image. Had he attempted the latter, Thoas would have ordered a fight to the finish with the Greek robbers, as he indicates in no uncertain terms. Orest's interpretation is central to the drama.[43] The entire action of the play is shaped by the need to hear and interpret personified voices. Dieter Borchmeyer has an intriguing reading of this resolution of the oracle's words, seeing in it the relationship between a just ruler and a free citizen in enlightened states.[44] The relationship between religion and human agency is explored from an Enlightenment perspective for it seems that it is the human actors, and not the gods, who are responsible for solving the dramatic problems.

Iphigenie declines Thoas's marriage proposal by telling him that the gods do not approve, implying that she knows this because they speak through the heart. When Thoas claims that for his part he has not heard anything from the gods, Iphigenie tells him it is a gentle voice that can be drowned out easily; he replies that it is only the priestess that perceives the voice.[45] Different ways of hearing are implied, just as there are different voices. Thoas accuses Iphigenie of not listening to the voice of good counsel and reason — his voice — and to what he holds to be common sense.[46] And throughout the drama Pylades has been a well-meaning yet error-filled voice to Orest.[47]

Most famous is the moment of pitched dramatic tension when Iphigenie exposes the Greek plot to Thoas. Thoas doubts whether Iphigenie really trusts a barbarian to be able to perceive the voice of truth. Nonplussed and earnest, Iphigenie insists that the voice of truth can bridge cultural differences, implying that the ability to recognise truth is not a prerogative of the Greeks.[48] Here a claim is made that the tension between Enlightenment universalism and Herderian cultural particularism can be resolved, through what Herder called "die Anerkennung der Menschheit im Menschen" [the recognition of humanity in human beings].[49] Cultural differences divide people; however, the assumption is that people ought to respect each other, and that they hold certain values in common. Ritchie Robertson concludes: "By subsuming the antithesis between Greeks and barbarians under a common humanity, Goethe shows that toleration is now a cultural as well as a religious issue."[50] But knowing the truth is sometimes not enough, especially when other voices compete for our attention; Thoas admits, near the end of the play, that he is filled with anger.[51] Iphigenie supplicates him to hear "der Billigkeit / Gelinde Stimme" [the mild voice of fairness] as he confronts Orest.[52] Wierlacher points out that *Billigkeit* has a long legal history, and is used similarly by Grotius, Herder, and Goethe in connection with *humanitas* [humanity] and *clementia* [clemency].[53]

Billigkeit creates enough time for Orest to explain why he, Fury-driven and nearly demented, came to Tauris, and to apologise for the near-disasterous confusion over the Diana image. Orest witnesses Iphigenie's bravery, which leads to his inspired rereading of the oracle as referring to his sister, not Apollo's and to the more civilised request of peaceful passage for his priestly sister so that she may purify their cursed lineage.[54] Iphigenie promises Thoas that should she meet someone in Greece who speaks or dresses like a Taurian, she will receive him with reverence and honour. In the moment Iphigenie is about to depart (and subject no longer to being threatened and pressured by Thoas), she realises how attached she has become to this people and their king.[55] She has, by prolonged exposure, become fond of the Taurians. Her comments on the Taurian tongue ring with a similar affection to the relief Pylades felt when he first spoke in Greek with Iphigenie and heard the sweet "Muttersprache in einem fremden Lande" [mother tongue in a foreign land].[56]

Iphigenie has come to understand the ways of her host people, and a dialogue can continue because there is respect at the level of language and culture. She has invited King Thoas to make a "Gastrecht" [convention of hospitality] between their peoples because she wants to preserve the possibility of future contact.[57] She may not be able to make the foreign land her fatherland, but it is now the land of her second father and although her mother tongue is Greek, she is capable of adopting the foreign tongue.

Gastrecht, an important Greek social concept, raises another major issue in the drama, for it identifies certain responsibilities that the native has vis-à-vis the foreigner in a guest-host relationship. Thoas invokes this role when he asks Iphigenie to trust him, her "Wirt" [host].[58] Iphigenie hesitates to follow Pylades because she cannot betray the man who extended hospitality to her.[59] And she continues to have doubts about doing an injustice to her host.[60] *Gastrecht* is a defined starting point for developing a relationship between cultures because it prescribes basic roles of hospitality, which in turn nurture a climate for achieving greater understanding. It is, like the environment in a greenhouse, an artificial atmosphere, but similarly it gives things that otherwise could not exist in the host climate a chance to survive. Thoas may have given his blessing with some bitterness, yet he has provided a context for future friendly contact as well as for differences to be aired in a less hostile manner than has heretofore been the case.

The question about a foreign country becoming a fatherland is answered ambiguously, however, it can at least become a familiar land. A similar ambivalence is voiced by Goethe in a letter to Herder during his sojourn in Italy: "Die Fremde hat ein fremdes Leben und wir können es uns nicht zu eigen machen, wenn es uns gleich als Gästen gefällt" [A foreign land has a foreign life and we cannot make it our own, even if we enjoy being guests].[61] Nevertheless, there is a mediating acknowledgement that Iphigenie, Orest, and Thoas have constructed a familial relationship, thus making cultural adoption and adaptation a real possibility. Long-held prejudices are being overcome on both sides through recognising their common humanity despite religious and cultural differences. This relationship is strengthened through something like a treaty of friendship that brings the Greeks and Taurians into a peaceful international relationship with each other. Having treated the issues of tolerance and recognition in an ancient story, in *Egmont* Goethe goes on to explore them in a real historical setting.

Notes

[1] Hartmut Reinhardt: MA 3.1, 730. Lamport views *Iphigenie* as a part of a triptych, along with *Nathan der Weise* and *Don Carlos*, depicting "the triumph of humanity." Francis John Lamport, *German Classical Drama: Theatre, Humanity and Nation 1750–1870* (Cambridge: Cambridge UP, 1992), 65. Cf. James Boyd, *Goethe's Iphigenie auf Tauris* (Oxford: Blackwell, 1942).

[2] T. J. Reed, "Iphigenies Unmündigkeit: Zur weiblichen Aufklärung," in *Germanistik: Forschungsstand und Perspektiven: Vorträge des Deutschen Germanistentages 1984*, ed. by Georg Stötzel (Berlin: De Gruyter, 1985), 505–24, (506).

[3] Alois Wierlacher, "Ent-fremdete Fremde: Goethes Iphigenie auf Tauris als Drama des Völkerrechts," *Zeitschrift für deutsche Philologie* 102 (1983): 161–80.

[4] Lamport, *German Classical Drama*, 67 and 76.

[5] I, ii, line 76: FA 5, 557.

[6] I, ii: FA 5, 152.

[7] I, i: FA 5, 151–52.

[8] I, ii: FA 5, 152. King Thoas, after hearing Iphigenie's gruesome family history, calls her "die Vertriebene" [the expellee] (only in prose version: I, iii: FA 5, 159) and she calls herself "die Flüchtige" [the refugee] (I, iii, line 252: FA 5, 562).

[9] I, ii: FA 5, 152.

[10] I, ii: FA 5, 152–53.

[11] I, ii: FA 5, 153.

[12] I, ii, line 100: FA 5, 558.

[13] I, ii: FA 5, 153.

[14] I, ii, line 101: FA 5, 558.

[15] "Ent-fremdete Fremde," 165.

[16] Stahl contends that Iphigenie's soliloquies should be understood not as monologues, but prayers. E. L. Stahl, *Goethe: Iphigenie auf Tauris,* Studies in German Literature, 7 (London: Arnold, 1961), 27. The role of the gods is discussed in: Terence James Reed, "Iphigenie auf Tauris," in *Goethe-Handbuch,* ed. by Bernd Witte and others, 4 vols (Stuttgart: Metzler, 1996–1998), 2: ed. by Theo Buck (1996), 195–228, (218–22).

[17] I, ii: FA 5, 154.

[18] I, iii: FA 5, 159.

[19] Ibid.

[20] IV, iv, lines 1640–642: FA 5, 603.

[21] II, ii: FA 5, 169. Iphigenie's hopes were raised temporarily when she inferred wrongly that her father was not amongst the fallen Greek heroes of the Trojan War: II, ii: FA 5, 168.

[22] III, i: FA 5, 170.

[23] V, iv: FA 5, 193. In the verse version she calls him a second father: V, iv, lines 2004: FA 5, 614.

[24] V, vii: FA 5, 197. Cf. When Jacob (Israel) blesses Joseph and his grandsons, Ephraim and Manasseh (Genesis 48 and 49).

[25] I, iii: FA 5, 160.

[26] Reed, "Iphigenie auf Tauris," 224.

[27] V, ii: FA 5, 188.

[28] V, ii, lines 1798–799: FA 5, 608. Theodor W. Adorno, "Zum Klassizismus von Goethes Iphigenie" in *Gesammelte Schriften,* ed. by Rolf Tiedemann et al., 20 vols. (Frankfurt am Main: Suhrkamp, 1970–1986), 11: *Noten zur Literatur,* ed. by Rolf Tiedemann (1974), 495–514, (508). Cf. Wolfdietrich

Rasch, *Goethes "Iphigenie auf Tauris" als Drama der Autonomie* (Munich: Beck, 1979).

[29] I "Palast der Regentin": FA 5, 468.

[30] V, ii: FA 5, 189.

[31] V, vii: FA 5, 196.

[32] I, ii: FA 5, 152.

[33] Cf. Wierlacher, "Ent-fremdete Fremde," 163–64 and 170.

[34] I, iii: FA 5, 160 and V, iii, line 1937: FA 5, 612. Cf. Edith Hall, *Inventing the Barbarian: Greek Self-definition through Tragedy* (Oxford: Clarendon Press, 1989).

[35] IV, iv, lines 1602–603: FA 5, 602. These phrases are not in the 1779 version.

[36] II, i: FA 5, 166. The phrase "unworthy people" is not used in the 1787 version. Cf. Herder in *Briefe zur Beförderung der Humanität* (1793–1797, Letters on the Promotion of Humanity), Letter 115 argues that peoples labelled "barbaric" were often more humane than the Europeans. *Johann Gottfried Herder Werke,* ed. by Martin Bollacher and others, 10 vols. (Frankfurt am Main: Deutscher Klassiker Verlag, 1985–2000), vol. *7: Briefe zur Beförderung der Humanität,* ed. by Hans Dietrich Irmscher (1991), 688.

[37] II, i, line 735: FA 5, 576 and II, i: FA 5, 166.

[38] II, i, line 784: FA 5, 577.

[39] V, vi: FA 5, 194–95.

[40] Robert T. Clark, Jr., "The Noble Savage and the Idea of Tolerance in Herder," *Journal of English and Germanic Philology* 33 (1934): 46–56, (56).

[41] V, vi, line 2167: FA 5, 618–19. The prose version contains neither "Milde" nor "edler Mann."

[42] V, vii: FA 5, 196.

[43] V, vii: FA 5, 195–96.

[44] Dieter Borchmeyer, "Iphigenie auf Tauris," in *Goethes Dramen: Interpretationen,* ed. by Walter Hinderer (Stuttgart: Reclam, 1992), 117–57, (147).

[45] I, iii: FA 5, 160. Iphigenie knows that there can be a confusion of voices: IV, iv: FA 5, 186.

[46] I, iii: FA 5, 159.

[47] V, vii: FA 5, 196. Orest does not mention Pylades's misinterpretation in the verse version.

[48] V, iii: FA 5, 191–92. The famous "Stimme . . . der Menschlichkeit" [voice of humanity] occurs only in the 1787 text (V, iii, lines 1937–38: FA 5, 612). Goethe does not make Christianity the epicentre of the moral law, and in this sense differs from Herder. After arguing for universal *Menschlichkeit* [humanity] in *Briefe zur Beförderung der Humanität* (Letters on the Promotion of Humanity), Herder writes in Letter 124, the conclusion of the work, that Christianity is the purest form of humanity (FA 7, 752).

[49] *Briefe zur Beförderung der Humanität* (Letters on the Promotion of Humanity), Letter 115: FA 7, 688 (Cf. footnote 227). Herder quotes James Dunbar who, upon reading Josiah Tucker, is said to have exclaimed: "when the benevolence of this writer is exalted into charity, when the spirit of his religion . . . corrects the *rancour of his philosophy*, he will *acknowledge in the most untutored tribes some glimmerings of humanity, and some decisive indications of a moral nature.*"

[50] Ritchie Robertson, "Freedom and Pragmatism: Aspects of Religious Toleration in Eighteenth-century Germany," *Patterns of Prejudice* 32 (1998): 69–80, (76).

[51] V, vi, line 2096: FA 5, 617. There is no mention of anger at this point in the prose text.

[52] V, vi, lines 2029–2030: FA 5, 615.

[53] "Ent-fremdete Fremde," 174.

[54] V, vii: FA 5, 196.

[55] V, vii: FA 5, 197.

[56] II, ii: FA 5, 167.

[57] V, vii: FA 5, 197.

[58] I, iii: FA 5, 156.

[59] IV, iv: FA 5, 185. When they first meet in Tauris, Orest thinks that Iphigenie (who has not yet identified herself) may have known his family (III, i: FA 5, 171). The Greeks had diverse opinions about telling lies, which may mean that Orest does not view his own deception as morally wrong. Cf. Wolfgang Speyer, *Die Literarische Fälschung im Heidnischen und Christlichen Altertum: Ein Versuch Ihrer Deutung* (Munich: Beck, 1971), 95.

[60] IV, iv: FA 5, 186. This important phrase does not appear in the 1787 version.

[61] 14 October 1786 (as quoted in Wierlacher, 164).

3: An Enlightenment Coign of Vantage: The Intersection of History, Literature, and Belief in *Egmont*

IN THE DRAMA *EGMONT* (1787) Goethe combines elements of history, literature, and questions about belief. The play chronicles the sixteenth-century revolt of the Netherlands against Spanish rule. Although an exact date for the drama's action is not given, the events indicate that it occurs between 1566 and 1568, the year of Egmont's execution. Goethe chose a historical event that would vindicate his eighteenth-century Enlightenment heritage. King Philip II of Spain was not an uncommon historical target, and to modern sensibilities — shaped by men like Goethe and his friend the historian and author Friedrich Schiller, who wrote a history of the Thirty Years' War as well as a play, *Don Carlos*, involving the Dutch Revolt — he seems overzealous, as the following extract from a 1585 letter from the king to Parma illustrates:

> In spite of everything I would regret very much to see this toleration conceded without limits. The first step [for Holland and Zealand] must be to admit and maintain the exercise of the Catholic religion alone, and to subject themselves to the Roman Church, without allowing or permitting in any agreement the exercise of any other faith whatever in any town, farm or special place set aside in the fields or inside a village . . . And in this there is to be no exception, no change, no concession by any treaty of freedom of conscience . . . They are all to embrace the Roman Catholic faith and the exercise of that alone is to be permitted.[1]

This was a period of immense religious and therefore political change in Europe.[2] In 1555 the Peace of Augsburg had led to the official recognition of the *Confessio Augustana* (Lutheranism) in the constituent States of the Holy Roman Empire according to the formula *cuius regio, eius religio* [in a (prince's) country, the (prince's) religion]. The Council of Trent (1545–1563) signalled an attempt to renew the Church spiritually and respond to Protestant objections. It also set in motion the Counter-Reformation (*Ecclesia semper reformanda*) — in 1559 Pope Paul IV introduced the *Index librorum prohibitorum*, a list of forbidden books and authors. In 1560 Elector Friedrich III of the

Rhine Palatinate converted to Calvinism. Although Calvinism would be recognised after the 1648 Treaties of Westphalia, achieving the right to public worship would be a struggle.

Goethe prided himself on his historical studies and used a German translation of the *Historia belgica* (History of Belgium, 1597, Antwerp) by Emanuel van Meteren (1535–1612) for the Protestant perspective and *De bello Belgico* (The Belgium War, 1640, Rome) by the Jesuit Famianus Strada (1572–1649) for the Catholic.[3] Critics aknowledge that religion and questions of faith are important elements in the drama.[4] Egmont, around whom the play "spirals,"[5] is seen as a "tolerant character,"[6] Margarete of Parma as preferring a "humane approach to religious bigotry and zealotry,"[7] and Machiavell as a potential representative of Goethean tolerance[8] — but this idea is often referred to rather than explored. In this chapter we will focus on key dialogues in which the revolt, with its religious, social, political, economic, and cultural implications, is discussed by the drama's main figures. Readers thus eavesdrop on historical positions as Goethe saw them, which has the effect of highlighting the ethical elements of the conflict and bringing Enlightenment politics into view. In drama a discussion between the State and the philosophers could at least be staged, as T. J. Reed has shown.[9] Thus drama itself is a strategic choice for Goethe, who wrote: "der Despotismus befördert keine Wechselreden" [despotism does not nurture dialogue].[10] Drama insists upon dialogue, and dialogue rests upon the possibility of people expressing and sharing their thoughts openly (a right that becomes endangered through the course of *Egmont*).

The Netherlanders

The central conflicts of the play are brought into view during the opening scene at an archery range. As the conversation turns to politics, Jetter, a tailor in Brussels, comments on the Regent in the Netherlands, Margarete of Parma, Philip II's half sister. He suspects that her reason for appointing so many foreign bishoprics in the land is politically rather than religiously motivated, although he considers her a moderate ruler. Jetter voices further grievances, including those directed toward the prohibitions against singing psalms or listening to the sermons of German preachers. Soest, a shopkeeper, hesitates to accuse the regent and instead blames the king for most changes. And Buyck, a soldier, responds that in his province, Count Egmont, the *Statthalter* (governor), does not care what they sing. These three represent a cross-section of the rank and file in the Netherlands and their view of what is happening. Jetter exposes the real issue, the power of the Inquisition to intimidate and to suppress freedom of conscience. Soest feels that the Dutch are not made like the Spanish and will not allow such tyranny. Jetter summarises this discussion in terms of religious freedom: "Und was ist's denn nun man kann ja einen jeden predigen lassen nach seiner Weise" [And what's the matter, then, one can allow a man to preach after his own way].[11]

The comments of Jetter, Soest, and Buyck echo the Protestant approach of the time: preaching in the people's language as opposed to Latin; criticism of a distant clergy; direct appeals to the Bible as a proof text; and the introduction of new hymns.[12] The revolutionary potential of Protestantism is here shown to be a confluence of religion and politics, but these men do not comprehend this fully. Moreover, they do not understand why singing non-sanctioned hymns or listening to itinerant foreign preachers teaching from the Bible in their own tongue causes Catholic ecclesiastical leaders to brand them heretics. Their fears and frustrations reflect the confusion of individuals trying to define the overlapping frontiers of religious, political, and personal life, even as they are caught in the greater geopolitical vortex that is changing such borders.

Margarete and Machiavell

From the Catholic perspective Protestantism was seen as inherently oppositional and parasitical. The reader is initiated into the ruler's outlook in the palace scene. In her soliloquy, Margarete of Parma frames the problem in religious language, for she speaks of blasphemy against sacred tenets. The foreign teachers, in her view, are confusing the rabble, and she must put an end to the "Übel" [evil].[13] When Machiavell, her servant and secretary, appears on the scene, he reads her his report, which will be sent to the king, on the iconoclastic destruction of chapels, churches, monasteries, an ecclesiastical library, and a cathedral.

The Protestant iconoclasts are described as a wild mob that cares nothing for that which is holy, human, artistic, or intellectual. The foreign teachers and a part of her people seem to have formed a conspiracy to overthrow and destroy the traditional order. Margarete feels that she has ruled temperately, and is therefore worried that the King will decide that the tumult is a consequence and an indictment of her "Güte" and "Nachsicht" [kindness and forbearance].[14] The implication is that he will retaliate without clemency, so she faces the problem of applying the right measures.

When Margarete obliges Machiavell to reveal his thoughts on the current difficulties, he recommends a policy of tolerance to ensure socio-political stability:

> Ihr unterdrückt die neue Lehre nicht. Laßt sie gelten, sondert sie von den Rechtgläubigen, gebt ihnen Kirchen, faßt sie in die bürgerliche Ordnung, schränkt sie ein und so habt Ihr die Aufrührer auf einmal zur Ruhe gebracht. Jede andre Mittel sind vergeblich und Ihr verheert das Land.[15]

> [Do not suppress the new teachings. Let them be, separate them from the true believers, give them churches, embrace them in the civil order, restrict them and you will have hushed the rebels all at once. Every other measure is useless and you will devastate the land.]

Machiavell's solution seems modern: limited tolerance imposed from the top by the rulers is one way of interpreting the Peace of Augsburg, a final effort to spare the Empire the ravages of war. Machiavell can be seen as one of the modernisers whom Pamela Currie identifies as having come into existence between 1550 and 1650: "The supreme lesson which the lawyer-historians drew from history, in France, Holland and Germany, was that sectional and confessional divisions in traditional society caused conflict and threatened anarchy."[16]

Machiavell touches upon a new conception of the relationship between church and state, namely, that their affairs can be distinguished. He propounds a proto-Enlightenment thought, that religious pluralism is not necessarily a threat to the civil order. Goethe followed the course of the United States revolution; in 1791, three years after the publication of *Egmont*, the United States Bill of Rights was ratified and the first sentence of the First Amendment includes the guarantee: "Congress shall make no law respecting an establishment of religion, or prohibiting the free exercise thereof."[17] Machiavell argues that the citizens may believe as they wish, for the primary duty of the State is to regulate political, not religious affairs.

Margarete reminds him that Philip rejects the idea of tolerance.[18] She describes the inextricable relationship between Catholicism and the State in Philip's medieval worldview; even societal peace and unity are secondary values to him. What Philip's father, Karl V, could not achieve throughout the Empire — stopping the Reformation — Philip demands throughout his kingdom at all costs.

Machiavell, arguing with a for once benevolent *raison d'état*, points out that the new religion is practically a *fait accompli* and therefore suggests tolerating it. Foreseeing the utter destruction that Philip's course will lead to, he appeals to his regent to intervene and communicate to the king that from a governing and economic perspective, as well as from a humane one, it is better to spare the populace a religious war.[19] What Machiavell does not understand is that his modern worldview is years ahead of Philip's and to some extent Margarete's.

Goethe portrays Margarete as a committed, even orthodox, religious woman. She demands that her religion maintain its hegemonic societal status.[20] Added to this is her delight in ruling.[21] In the spectrum of religious sympathies, Philip II, not Margarete, occupies the position of zealot. She is a believer in the religious tradition for which she knows many have sacrificed themselves and become martyrs. She senses that the present troubles are not merely about a band of iconoclasts, as serious as that is from a Catholic standpoint, but suspects that there is a deeper problem, something betrayed by her use of the word *Übel*, a term she returns to at the conclusion of her conversation with Machiavell.[22] *Übel* is often used to describe terrible and incomprehensible plagues, and implies that the new religion is not only heterodox and theologically evil, but is a malady or virus that has been introduced into the Provinces from German lands and France. Machiavell's word, "angesteckt" [infected], supports this interpretation as well.[23] The recent ills that have seized violently both the Netherlandic *ecclesiasticum corpus* (Catholicism) and the body politic (Flanders), are quickly spreading to the brain (Brussels).[24] Margarete's reaction to Machiavell's pragmatic humanism is motivated in part by the fear of the chaos that could be unleashed in religious revolution. Her problem is that of choosing the proper means to control what she perceives to be a kind of plague that will ravage her people and the Church.

Margarete may be justified in her fear, since thirty years earlier (1534–1535) Münster was besieged when radical religious reformers gained control of the city. This event confused and frightened European monarchs. While Margarete seems to intuit that the dream of a religiously unified Empire cannot be realised even in the much smaller-scale setting of the Netherlands, and "has grasped the futility of suppressing disaffection by force,"[25] yet she must ultimately oppose the new religion. This paradox reflects the great difficulty practising Catholic rulers had in coming to terms with Protestantism, for as a devout Catholic ruler the doctrine of *prudentia* [prudence] plays a role in her actions. In fact, Philip II held similar views and was willing to employ deadly force to ensure the supremacy of Catholicism, as this excerpt from a 1566 letter to Pope Pius V shows:

> If possible I will settle the religious problem in those states [i.e. the Netherlands] without taking up arms, for I know that to do so would result in their total destruction; but if things cannot be remedied as I desire without recourse to arms, I am determined to take them up and go myself to carry out everything; and neither anger nor the ruin of these states, nor all of the others which are left to me, will prevent me from doing what a Christian prince fearing God ought to do in his service, [and for] the preservation of the Catholic faith and in the honour of the apostolic see.[26]

The regent believes that she, preferably with Egmont and Orange, must combat the disease that threatens her political authority and her personal religious worldview, which, in the end, is the only officially sanctioned view.[27] Isaiah Berlin reminds readers of the gap between modern views, which have been shaped in part by the Enlightenment, and those of previous centuries:

> Again, what Catholic in, let us say, the sixteenth century would say "I abhor the heresies of the reformers, but I am deeply moved by the sincerity and integrity with which they hold and practise and sacrifice themselves for their abominable beliefs"? On the contrary, the deeper the sincerity of such heretics, or unbelievers — Muslims, Jews, atheists — the more dangerous they are, the more likely to lead souls to perdition, the more ruthlessly should they be eliminated, since heresy — false beliefs about the ends of men — is surely a poison more dangerous to the health of society than even hypocrisy or dissimulation, which at least do not openly attack the true doctrine. Only truth matters: to die in a false cause is wicked or pitiable.[28]

Furthermore, Margarete's half brother demands that no boundary be accepted between the Church and the State; thus any real or perceived ill in one is by definition an ill in the other. Machiavell, in contrast, distinguishes between these two spheres, the religious and the secular, if only because the *Übel* has already transformed their relationship, a view he urges his regent to accept. Yet Margarete is unprepared and unwilling to enter the new socio-political field that Machiavell's proto-Enlightenment ideas map out: toleration and limited official recognition of the new religion. Tolerating and recognising the new religion (one that she views as uncertain and contradictory), even only tactically, would in her view be tantamount to religious indifference. Catholicism must not only inform her personal behaviour and attitudes, but it must also be enforced as the sole faith in the Netherlands.

Though not given to her brother's stridency, and able to be lenient for a time, she cannot in the end suspend her belief in order to tolerate and incorporate the new religion within the Dutch polity. It is thus unsurprising that she accuses Egmont of indifference and frivolity regarding the religious unrest.[29]

The regent fumes over Egmont's reaction to the religious tumult and vents her feelings on Machiavell.[30] She believes that Egmont, a Catholic ruler, has been far too indulgent and fears that he may even sympathise secretly with the new religion.[31] He has suggested that the Spanish recognise the local constitutions of the provinces and that such a move would calm the social turbulence. This reveals that he can separate the political and religious issues. Machiavell is able to see the wisdom in Egmont's proposition:

> Vielleicht hat er wahrer als klug und fromm gesprochen. Wie soll Zutrauen en[t]stehen und bleiben wenn der Niederländer sieht daß es mehr um seine Besitztümer als um sein Wohl, um seiner Seelen Heil zu tun ist. Haben die neuen Bischöfe mehr Seelen gerettet als fette Pfründen geschmaust? und sind es nicht meist Fremde? Noch werden alle Statthalterschaften mit Niederländern besetzt, lassen sich es die Spanier nicht zu deutlich merken daß sie die größte und unwiderstehlichste Begierde nach diesen Stellen empfinden? Will ein Volk nicht lieber nach seiner Art, von den seinigen regiert werden als von Fremden, die erst im Lande sich wieder Besitztümer auf Unkosten aller zu erwerben suchen, die einen fremden Maßstab mitbringen und unfreundlich und ohne Teilnehmung herrschen.[32]

> [Perhaps he spoke more truly than piously and wisely. How can confidence be established and endure when the Netherlanders see that there is more concern with their possessions than with their well-being or salvation? Have the new bishops saved more souls than they have feasted on fat benefices — and are not most of them foreigners? Still all the town governorships are held by Netherlanders — do not the Spaniards allow it to be noticed that they feel the greatest and most irresistible desire for these positions? Does not a people want to be ruled by its own kind, after its own fashion, rather than by foreigners who start by seeking to obtain property in the land at everyone's expense, who bring strange standards with them and who rule without sympathy and understanding?]

Machiavell's best interest is not served by criticising established absolutist decrees; nevertheless he cites a central hypocrisy in Spanish religious policy, namely that materialism and political power, not spiritual welfare, are its goals. This insight, similar to Jetter's impressions, foreshadows Egmont's later complaints to Alba. Machiavell observes that the Netherlanders appraise Spanish religious policy as Spanish foreign policy, as the actions of a self-interested, avaricious foreign power imposing its ways upon an existing civil order. Given that the monarch and regent cannot tolerate the new religion, Machiavell seems to suggest three policy changes that may allay fears and establish a foundation for improved relations between the Spanish and the Dutch:

1. Rein in the imposed, self-aggrandising bishops

2. Recognise that the Netherlanders need to be governed after their own way

3. Rule with sympathy and understanding, perhaps even delegate authority to the Dutch nobility

Machiavell's relatively modern statecraft is striking, as is his continued plea for (primarily) humane principles, in this case sympathy and understanding, important eighteenth-century ideals. When Margarete chides him for taking the side of the "Gegner" [opponent], a word that reflects the regent's mindset, he lets her know that his sympathies lie decidedly with Madrid, but that his reason cannot support unreservedly Spanish policy.

Vansen

Act II opens in Brussels, where a carpenter (whose name is never given) makes his first appearance. As a citizen and master of a guild opposed to the religious upheaval, he is an important representative figure. His opinion of the situation appears to be, at least partially, class-related. He sees the iconoclasts as riffraff, drunkards, and idlers who, unlike himself, have nothing to lose.[33] A soap boiler who joins the conversation represents a Catholic citizen's perspective on such events: shock. He cannot believe that there are faithful subjects and sincere Catholics who sympathise with the Protestant cause.[34]

Vansen, a legal clerk, begins to inform the gathered people about their constitutional privileges and freedoms. He tells the crowd that King Philip II is bound to respect their laws and traditions and he paraphrases significant excerpts from their constitution.[35] This incites the gathered citizens, and they react with indignation.[36] He then agitates the crowd further by declaring that they could throw off the Spanish yoke and points to the precedent in Flanders.[37] This triggers chaos in the street and makes for a visually busy scene (the stage directions are among the lengthiest of the play). Elizabeth Wilkinson has pointed out that "much of what [Vansen] advocates is a necessary condition for the preservation of liberty," and she notes the complexities of the arguments: "At each moment of this scene we face the challenge of where to draw the line, at what precise point to stop putting up with restrictions on liberty and begin to insist on traditional rights."[38]

A telling parallel emerges, for the people now break out in shouting, "Freiheit und Privilegien! Privilegien und Freiheit!" [Freedom and privileges! Privileges and freedom!],[39] echoing yet also transforming the words shouted joyfully and harmoniously in the first scene of the drama: "Sicherheit und Ruhe! Ordnung und Freiheit!" [Security and peace! Order and freedom!][40] This signifies more than a shift in slogan for the Netherlanders; it raises the question of whether they are willing to defend their constitutional privileges at the expense of their security, peace, and the civil order.

Egmont

As Count Egmont and his entourage happen upon the gathered crowd, he disperses them, orders them back to work, and charges them to remember that peace is best for the economy. Egmont understands basic power politics, for he knows that the king has the force of arms on his side. His harsh words to the crowd must be understood in their context, spoken in Brussels near the regent.[41] Perhaps this is a tactical exhortation, for, as Emil Staiger observes, he speaks differently when confronting Alba.[42]

In Egmont's apartment the reader is given deeper insights into his personal views on how to handle the recent unrest. It is broadly symmetrical with the conversation between Machiavell and the regent. Egmont's secretary begins by giving Captain Breda's report on the actions of the iconoclasts and asks whether six persons caught are to be hanged as others have been. Egmont tells his secretary that he is tired of hangings and orders that they be flogged and released.[43] At first this appears arbitrary, but Egmont's punishment may be both an act of mercy and a subtle relaxing of Spanish martial law. When he is told that two women are in the same group, his instructions are that they merely be warned and released. Later, Vansen, whom Goethe portrays in a negative light, cites Egmont's tolerant attitude.[44]

The secretary continues his report and asks what is to be done with a foreign teacher who has been apprehended, for the orders state that he ought to be beheaded. Egmont counteracts these regulations and commands that the teacher be taken to the border and released quietly with only a stern warning.[45] Perhaps Egmont does not want to create a precedent for clemency that might embolden other Protestant preachers. Or he may desire to keep the teacher's release quiet because he is contravening Spanish regulations. The vast difference in severity of punishment between beheading and release indicates the widening gulf between Spanish policy and Egmont's and functions as an ironical auguring of his own beheading.

The Dutch attitude of live and let live and the Spanish "Hof Kadenz" [court cadence] to which Egmont refuses to walk are differences of culture.[46] Egmont cannot be swayed by a letter of warning he receives from a friend at the Spanish court because he will not alter his nature. His refusal to step in time with Madrid's dictates shows that he wants to lead his own life and this Enlightenment thought — Kant calls it "den Schritt zur Mündigkeit" [the step to maturity] — is a recurring motif in the drama, namely, the ability to walk and move freely.[47] This metaphor stands for both maturity and freedom. Of course, as a nobleman, Egmont's movements are already granted greater range than those of the common people.

Machiavell observes that the count walks as if the world belonged to him. Egmont's attitude is expressed in his own words: "Laßt jeden seines Pfades gehn" [Let every man go his own way] and he maintains that "ein selbst verfehlter Schritt" [a misplaced step] is a part of life's experiences.[48] Duke Alba, who is sent to the Netherlands to put down the iconoclasm by force of arms, symbolically disempowers Egmont: he watches from a balcony window as the count dismounts from his horse before their first meeting — a meeting at which he plans to place Egmont under arrest — and imagines "Steig ab! — so bist du mit dem Einen Fuß im Grab! und so mit beiden! — " [Dismount! — Now you have one foot in the grave; and now both! —][49] William of Orange, in an earlier conversation, perceived the precarious position that he and Egmont occupy: "Wir haben nicht für den leisesten Fußtritt Platz mehr, der Abgrund liegt hart vor uns" [We have no place for even the quietest footstep; the abyss lies directly in front of us]. Even the ground they are on, Orange warns, is slippery.[50] Alba enforces the Spanish "court cadence" by the military boot, and Jetter describes the Spanish army of occupation as a machine, marching in "Ein Tritt" [one step]. Alba's plan to intimidate the citizens is successful, as his lieutenant, Silva, triumphantly reports: "keiner wagt einen Schritt" [no one dares take a step].[51] Egmont's movements are completely restricted, of course, when he is seized, something that is to be visually represented, as the stage notes specifically direct.[52] Nevertheless, the physical inability of Egmont to move is replaced in the last scene by a spiritual ability to know that although he cannot as in bygone days charge into the battlefield, his sacrifice is meaningful as the Enlightenment metaphor of walking is merged with the concept of freedom: "Auch ich schreite einem ehrenvollen Tode aus diesem Kerker entgegen, ich sterbe für die Freiheit für die ich lebte und focht, und der ich mich jetzt leidend opfre" [I too march from this dungeon to meet an honourable death; I die for freedom, for which I lived and fought and for which I now sacrifice myself].[53]

In act III Margarete confides in Machiavell that Alba is to prevent the citizens from making any "große Sprünge," that is, great leaps. By act IV her words have come to pass. The carpenter sees that the Netherlands is now under marshal law and the citizens bemoan the trampling of their freedoms and constitutional privileges — Alba initiates a reign of terror.[54]

Alba and Egmont

Margarete describes to Machiavell how some of the court counsellors in Madrid (especially Alba) look upon her as a poor rider (i.e., leader).[55] Thus the Netherlanders are likened unto a horse. Egmont is associated with horses from the first act as Buyck recalls the victory at Gravelingen in which Egmont's horse was shot from under him. He further describes the raging battle as not only man against man, but also horse against horse.[56] In a metaphorical sense, then, the French and the Netherlanders are horses fighting against each other: the rulers are the riders. Clärchen, Egmont's beloved, remembers him riding by on a horse. Silva reports to Alba that since the duke's arrival Egmont's behaviour has not changed, in stark contrast to the citizens, for he continues to ride his horses freely. The duke's natural son, Ferdinand, encounters Egmont on an unbroken horse, reflecting symbolically the Spanish view of the uncontrollable Netherlanders. And Egmont considers presenting Ferdinand (who has by this time become a tacit accomplice to his demise) with the fine horse that his people have brought to escort him following his meeting with Alba.[57]

Egmont's love for horses is a symbol of his sympathy for the people. Alba mocks this upon the count's arrival at the Palace: "Trug dich dein Pferd so leicht herein, und scheute vor dem Blutgeruche nicht, und vor

dem Geiste mit dem blanken Schwert, der an der Pforte dich empfängt?
... Ja, streichl es nur, und klopfe für seinen mutigen Dienst zum letzten Male den Nacken ihm" [Did your horse carry you in so easily,
without sensing the smell of blood or the spirit with drawn sword who
receives you at the gate? ... Yes, go on and stroke it, pat for the last
time its neck for serving you so bravely].[58] In fact, the image of horse
and rider is perhaps the central image of Egmont's climactic discussion
with Alba. It is, of course, an exercise in rhetoric on the duke's part, as
he has called this meeting with Egmont and Orange (who has strategically bowed out) in order to imprison and execute them. His lengthy
conversation with Egmont is a necessary façade, a time-consuming ma-
noeuvre to put Egmont at ease even as his associates are being arrested
and Spanish soldiers cover all the exits. The stage directions for Alba
are meant to give an audience the distinct visual impression that he is
distracted and not so much interested in the conversation as waiting for
the word that he can end the diversionary dialogue and get on with the
real business of seizing Egmont.[59] But Egmont has come to discuss the
current state of affairs; his description of the Netherlanders as a noble
horse, as opposed to an ox or a flock of sheep, brings together several
strands of the drama as he makes his plea to Alba to allow them to re-
tain their constitutional privileges.

Egmont echoes Machiavell's earlier thoughts when he pleads for the
Spanish to rule with sympathy and understanding. He also relates how
some citizens suspect that greed and selfishness are at the heart of
Spanish policies. The suggestion that foreign tyranny being exercised
upon the citizens despite their constitution strikes a nerve with Alba.
Egmont explains that a citizen wants to be ruled by one who was born
in the land and who has similar ideas on justice.[60]

Egmont does not reject Spanish rule outright. He is not suggesting
that Madrid acquiesce to a rebellion, but rather respect local traditions
and laws. The Netherlanders, too, can learn to trust and co-operate, as
he compares working with the people to riding a horse. Egmont's image is one of applying subtle pressure, working together, being mutually responsive — although the rider is still ultimately in charge. Alba
has earlier argued that the king should have the power to change traditions and to centralise government for the sake of progress. He now
drops this line of argument and states plainly a second time that the
king demands his way. Alba, in the manner of the conceptually paradoxical "enlightened despots" such as Friedrich II and Joseph II, es-
pouses absolute authority. He argues that the king will restrict the

people for their own good — and root out harmful citizens for the harmony of all.[61]

This amplifies what he has already told Egmont, that the people are like children and that one needs to treat them as such. Egmont, as Reinhardt argues, is not free from viewing the people as "unmündig" [immature], but the picture is a complex one. They are in some ways not yet of age politically, although, with historical hindsight, they were on the verge of it.[62] The cry of the people in act II suggests that they still rely on their rulers who take care of their best interests.[63] And later, after the citizens learn that the regent is departed and Orange has fled, they feel helpless and rely completely on Egmont. In act V, after they learn that Egmont is imprisoned, they are impotent (as Vansen predicts).[64] Thus Clärchen's courageous call for the citizens to arm themselves in order to oppose Madrid's tyranny falls on intimidated and unreceptive ears.[65] On the other hand, Egmont tells Alba that the people tolerate the Dutch aristocracy's privileges, implying that they are used to it, but at the same time acknowledging that this is not a just circumstance.[66] Egmont realises he has the people's trust not only because he cares for them and has fought for them, but also because of their "guter Wille" [good will].[67] Inherent in this relationship is an implicit social contract, akin to Rousseau's *Le Contrat social* (The Social Contract, 1762).

The difference of perception regarding the people's maturity is a matter of degree between Egmont and Alba, the difference between pressing, as a rider might press a horse with his knees, and oppressing; between a respect for the Netherlanders as an individual people and seeing them as Alba does, as "Tiere und Ungeheuer" [animals and monsters].[68] In Egmont's opinion the King has ignored this difference:

> So hat er denn beschlossen was kein Fürst beschließen sollte! Die Kraft seines Volks, ihr Gemüt, den Begriff den sie von sich selbst haben, will er schwächen, niederdrücken, zerstören, um sie bequem regieren zu können. Er will den innern Kern ihrer Eigenheit verderben, gewiß in der Absicht sie glücklicher zu machen. Er will sie vernichten damit sie Etwas werden, ein ander Etwas.[69]

> [So he has decided what no prince ought to decide. In order to rule more comfortably, he wants to weaken, oppress, destroy the strength of his people, the conception they have of themselves. He wants to corrupt the very core of their individuality, surely with the intention to make them happier. He wants to destroy them so that they will become something, a different something.]

The major difference in their claims (certainly Alba's actions undermine some of his more principled claims) is their conception of a people's right to be itself. Egmont does not question the king's right to rule, neither does he dispute that Catholicism should remain the official religion of the land. He wishes that the king would respect the Dutch constitution and the distinctiveness of the Dutch people, something more fundamental and permanent than the historically recent occurrence of new beliefs. Egmont's argument and his use of the idea of "Eigenheit" [individuality] ring with Herderian historicism.[70]

Furthermore, he asks that the king proclaim a general pardon for the iconoclasts and thus secure the people's loyalty, love, and trust. His plea is that an ounce of tolerance is worth a pound of repressive measures. But Madrid will not sanction the Dutch claim to historical and cultural uniqueness, nor will it suffer religious deviance. Alba rejects flatly Egmont's request, claiming that it would set a poor precedent. Of course, Alba's repressive measures have gone far beyond punishing the unruly, thus undermining his argument, and he does not address the substance of Egmont's idea: how to secure the people's confidence. Egmont appeals finally to something that he believes will get Alba's attention, the economic issue, for he predicts that the wealthy will flee the country. Alba's answer is to prevent them from leaving.[71]

Egmont now makes his case boldly, but he protects himself by implicitly calling upon King Philip to assume a King Solomon-like role and hear all sides of the argument. He relates to Alba that some suspect the religious issue is merely a smoke screen behind which all of their freedoms are being crushed. Egmont summarises the two major issues that vex the Netherlanders, their double yoke: they fear cultural assimilation through total Spanish political domination, as well as enforced religious conformity.[72] He has put forth propositions and argued his case for limited tolerance, but he knows he has been unsuccessful; in Enlightenment manner he looks forward optimistically to another moment, another conversation, in a more public forum with his peers, the other rulers. He places his hope in open discussion — but he has been deceived and trapped.[73]

History affords modern readers the benefit of knowing that the Dutch Revolt was successful and act V of *Egmont* does not leave even an uninformed reader in doubt of the outcome. A "Victory Symphony" concludes the work and Clärchen appears in a dream sequence as the symbol of freedom.[74] All of these promise allegorically a vindication of Egmont. The ample stage directions give a theatre director enough licence to create a visually spectacular finale, as Schiller implied.[75] But where does this get us? The play is not an actual history of the Dutch Revolt, although historical texts informed Goethe. And what of Goethe's oft-quoted words about the daemonic in *Egmont*? Has he brought us this far only to tell us that we are impelled by fate to our destinies — certainly Egmont appears to ride comfortably, even defiantly, in Destiny's chariot.[76]

But something occurs before the triumphant vision of the finale that motivates Egmont, who faces execution, to declare that he is free from worry, pain, and fear.[77] While his vision of freedom confirms to him that his sacrifice will not have been in vain, something has calmed and perhaps even prepared him to receive the vision. Discovering this provides an integral continuity to the drama and redeems an otherwise failed instance of intercultural understanding.

The final act opens ominously with the stage description that it is now dusk.[78] Egmont is in prison. His hope flickers much like the lamp must next to his prison bed. Sleep, his old friend, has fled him; he tries vainly to fight off care and he feels utterly alone and abandoned. He doubts himself. He is stunned that the king has tacitly approved his incarceration; he recalls his friendship with the regent, who has nevertheless abandoned the provinces. He imagines vainly that Orange, who has saved himself, might be coming to his rescue at the head of an army of people to whom Egmont has urged restraint with the words, "Reizt den König nicht mehr" [Don't provoke the king any longer] and the injunction to be "ordentliche Bürger" [orderly citizens].[79] He imagines that thousands of prayers are being sent heavenward, petitioning for a miracle, even an angel to come to his rescue, despite the fact that religion has not played an overt role in his life. He thinks of Clärchen, but in the grammatical subjunctive "wärst du Mann" [if you were a man], signifying the wishful nature of all of these thoughts.[80] Later, he — a man who believes in open discussion and in his right to a judgement by a jury of peers — must listen helplessly to his death sentence on trumped up charges of high treason, and hear the apparent annulment of his rights as a member of the Order of the Golden Fleece.[81]

Egmont is disconcerted because he believes in a hitherto secure world, as he explained to Clärchen, who admires his chain and pendant that signify membership in the Order of the Golden Fleece: "Und Kette und Zeichen geben dem der sie trägt die edelsten Freiheiten" [And the chain and sign grant the bearer the noblest freedoms].[82] Similarly, he asked the rioting citizens to identify themselves according to their professions.[83] He has learned to trust that people are as they say they are. Hence he cannot discern the political patterns that Oliva and Orange do, and is completely taken in by Alba's deception.

Ferdinand and Egmont

It is at this moment of deepest despair that Egmont perceives that Ferdinand, Alba's natural son, has been observing him. If length is any indication of importance, then the conversation between Egmont and Ferdinand is more important than most of the other long dialogues in the drama. Yet it differs in content from the other lengthy dialogues, such as those between the regent and Machiavell, or Egmont and Orange, or Alba and Egmont. One reason for this is that much of the dramatic tension is resolved by this time. The regent is gone, Orange escaped, and Alba's trap has been sprung successfully. The citizens are paralysed and Egmont's beloved Clärchen has taken her life in desperation. Even Egmont's fleeting hopes that perhaps his judgement is merely a humiliating threat or that Ferdinand might assist him in an escape attempt are not given the stage time to gestate into dramatic tension, for they are quickly dashed as Ferdinand informs Egmont that his condemnation is real and there is no escape from the well-guarded prison.[84] What then is the purpose of this final dialogue?

Ferdinand confesses that he has been an ignorant and unwilling participant in Egmont's demise. This surely helps to regain Egmont's trust, and he hears something else in the young man's admission: "Welche sonderbare Stimme welch ein unerwarteter Trost begegnet mir auf dem Weg zum Grabe" [What strange voice, what an unexpected comfort meets me on my way to the grave].[85] This voice is evident in *Iphigenie auf Tauris* as "die Stimme der Wahrheit und der Menschlichkeit" [the voice of truth and humanity].[86] Ferdinand attempts to explain himself, but he is overcome with emotion and cries that Egmont does not understand him. Words fail Ferdinand, therefore the stage directions indicate gestures — he embraces Egmont. The count then asks him a crucial question: "Wie bewegt dich so tief das Schicksal eines fremden Mannes?" [How is it that the fate of a foreign man moves you so deeply?][87] The idea of foreignness is crucial to the play. The foreign teachers of religion (French and German) are seen as doubly foreign by the Spanish and Dutch Catholics; Spanish rule is foreign to the Netherlanders, and Egmont petitions Alba to at least attempt to respect Dutch cultural difference. In act V the international macrocosm is concentrated in the microcosm of the relationship between Egmont and Ferdinand.

Ferdinand first replies to Egmont that he is "Nicht fremd! Du bist mir nicht fremd" [No foreigner. You are no foreigner to me].[88] He had learned about Egmont prior to their first meeting. This is in a sense what Egmont has suggested to Alba, that the Spanish take the time to gain an understanding of Dutch needs. It also harks back to Machiavell's suggestion to the regent that the Spanish come to the Netherlands with an attitude of sympathy and understanding. Egmont's qualities as a mature and sensitive man now reveal themselves. Although he faces execution, he nevertheless comforts Ferdinand:

> Junger Freund . . . du verlierst mich nicht. . . . Die Menschen sind nicht nur zusammen, wenn sie beisammen sind, auch der Entfernte, der Abgeschiedne lebt uns. Ich lebe dir, und habe mir genug gelebt. Eines jeden Tages hab ich mich gefreut, an jedem Tage mit rascher Würkung meine Pflicht getan wie mein Gewissen mir sie zeigte. . . . so leb auch du mein Freund gern und mit Lust.[89]

> [Young friend . . . you do not lose me. . . . People are not only together when they are with each other; even the most distant, the departed lives in us. I live for you and have lived long enough for myself. Each day I was happy to have done my duty that day with swift effectiveness, as my conscience showed me. . . . so live too, my friend, gladly and with joy.]

The embrace, the transformation of *Fremder* into *Freund*, represents what Spanish-Dutch relations might have been. Martin Swales suggests that in this scene Egmont is reborn, that the "ideal image of human freedom" emerges "from the husk of the actual man."[90] Not only do Egmont's words stress human interconnectedness, they identify his ethical framework, duty and conscience. His words incorporate an ethical model that reveals itself to be one of living and letting live, for in citing one's conscience as the measure of duty one cannot disallow others that same measure. And this is precisely Margarete of Parma's difficulty, why she is so sympathetic to the Netherlanders and to the readers, for she is doing her duty as a faithful Catholic regent, according to her conscience, even when it has run contrary to the crown's demands.[91] Conscience can induce a reflective pause that mitigates the instant judgements of prejudice. This scene also highlights an irony, as T. J. Reed remarks: "if Alva and his commitment to atrocity are beyond Goethe's power to humanize, the appearance in the last act of Alva's son, who suffers and grieves for the Egmont he has always admired, is a chink in the armour of the father's inhumanity."[92]

The vision of freedom reassures Egmont that his blood and that of others will not have been spilt in vain and redeems the historical moment. But it is the understanding between Egmont and Ferdinand that preserves the flame of future peaceful co-existence, despite the failure of intercultural relations in the drama's main plot. Their friendship vindicates Egmont's faith in humanity and serves as a symbol of the possibility of a universal brotherhood.

Eckermann reports that Goethe was fascinated that, ten years after he had finished writing *Egmont*, history repeated itself: the revolt of the Netherlands under the Austrian Hapsburg rule of Joseph II occurred. Goethe later commented in relation to *Egmont*: "Und wozu wären denn die Poeten, wenn sie bloß die Geschichte eines Historikers wiederholen wollten! Der Dichter muß weiter gehen und uns wo möglich etwas Höheres und Besseres geben" [And why would there be poets if they only wanted to repeat the history of a historian! The poet must go further and where possible give us something higher and better].[93] *Egmont* is Goethe's fruitful anachronism: he utilises sixteenth-century history in order to address eighteenth-century concerns. The interplay of history, literature, and religion in *Egmont* throws into vivid relief the ethics of the Enlightenment.

Notes

[1] Peter Limm, *The Dutch Revolt 1559–1648* (London: Longman, 1997), 122–23. Cf. Gerhard Güldner, *Das Toleranz-Problem in den Niederlanden im Ausgang des 16. Jahrhunderts,* Historische Studien 403 (Lübeck: Matthiesen, 1968).

[2] Cf. Malcolm R. Thorp and Arthur J. Slavin, editors, *Politics, Religion and Diplomacy in Early Modern Europe: Essays in Honor of De Lamar Jensen,* Sixteenth Century Essays and Studies 27 (Kirksville, MO: Northeast Missouri State University, 1994).

[3] FA 5, Borchmeyer and Huber, 1246–247. Cf. DuW IV/20: FA 14, 840.

[4] Georg-Michael Schulz, "Egmont," in *Goethe-Handbuch,* ed. by Bernd Witte et al., 4 vols. (Stuttgart: Metzler, 1996–1998), vol. 2: *Dramen,* ed. by Theo Buck (1996), 154–72, (158).

[5] Benjamin Bennett, *Modern Drama and German Classicism: Renaissance from Lessing to Brecht* (Ithaca: Cornell UP, 1986), 122–23.

[6] Martin Swales, "A Questionable Politician: A Discussion of the Ending of Goethe's 'Egmont,'" *Modern Language Review* 66 (1971): 832–40, (834).

[7] Hans Reiss, "Goethe, Möser and the Aufklärung: The Holy Roman Empire in 'Götz von Berlichingen' and 'Egmont,'" *Deutsche Vierteljahresschrift für Literatrurwissenschaft und Geistesgeschichte* 60 (1986): 609–44, (636). Goethe read Möser's *Patriotische Phantasien* (1774–1778) and Herder published a part of his *Osnabrückische Geschichte* (1768) in *Von deutscher Art und Kunst* (1773).

[8] Emil Staiger, *Goethe*, 4th ed., 3 vols. (Zurich: Atlantis, 1952–1959), vol. 1: *1749–1786*, 296.

[9] T. J. Reed, "Talking To Tyrants: Dialogues with Power in Eighteenth-Century Germany," *The Historical Journal* 33 (1990): 63–79.

[10] *Besserem Verständnis* ("Nachtrag"; Supplement): FA 3/1, 208.

[11] I "Armbrustschießen": FA 5, 465–66.

[12] John Calvin (1509–1564) commissioned the French poet Clément Marot (1496–1544) to compose new hymns; church bodies later decreed them to be heretical.

[13] I "Palast der Regentin": FA 5, 468.

[14] I "Palast der Regentin": FA 5, 468–69.

[15] I "Palast der Regentin": FA 5, 469.

[16] Currie, *Literature as Social Action*, 47–48.

[17] As quoted in James MacGregor Burns et al., *Government by the People*, 16th ed. (Englewood Cliffs, New Jersey: Prentice Hall, 1995), insert of The Constitution of the United States of America.

[18] I "Palast der Regentin": FA 5, 470.

[19] Ibid.

[20] I "Palast der Regentin": FA 5, 470.

[21] III "Palast der Regentin": FA 5, 501.

[22] I "Palast der Regentin": FA 5, 474.

[23] I "Palast der Regentin": FA 5, 470.

[24] II "Platz in Brüssel": FA 5, 481.

[25] Reiss, "Goethe, Möser and the Aufklärung," 636.

[26] Limm, *The Dutch Revolt 1559–1648*, 119. Goethe casts the King as one who interprets politically and ecclesiastically the Pauline conception: "That there should be no schism in the body" (1 Corinthians 12: 25).

[27] I "Palast der Regentin": FA 5, 474. Cf. Schulz, "Egmont," 153. Margarete seeks and apparently receives some assurances from Egmont (and possibly Orange) that they will assist her.

[28] Berlin, *The Crooked Timber of Humanity*, 208.

[29] I "Palast der Regentin": FA 5, 471.

[30] Ibid.

[31] II "Platz in Brüssel": FA 5, 473.

[32] I "Palast der Regentin": FA 5, 471.

[33] I "Palast der Regentin": FA 5, 481; and II "Platz in Brüssel": 487.

[34] I "Palast der Regentin": FA 5, 482. The carpenter and soap boiler, who both oppose the religious unrest and later the revolutionary words of Vansen, remain unnamed throughout the play.

[35] II "Platz in Brüssel": FA 5, 482–85. Cf. "The new 'legal experts' called on the prince not only to head a new kind of state but to involve all sections of society in common activity for the good of that state" (Currie, *Literature as Social Action*, 49).

[36] II "Platz in Brüssel": FA 5, 485.

[37] II "Platz in Brüssel": FA 5, 482–85.

[38] "The Relation of Form and Meaning in Egmont," in *Goethe: Poet and Thinker* (London: Arnold, 1962), 55–74 (67), first published in *Publications of the English Goethe Society*, 18 (1949): 149–82.

[39] II "Platz in Brüssel": FA 5, 486.

[40] I "Armbrustschießen": FA 5, 467.

[41] II "Platz in Brüssel": FA 5, 486–87.

[42] Staiger, *Goethe*, 295.

[43] II "Egmonts Wohnung": FA 5, 489.

[44] IV "Strasse": FA 5, 515.

[45] II "Egmonts Wohnung": FA 5, 490.

[46] I "Armbrustschießen": FA 5, 463 and II "Egmonts Wohnung": FA 5, 491–92.

[47] Kant, *Was ist Aufklärung?*, 53.

[48] I "Palast der Regentin": FA 5, 472; II "Egmonts Wohnung": FA 5, 492–93. Kant writes that it is only "durch einigemal Fallen," that is through falling a few times, that one learns to walk, meaning think (*Was ist Aufklärung?*, 54).

[49] IV "Culenburgischer Palast": FA 5, 521.

[50] II "Egmonts Wohnung": FA 5, 499.

[51] IV "Strasse": FA 5, 511 and IV "Culenburgischer Palast": FA 5, 518, Kant writes that a human is "Mehr als Maschine" [more than a machine] and needs to be treated according to "seiner Würde" [his worth] (*Was ist Aufklärung?*, 61). Thus, Jetter's description of the Spanish soldiers as machines is a particularly incisive critique from an Enlightenment perspective.

[52] IV "Culenburgischer Palast": FA 5, 518 and 529. The planned capture is likened by Silva to a "Sonnenfinsternis" [eclipse]. This can be understood as the blotting out of an Enlightenment metaphor, the sun (517).

[53] V "Gefängnis": FA 5, 550–51.

[54] III "Palast der Regentin": FA 5, 502 and IV "Strasse": FA 5, 510.

[55] III "Palast der Regentin": FA 5, 503.

[56] I "Armbrustschießen": FA 5, 464. Not only are the people singing about Egmont in the streets, but Clärchen reads a description in a history of the battle and discovers his role (I "Bürgerhaus": FA 5, 478).

[57] I "Bürgerhaus": FA 5, 476 and IV "Culenburgischer Palast": FA 5, 518–19 and 528.

[58] IV "Culenburgischer Palast": FA 5, 521.

[59] IV "Culenburgischer Palast": FA 5, 525 and 527.

[60] IV "Culenburgischer Palast": FA 5, 526–27.

[61] Ibid. Joseph II argued similarly about the Austrian Netherlands (Reiss, "Goethe, Möser and the Aufklärung," 632–33).

[62] IV "Culenburgischer Palast": FA 5, 525; Hartmut Reinhardt, "Egmont" in *Goethes Dramen: Neue Interpretationen,* ed. by Walter Hinderer (Stuttgart: Reclam, 1980), 122–43, (133).

[63] I "Platz in Brüssel": FA 5, 485.

[64] IV "Strasse": FA 5, 512–13.

[65] V "Strasse": FA 5, 530–31.

[66] IV "Culenburgischer Palast": FA 5, 527.

[67] III "Clärchens Wohnung": FA 5, 507.

[68] III "Palast der Regentin": FA 5, 503.

[69] IV "Culenburgischer Palast": FA 5, 527–28.

[70] Egmont expresses that the "peculiarity" of the Dutch is essential to their character. In this respect, Goethe comes close to Herder's position of "Eigenheit." Cf. *Auch eine Philosophie der Geschichte,* in: Johann Gottfried Herder, *Werke,* 10 vols, ed. by Günter Arnold and others (Frankfurt am Main:

Deutscher Klassiker Verlag, 1985–2000), 4: *Schriften zu Philosophie, Litera-tur, Kunst und Altertum 1774–1787,* ed. by Jürgen Brummack and Martin Bollacher (1994), 9–108 (32–35).

[71] IV "Culenburgischer Palast": FA 5, 523–24. In 1570 a large group of Dutch traders fled to Germany (Emden). Egmont implores Orange to con-sider the economic devastation that war would bring to the Netherlands (II "Egmonts Wohnung": FA 5, 498). He also believes that the citizens have a right to defend their belongings: "Schützt eure Güter!" [Protect your posses-sions!] (V "Gefängnis": FA 5, 551).

[72] IV "Culenburgischer Palast": FA 5, 524–55. These could be compared to the "Joch der Unmündigkeit" [Yoke of immaturity] to which Kant refers (*Was ist Aufklärung?*, 54).

[73] IV "Culenburgischer Palast": FA 5, 529.

[74] V "Gefängnis" (b): FA 5, 549–51.

[75] "Salto mortale in eine Opernwelt" in "Über Egmont: Trauerspiel von Goethe," in Friedrich Schiller, *Sämtliche Werke,* ed by Helmut Koopman, 5 vols. (Munich: Winkler, 1968), vol. 5: *Philosophische Schriften und Vermischte Schriften,* 637–46, (646).

[76] V "Gefängnis" (b): FA 5, 548 and II "Egmonts Wohung": FA 5, 491; Cf. DuW IV/20: FA 14, 841–52.

[77] V "Gefängnis" (b): FA 5, 549.

[78] V "Strasse": FA 5, 530.

[79] II "Platz in Brüssel": FA 5, 487.

[80] V "Gefängnis" (a): FA 5, 534–36.

[81] II "Egmonts Wohnung": FA 5, 496 and V "Gefängnis": FA 5, 542.

[82] III "Clärchens Wohnung": FA 5, 507.

[83] II "Platz in Brüssel": FA 5, 486.

[84] V "Gefängnis" (b): FA 5, 543.

[85] V "Gefängnis" (b): FA 5, 544. Ferdinand reveals that he has pleaded for Egmont's life (546). Schings points out that with Ferdinand's help, Egmont is able to withstand this crisis and regain his "Lebensgefühl" [feeling for life]. Hans-Jürgen Schings, "Freiheit in der Geschichte: Egmont und Marquis Posa im Vergleich," *Goethe Jahrbuch* 110 (1993): 61–76, (75).

[86] V, iv, lines 1937–938.

[87] V "Gefängnis" (b): FA 5, 545. Similarly, Iphigenie asks Thoas to sympa-thise with a foreign family.

[88] V "Gefängnis" (b): FA 5, 545.

[89] V "Gefängnis" (b): FA 5, 547.

[90] Swales, "A Questionable Politician," 840.

[91] I "Palast der Regentin": FA 5, 468.

[92] Reed, "Talking to Tyrants," 79.

[93] *Gespräche mit Goethe*: 10 January 1825: FA 39, 134 and 31 January 1827: FA 39, 226.

4: Healing the Wounds of War: The *Sankt-Rochus-Fest zu Bingen*

THE NAPOLEONIC WARS reshaped Germany, not least the French-occupied Rhine region.[1] The influence of the Catholic Church was curtailed even further after the Congress of Vienna. As Eda Sagarra has summarised,

> Only three territorial rulers survived: the Archbishop of Mainz, now however virtually landless, the Grand Master of the Teutonic Order, and the Master of the Knights of St. John. In 1815, at the end of the Congress of Vienna, there was no Catholic German state; even Bavaria was partly Lutheran, through its acquisition of Franconia and Bayreuth-Ansbach; the Catholic Rhineland had been given to Prussia, while the many Catholic principalities and abbeys in and near its territory had gone to Württemberg.[2]

Goethe had put off visiting the Rhineland due to the uncertainty of the Napoleonic Wars, although he hailed from nearby Frankfurt, but decided finally in 1814 to make the journey. His *Sankt-Rochus-Fest zu Bingen* (Saint Roch Festival at Bingen) is often classified as an autobiographical piece, but it was first published in his journal *Ueber Kunst und Alterthum in den Rhein- und Mayn-Gegenden* I/2 (On Art and Antiquity in the Rhine and Main Regions, 1817). The piece is a literary tour de force; Emil Staiger even makes the astounding (and perhaps overstated) claim that if all of German prose were to become lost, it could be restored through the *Sankt-Rochus-Fest zu Bingen*.[3]

The essay describes a two-day excursion through the Rhine Gorge that Goethe undertook in the company of friends in 1814. On one level it provides a historical snapshot of the war-rent region and gives a rare glimpse of Goethe's social and political reflections as he observed how the Germans along the Rhine were attempting to regenerate their lives. An editorial in the first edition of *Ueber Kunst und Alterthum* (I/1, 1816) voices gladness about the return of library holdings that had been taken from the Vatican to Paris by Napoleon to their original library in Heidelberg thanks to the good offices of the Austrian Kaiser, the Prussian King, and the Pope.[4] There are other signs of regeneration. Goethe stumbles onto the rededication of the Saint Roch chapel.

The ruined chapel may have come to his attention through a child correspondent, Bettine Brentano, who had described it to him in a letter dated 20 June 1808.[5] The sacred edifice had been desecrated and plundered by the occupying French military forces, who also forbade its use and turned the strategically situated chapel into a stall for horses; eventually it was devastated by fire. Saint Roch lay in ruin for nearly twenty years, and only the most tenacious and courageous undertook pilgrimages there. Goethe's account of its restoration is a meaningful contribution to the social history of the religious and political communities on the Rhine.[6] Later, rebuilding churches became a tool of Prussian policy for improving relations in their newly acquired Rhine territories. In 1837 when the Prussian authorities clashed with Rhenish Catholics, Friedrich Wilhelm IV organised interdenominational contributions to complete the Cologne cathedral.[7]

Goethe uses the rebuilding of the destroyed chapel as a metaphor for the healing of the region, and his essay is itself an act of recovery and creation. As an immediate post-occupation piece, the *Sankt-Rochus-Fest zu Bingen* serves as a surprising counterweight to religious nationalism; Napoleon and the French military are never mentioned directly and Goethe's tone is not vindictive, only saddened over the misery caused by the war.

Goethe's journal entry for 15 August 1814 lends force to his claim that the decision to explore the Rhine valley was a spontaneous one: after bathing at the Wiesbaden spa, the idea suddenly came to him.[8] He and his two friends leave the recuperative amenities of the spa and set off. The brightest point of light on the horizon is the secularised Johannisberg monastery.[9] The themes of journeying and exploration, which heighten the reader's expectation of encounter, are immediately set in motion as the friends ride off into the sun, a typical Enlightenment emblem, auguring the further light and knowledge ahead.

Goethe introduces the bellwether word, "fromm," employed not less than fifteen times in the text, with nuances of meaning that range from meekness to uprightness. Polysemy plays an important part in the essay, especially with such words as *erbauen, erquicken, schirmen,* and *Wiederherstellung.* His party discover that they are in "ein frommes Land" [a pious land] as the trio meet an Italian man carrying colourful Catholic figurines, including one of Saint Roch, who is thus foreshadowed. Although he does not identify with the images, Goethe contrasts them to northern ones he has seen before and by so doing assumes a comparative position. This allows a religion to define itself ideally, on its own terms. Goethe outlines the believer's hierarchy of these icons by observing that the Mother of God reigns over the "Nothelfer" [Helpers in need or auxiliary Saints].[10] A subtle and generous artistic-anthropological assessment occurs, as he is able to convey aesthetically a Catholic's hierarchical reverence for the Holy Virgin. That Goethe does not share this awe is clear; it is, however, the worshipper's taxonomy that matters.

The trio travel through the Rhine Gorge and enter a land of promise. The fecundity of nature, the fruitful abundance and fertility of the region are everywhere in evidence as the companions pass cornfields, fruit and nut trees, lush meadows, and rolling hills brimming with vineyards.[11] A biblical image of the Passover is inverted as the narrator observes that the "Einquartierungskreide" — the chalk marks left on the doors of homes where the French were billeted — has not yet faded.[12] While this area represents the promised land for the journeying friends, it has been the place of servitude for the local inhabitants, as the meaning of the Israelites' marked doors is transformed from bypassing to one of bondage.

Goethe next comments on that most banal of topics, the weather. The inclusion of a weather report is by no means unexpected, as it features prominently in many of his travel pieces,[13] and his dry and cumulus-droll observation about the heat of the day and the dust eventually breaks nimbus-like over several planes of narrative. For the initial report of aridity sets up a sharp contrast with his final weather report of refreshing rain at the festival's conclusion.

This process of drought followed by rain symbolises the socio-political context of this wounded region. The "Wiederherstellung" [restoration] of the Saint Roch chapel stands not only for the literal restoration of personal life, as enemy troops no longer command the area; it is the catalyst to the restoration of Rhine valley community life, disrupted by the long war. Restoration is a powerful motif, linguistically as well as metaphorically linked to the community's physical and spiritual needs. Just as the coming rain "erquickt" [refreshes] the natural environment, so will the restoration of the chapel refresh the economic and socio-cultural environments through the restored "Wechselverkehr" [trade] between the Rhine communities.[14]

The restoration of the chapel and what it means to the believer, like the restorative rain, will renew, cleanse, and help heal individuals and communities. Goethe identifies the tradition of pilgrimages to Saint Roch as a religious need and social outlet: the spiritual drought is assuaged as believers are able to practise their religion in freedom and as friends are restored to each other. This is a cause for great rejoicing, as the travellers learn upon meeting residents from neighbouring towns who express their elation at the imminent festival. Enlightenment exactness does not preclude respect or even sympathy for the religious faith of others. Rather than superimpose personal standards on the Catholic perspective, the explorers warmly accept the invitation to see things from another point of view. For when some of the local residents assume that the friends have visited at this particular time to take part in the rededication of the Saint Roch chapel, the trio avail themselves of the opportunity to join in. They will cross the Rhine and scale the steep hill in order to inhabit the Catholic coign of vantage by observing this slice of religious life and perchance glimpsing the world from the perspective of the pilgrim.

Goethe performs the role of an anthropological chronicler. He does not presume to render transparent or fathom fully the faith of the believer by attempting to locate an Archimedean point. Rather than theorise Goethe, with not a little physical exertion as he admits, joins hundreds of pilgrims pressing up the hill. Moreover, he has already confessed metaphorically that he is having problems with his vision: the blinding sun and bothersome dust impair his sight.[15] Only after Goethe participates to an extent with the pilgrims do the air-cleansing rains fall, which remove the dust that has clouded both observer and observed, signifying clearer understanding all round. This is the experiential hermeneutics of Dilthey with a twist. The narrator does not attempt to render transparent the believer's perspective, and later in the essay he removes himself from participation in ritual, the most intimate practice of religion, by not joining in the Mass. Goethe's anthropological approach has shown itself earlier in *Das Römische Karneval* (The Roman Carnival, 1789), in which he captures the enlivening spirit of another festival.[16]

As dusk falls and the friends survey the landmarks of their travels from the walls of a castle ruin, they look wistfully at the secularised Johannisberg monastery, set beautifully amidst hillside vineyards. This edifice defines paradigmatically Goethe's cultural mapping of the region as a sacred-secular blend within nature. And with the onset of twilight, he perceives wistfully the totality of the topography: "In Dämmerung versank nach und nach die Gegend. Auch das Verschwinden so vieler bedeutender Einzelheiten ließ uns erst recht Wert und Würde des Ganzen fühlen, worin wir uns lieber verloren hätten; aber es mußte geschieden sein"[17] [The disappearance of so many important individual objects allowed us only then to feel the value and worth of the whole, in which we would have liked to have lost ourselves; but we had

to depart]. Although Goethe feels the pull to merge romantically subject and object, he is able to divorce himself from the scene and interpret important individualities, like the socio-political or cultural-
religious artifacts of the area, within their discursive settings. This scene
shows the operation of Goethe's hermeneutics as a mediation between
eighteenth-century rationality and sensibility, a movement hinted at in
one of his epigrams: "Willst du in's Unendliche schreiten, / Geh nur
im Endlichen nach allen Seiten" [Would you stride into infinity? Just
explore finite things in all directions].[18]

The shape of Goethe's hermeneutics may be the spiral, as suggested
in a botanical essay positing the spiral tendency as a basic law of life.[19]
The spiral shape captures the effect of looping back to a recognisable
yet different position, thereby allowing the interpretation of events,
objects, and experiences from a different, yet recognisable perspective.
It is, then, not unexpected that the words "Unser Rückweg" [our way
back] begin the next scene in Goethe's essay. He and his friends progress only by recovering ground they have already traversed, and it is
precisely this recovery that further opens up the narrative to Goethe's
hermeneutics. They realise that they have actually seen the Saint Roch
chapel at different points on their journey, yet they did not recognise it
as such, and only upon recollecting their steps and seeing from the
same points again can they reform their composite vision of the chapel.
In other words, they remember the scene and put together again the
panoramic context in which the holy house originally appeared as a
white point, but now discloses itself as a chapel. Still, this idealistic
translation gives way to momentary yet real transformation, as the narrator notes that the Catholic faithful credit Saint Roch with restoring
the one-time military station into a place of peace and reconciliation.[20]
The shifting perspective reveals multiple images of Saint Roch: white
point, chapel, symbol of peace and reconciliation. The perspective of
the reader is not only subjective, incarcerated by its own myopic perceptions, it is also objective, emancipated by an infinitely diverse number of objects and perspectives that demand constant re-evaluation of
opinion and compel openness.

After the friends stay overnight in the guest house Adler, at the earliest opportunity the next morning (Goethe calls it a "pure sunrise")
they visit a collection of minerals from the region's woods and mines.[21]
They do this before joining the pilgrims for the day, and they are
stimulated by a passion to study nature, revealing Goethe's predilection
for geography over hagiography. Upon completing their visit and being
joined by the owner of the mineralogical collection, Goethe mentions

that the scientific excursion could have spoiled their day, for the pilgrimage has already begun. Masses of pilgrims are flocking onto boats that are ferrying them across the Rhine to the far shore so they may ascend the hill to the Saint Roch chapel, which is over 140 meters above Bingen.[22]

After ferrying across the river, the party disembarks and Goethe's naturalist instincts again take over, as his fondness for geology leads him to examine the curious rocks at the base of the hill. He adds: "Der Naturforscher wird von dem heiligen Pfade zurückgehalten" [The naturalist is held back from the holy path].[23] At the hill's foot lay the true wonder for Goethe, in contrast with yet also allusive to the miracles and signs associated with Saint Roch at the crown of the hill.[24] With scrutinising enthusiasm and a hammer he gets to work, excavating the hill's contents for the reader, even making suggestions for further mineralogical study. Impatient with Moses' delayed descent from the mount (and not too quick to follow in his footsteps) Goethe attempts to create his own subtext by hammering away at the hill itself, symbolically and literally undermining the mighty revelations occurring above. Yet, for the present at least, the prophet carries the day, as nature rebels against the zealous explorer, releasing only a few crumbs: "Ungeheure Festigkeit hindert uns, mehr als kleine Bröckchen zu gewinnen" [Unbelievable hardness prevented us from winning more than a few small bits].[25]

The friends, in good humour, rejoin the thronging pilgrims ascending the hill. This prompts a narrative allusion to the Pinax of Cebes, an allegory of life that has been rendered as a mass journey up a mountain in which many get sidetracked on paths that do not lead upward and only a few succeed in reaching the top. Goethe wryly adds that on this hill there are not so many misleading byways.[26]

As the foursome forge on and reach the hill's crest, they push with the pilgrims into the Saint Roch chapel. Once inside, Goethe's trained artistic eyes seize upon the sacral objects, cataloguing them for the reader and describing the affection and veneration shown by the pilgrims for holy relics.[27] Soon the reader learns that this artistic listing is not merely an aesthetic table of contents, but represents the pieces of a puzzle, for Goethe discovers an intriguing paradox. He knows that the holy edifice was ransacked and that the inside is new, yet the chapel's contents are beautiful, well-preserved older pieces. And he asks how this is so in a recently destroyed church.[28]

He learns that the Protestant citizens of Eibingen, the community on the other side of the Rhine, had for a nominal cost donated the contents of a former monastery — prayer and confession chairs, altars, an organ, and even the pulpit — to the Catholic parish of Bingen for the restoration of the Saint Roch chapel. This interdenominational generosity so inspired the Catholic inhabitants of Bingen that they vowed to haul the donated items across the Rhine. Goethe paints a colourful picture of the impressive sight that these pilgrims made in transporting the magnificent furnishings on their backs across the Rhine and up the steep hill to the Saint Roch chapel. Perhaps inspired by this event, Goethe would visit Eibingen himself in the following weeks. He is impressed with those who took the vow and the practical and long-lasting results achieved, "daß jeder, unter seiner Last und bei seiner Bemühung, Segen und Erbauung sein ganzes Leben hoffen durfte" [that each, under his burden and with his efforts, could hope for blessing and edification for his entire life].[29]

Goethe highlights another charitable act of interconfessional sensitivity as he adds that the remains of Saint Ruprecht, also at Eibingen and not included in the nominal sale of ecclesiastical furnishings, were generously and freely offered by the Protestants as a "fromme Zugabe" [pious addition] to their Catholic neighbours. He then exclaims: "Möchte man doch überall, in ähnlichen Fällen, mit gleicher Schonung verfahren sein!" [Would that people had always acted with the same consideration in similar cases!][30] He stresses not only the blessing for the believer as a result of this respectful treatment of each faith by the other, but the edification that all present at the rededication of the chapel — Catholic or not, religiously inclined or not — could enjoy because of the mildness and good will shown by the neighbouring Rhine communities to each other. The Saint Roch chapel restoration serves more than one purpose — Goethe plays on the word "erbauen" — for as the holy edifice was built up, so too were all who helped edified. It is a monument to international peace and interdenominational tolerance, commemorating the mutual good will and cooperation that contribute to the healing and unity of the war-torn communities on both sides of the Rhine, and as such is a hope-filled model for the future. This is accentuated symbolically by the changed location of an altar, for by being passed from one community to another, it has bound them together.[31]

Observing the diversity, activity, and vitality of the religious assembly, Goethe no longer stands outside the stream of life as an onlooker only. He blends his dual anthropological role of observer and participant and allows himself to be drawn into the festival life of the pilgrims. Although most are celebrating, Goethe notices that some of the young people who were born during the grim Napoleonic occupation appear indifferent. And when the main procession from Bingen is disrupted for a moment by a bizarre badger-chase, the idyllic scene is temporarily threatened as the animal is hunted and he reminds the reader that the human capacity for kindness can be matched by a capacity for cruelty.[32]

The friends soon find themselves enjoying a sort of secular sacrament of fresh bread and freely flowing Rhine wine, typifying the coming Catholic Mass. In a microcosm of the festival's neighbourly spirit, the narrator praises, in *pax vobiscum* fashion, the friendly people, pleasant company, and charming society that he discovers when everyone at a particularly crowded table makes room so that he and his friends may sit and partake.[33] A socio-political dimension can be read into this scene as Goethe stresses one of the great advantages of a "Volksversammlung" [gathering of the people], namely, that important knowledge may be shared rapidly.[34]

Socio-political allegory ferments into humorous political satire on German regionalism as the locals begin squabbling sourly over the relative merits of lesser-known Rhine wines. Goethe observes smugly that the well-established wines such as Hochheimer, Johannisberger, and Rüdesheimer do not envy each other as do the "Götter mindern Ranges" [lesser gods]. Yet he needs little prodding to descend from his Olympian heights when his party is invited to preside Paris-like at a *dégustation* of a less-known Nahe Valley wine called Monzinger. Though the friends have emptied their brown mugs a couple of times already, they bravely take their cue from a scripture quoted in a well-remembered local sermon on the vices of drunkenness delivered by a robust auxiliary bishop who considered it a divine gift that he could responsibly consume eight measures of wine: "Prüfet alles und das Beste behaltet" [Test all things; hold fast that which is good].[35]

At this point, Goethe inserts a brief biography of Saint Roch, as well as a list of local proverbs relating to the weather. Also included, at length, is his version of the rededication sermon delivered that day with its practical Christian counsel. During this outdoor sermon Goethe observes that individual pilgrims and community processions have laid aside their distinguishing flags and standards, and even internal Catholic hierarchies are abolished as the presiding bishop is swallowed up in the crowds.[36] Goethe elevates humanity above political and religious distinction by placing humankind itself in a continuum with nature, as the vast congregation merges into the setting of the bucolic landscape visible on the horizon.[37] This pastoral picture is a vision of harmony: peace among nations, peace among denominations, and peace with nature. This peace requires the ability to lay aside flags, to swallow up the enmity created by prejudices and pride through an expanded view.

Following the al fresco sermon, as pilgrims celebrate the Mass, Goethe and his friends decide it is time to go. When things get too mystical or too boring — when the friends have had enough religion — they leave the festival peacefully and let the faithful worship. With religion, especially sacred rituals, Goethe realises that much will remain hidden or appear confusing. This acknowledged lack of understanding forms a basis for tolerance rooted in intellectual humility.[38]

Without interfering in the internal mechanisms of the religious community, Goethe makes informed and constructive aesthetic suggestions, directed at improving the sacral and natural landscape. His "geübtes Kunstauge" [practised eye for art] observes the incomplete repair work on the chapel and imagines how thoughtful future architectural planning might make this place of pilgrimage one of the most beautiful places in the world.[39]

Earlier Goethe has surveyed the barren hill on which the chapel rests and expressed his pleasure that young nut trees had been planted. He advises that the pilgrims ought to take care of these trees so that their families and future thousands may enjoy them.[40] This practical proposal is intended not only to beautify the sanctuary's natural surroundings, but also to inspire further community cooperation. And as the citizens look after and protect ("schirmen") the young trees, as they care for nature, nature will in turn protect their future children by affording future shade (Goethe exploits the various meanings of *schirmen*). This act of nurturing reflects mimetically the caring nature of their patron saint as he looks after, protects, and helps the believers to grow. Thus, the faithful may rejoice in having emulated their intercessor.[41]

This is the crux of the priest's message to the congregation, to look to Saint Roch as a pattern by which to model and measure their individual growth.[42] But Goethe's mimesis reverses the traditional Catholic paradigm of the *Nachahmung* (*imitatio*) of the Divine by implying that mortals may be its preview and exemplification (*Vorbild*) through good deeds as in the poem, "Das Göttliche" (The Divine, 1783):

> Der edle Mensch
> Sei hülfreich und gut!
> Unermüdet schaff' er
> Das Nützliche, Rechte,
> Sei uns ein Vorbild
> Jener geahndeten Wesen.[43]

[The noble man is helpful and good! Untiringly he creates the useful,
the just. Be thou an example of those intuited beings.]

Human originality is preserved, as each individual is a creator and not
only an imitator of the useful and just. Goethe, too, goes beyond being
a passive spectator by memorialising the Saint Roch festival in writing.
But he also modulates his own response yet again, this time in a
touching Catholic register, as a human being who has been moved by a
festival of human healing. Less than a year after his visit, he initiated
and organised the benefaction of a painting to the ecclesiastical
authorities at Bingen for the Saint Roch chapel. He and Johann Heinrich Meyer (1760–1832) designed it and Caroline Louise Seidler
(1786–1866) produced the painting. Three years later, in *Ueber Kunst
und Alterthum* (I/2, 1817), an editorial announced that a painting of
Saint Roch had been donated — Goethe's name does not appear — to
the chapel above Bingen in remembrance of the peaceful restoration on
16 August 1814.[44] Goethe's further purpose and hope regarding the
painting, as expressed in a private letter, was to uplift and edify the believers.[45]

On one level the *Sankt-Rochus-Fest zu Bingen* is about the meanings
of an important "politisch-religiöses Fest" [political-religious festival]
that celebrates "Glaubensfreiheit" [religious freedom] and the winning
back of the German communities on the left bank of the Rhine.[46] But
there is another level that is embodied in the narrative style itself and
comes into view cumulatively, as the reader progresses through the essay.

Goethe shows with the *Sankt-Rochus-Fest zu Bingen* a kind of religious etiquette that must prevail precisely because freedom of belief
exists. George Steiner defines this sense of courtesy as follows: "The
informing agency is that of tact, of the ways which we allow ourselves
to touch or not to touch, to be touched or not to be touched by the
presence of the other."[47] For Goethe, as exemplified over and over
again in the essay, this is something akin to "Schonung" [considera-
tion].[48]

Another way that his piece exemplifies consideration, a way that
transforms tolerance from a negative gesture into a positive humane
act, is implied by the phrase "fromme Zugabe" [pious addition].[49]
Doing more than the minimum can be an act of service that will edify,
as denoted by the essay's strategic deployment of the word *erbauen*.
Such service may be as patently pedestrian as planting a nut tree, do-
nating a painting, or picnicking with pilgrims; but being pedestrian,

which evokes an important Enlightenment image of growth and maturity, requires learning how to walk peaceably with others.

As the friends finally leave the festival to take pleasure in an exhilarating Rhine boat ride, Goethe sadly observes further wartime destruction of the chapel grounds, specifically the stations of the cross, and suggests: "Bey Erneuerung dieser könnte frommer Geist und redlicher Kunstsinn mitwirken, daß jeder, er sey wer er wolle, diesen Weg mit theilnehmender Erbauung zurücklegte" [When these are renewed, a meek spirit and an honest sense of art could co-operate so that each person, whoever he might be, would walk this way with sympathetic edification].[50] As the friends leave the festival grounds, the refreshing rains fall, and Goethe links the salutary processes of healing and humour as he alludes, with a literary wink, to the blessings being sent down from the heavens by Saint Roch, who is probably exercising his influence on other saints.[51] Goethe counsels all who would walk this way — today it has been to a Catholic festival, tomorrow it may be to a Protestant or a Jewish or a Muslim one — to combine a meek spirit and an earnest creative sense, much as he has done in his account.

In a letter to Sulpiz Boisserée, Goethe confides that the *Sankt-Rochus-Fest zu Bingen* represents a "fromme Darstellung" [pious depiction].[52] The anthropological artist, the artist who would utilise beliefs as creative material, must employ the utmost aesthetic care and humility (a precondition of intellectual honesty) in creative representation. In this sense, the *Sankt-Rochus-Fest zu Bingen* is an example of the literary practice of tolerance. Goethe is considerate of the religious beliefs he describes, not least because such beliefs are held to be sacred by the believer. When Goethe draws contrasts between a believer's perspective and those of a sceptical naturalist, the key lies not in Goethe's preference, for he openly favours the latter, but in understanding how, given his strong preference, he negotiates the difference.

Goethe's essay not only foregrounds the events leading up to and including the festival, but the narrative itself is a subtle stylistic performance that frames, informs, and galvanises the content. In other words, *how* Goethe reports is just as important as what he reports. His attitudes and observations generate and establish an interpretative field within which the reader receives an impression of the multivalent meanings of the Saint Roch festival.

Goethe's account not only exhibits extraordinary narrative discipline, it also gives subtle clues to his hermeneutic approach, his way of understanding the world around him. The balance of reporting the facts, but recognising that they are only the facts as he sees them, is an example of how to overcome bias through maintaining a self-conscious descriptive distance, while not pretending that such distance implies a legitimising validity.

The gentle tone, the humour, and the good will of Goethe's narrative, invite readers to examine their own attitudes towards the beliefs of others. These are catalysts to an integrated approach that is both reverent and artistic, an aesthetic-ethical union that seeks to build and edify, to refresh and renew: "Denn am Ende sind wir alle / Pilgernd Könige zum Ziele." [Because in the end we are all kings on a pilgrimage to the goal].[53]

Notes

[1] Cf. Saine, *Black Bread — White Bread*, the section "Laukhard's Introduction to Revolutionary France" (299–308) for a picture of politics and religion in the Rhine region during the 1790s.

[2] Sagarra, *A Social History of Germany 1648–1914*, 224.

[3] Emil Staiger, *Goethe*, 3 vols. (Zurich: Atlantis, 1952–1959), 3, 72–73. Beginning with II/4, 1818 and until Goethe's death in 1832, the journal's title was *Ueber Kunst und Alterthum* (hereafter KuA).

[4] FA 20, 98.

[5] FA 20, 878–79.

[6] For a political analysis see: A. G. Steer, "Sankt-Rochus-Fest zu Bingen: Goethes politische Anschauungen nach den Befreiungskriegen," in *Jahrbuch des Freien Deutschen Hochstifts*, (1965), 186–236.

[7] Sagarra, *A Social History of Germany 1648–1914*, 228.

[8] "Gebadet. Einfall nach Rüdesheim zu gehen" (WA III/5, 126). Goethe was accompanied by the composer Carl Friedrich Zelter (1758–1832) and the mineralogist Ludwig Wilhelm Cramer (1755–1832).

[9] FA 20, 130. Secularised in 1802.

[10] FA 20, 131. Cf. Günter Niggl, *"Fromm" bei Goethe: Eine Wortmonographie*, Hermaea: Germanistische Forschungen 21 (Tübingen: Niemeyer, 1967), 57–62. From 1767–1786 *fromm* (excluding verb variants) occurs 36 times in Goethe's writings; from 1786–1805, 92 times; and from 1805–1832, the period of this text, no less than 525 times.

[11] Cf. *Hermann und Dorothea* (1797), which is situated historically at the beginning of Napoleon's occupation of the Rhine region, so that the landscape is constantly threatened.

[12] FA 20, 131. Goethe's parents and other citizens of Frankfurt had endured the "unerhörte Last" [outrageous burden] of French military billeting in 1759 (DuW I/3: FA 14, 94). The traditional Catholic blessing — marking the entrance to a home with the names of the three kings — is also inverted.

[13] Cf. *Italienische Reise* (The Journey to Italy, 1816) and *Reise in die Schweiz 1797* (Travels in Switzerland, 1833).

[14] FA 20, 158 ("erquicken") and 132 ("Wechselverkehr"). *Erquicken* has both spiritual and meteorological connotations.

[15] FA 20, 132.

[16] Bell puts forward that *Das Römische Karneval* is a literary manifestation of Goethe's anthropological thinking. Matthew Bell, *Goethe's Naturalistic Anthropology: Man and Other Plants* (Oxford: Clarendon Press, 1994), 184–88.

[17] FA 20, 136.

[18] FA 2, 380. Cf. Schiller's letter to Goethe, 23 August 1794.

[19] *Spiraltendenz der Vegetation* (The Spiral Tendency of Vegetation, 1831): FA 24, 789. Dieter Borchmeyer identifies the importance of the spiral for Goethe in his *Weimarer Klassik: Porträt einer Epoche* (Weinheim: Beltz/Athenäum, 1994), 507–509.

[20] FA 20, 137.

[21] This is the collection of Wilhelm Friedrich Götz (1763–1823), who led Goethe and Zelter to the castle ruin the previous evening and accompanies the three friends to the festival.

[22] FA 20, 138.

[23] Ibid. The naturalist is not always held back from the religious path, as Goethe notes in his *Travels in Switzerland 1797* (1 October), after having seen a path that served both pilgrims and mineralogists (FA 16, 217).

[24] FA 20, 142.

[25] Peter Ganz trenchantly illustrates Goethe's self-confessed geological predilection in "Sankt-Rochus-Fest zu Bingen," *Oxford German Studies* 10 (1979): 110–20.

[26] FA 20, 139. Goethe owned an engraving of the Pinax of Cebes by Matthaeus Merian (Birus: FA 20, 893).

[27] Ibid. Cf. *Venezianische Epigramme*, 21 (Venetian Epigrams 21, 1791): FA 1, 447–48.

[28] FA 20, 139–40.

[29] FA 20, 140 and FA 20, 199.

[30] FA 20, 141.

[31] FA 20, 140.

[32] FA 20, 143.

[33] FA 20, 144. Goethe was interested in the ritual of the sacrament in general. See DuW II/7 (FA 14, 321).

[34] FA 20, 144.

[35] FA 20, 145–46. Cf. 1 Thessalonians 5:21.

[36] FA 20, 155. In a letter written to his wife Christiane on 19 August 1814, Goethe estimates that 10,000 people were in attendance: WA IV/25, 19.

[37] FA 20, 155.

[38] FA 20, 157. For a religious interpretation of Goethe's essay see: Katharina Mommsen, "Der Unbequeme Goethe," *Publications of the English Goethe Society* 37 (1968): 12–42.

[39] FA 20, 154.

[40] FA 20, 152.

[41] Ibid.

[42] FA 20, 156.

[43] Lines 54–59: FA 1, 335.

[44] FA 20, 176.

[45] Letter to Sulpiz Boisserée, 24 June 1816: WA IV/27, 65.

[46] FA 20, 142.

[47] George Steiner, *Real Presences* (London: Faber and Faber, 1990), 148.

[48] FA 20, 141.

[49] FA 20, 141.

[50] FA 20, 158.

[51] Ibid. Goethe achieves here a symmetrical-motivic frame by alluding to auxiliary saints he learns about from the pilgrims, as well as from the Italian man he had met earlier.

[52] 27 September 1816: WA IV/27, 171.

[53] "Rhein und Main" in *Die Sammlung von 1827* [The Collection of 1827] number 97, Lines 7–8: FA 2, 619.

5: Goethe's *Morgenblatt* Essay on *Die Geheimnisse*

IN 1993 THE SECOND Parliament of the World's Religions convened in Chicago. Representatives of many denominations shared their beliefs with each other in an atmosphere of mutual respect. In 1893, in the same city, the first Parliament of the World's Religions had been held in conjunction with the spectacular Columbian Exposition. It was an event motivated by good will and the desire to understand the religious convictions of others.[1] The first Parliament of the World's Religions was not without intellectual predecessors. Peace among nations was the goal of Kant's treatise *Zum ewigen Frieden* (On Eternal Peace, 1795), written a century before the first Parliament. Peace among denominations was a vanguard principle of many Enlightenment thinkers. Prior to this, Europe had been at times a confessional battlefield. The Reformation, which has been typified as a "religious hurricane," swept through Europe in the sixteenth and seventeenth centuries and triggered social upheavals that caused widespread fear.[2] In 1534 a Protestant sect seized control of the city of Münster and attempted to establish by force the New Jerusalem.[3] The radicals held the city for a year and confirmed in many minds the dangers of heresy.

The French Wars of Religion (1559–1598), The Revolt of the Netherlands (1567–1648), and The Thirty Years' War (1618–1648) are some of the bloodied milestones on the trail of European religious history. But it was Louis XIV's infamous Revocation of the Edict of Nantes in 1685 that shocked the philosophers of the European Enlightenment:

> With regard to the remainder of the said "Religion Prétendue Reformée" [the so-called Reformed religion], until it please God to enlighten them, as he has the rest, they shall continue to dwell in the cities and places of our kingdom, . . . and may continue their business, and enjoy the possession of their property without being troubled or disturbed under the pretext of the said "Religion Prétendue Reformée," on condition . . . of having no exercise, nor assembling under the pretext of prayer, or of worship of said Religion, of any nature whatever, under the above-mentioned penalties of body and goods.[4]

Within earshot of the Revocation came the English Toleration Act of 1689, which, however, did not prevent Catholics and Non-Conformists from being legally discriminated against in Britain. Prussian rulers were sympathetic and calculating in their willingness to help the displaced and dispossessed French Huguenots, who were known for their industry.

Individuals, too, worked to end religious conflict. In London John Dury published his book, *A briefe revelation of that which hath been lately attempted to procure ecclesiastical peace amongst Protestants* (1641) and Count Nicholas Zinzendorf granted refuge to a branch of the persecuted Moravian Brethren in 1722 on his Herrnhut estate. Voltaire's *Traité sur la tolérance* (Treaty on Toleration, 1763) and Lessing's *Nathan der Weise* (Nathan the Wise, 1779) both helped to blaze the way for official tolerance, such as Emperor Joseph II's *Toleranzpatent* decreed in Vienna in 1781.

As has been shown, Goethe also contributed to the development of religious tolerance with his *Brief des Pastors* (1773). A lesser-known contribution was his 1784–1785 sketch for a religious epic poem that was to remain a fragment, entitled *Die Geheimnisse* (The Mysteries). Hans-Dietrich Dahnke views this piece as a continuation of the German Enlightenment legacy of Kant, Lessing, and Herder[5] and Wolfgang Dietrich posits that the epic fragment is a part of Goethe's general humanitarian vision, with links to the Rosicrucians, Freemasons, and Knights Templar.[6]

On 27 April 1816, more than thirty years after Goethe stopped working on *Die Geheimnisse*, he published an essay on the epic fragment in the newspaper *Morgenblatt für gebildete Stände* (Morning Paper for Cultured Classes). In the article Goethe reveals how he intended to conclude *Die Geheimnisse* by providing an outline of the narrative from the point he had ceased writing. The *Morgenblatt* essay is a late-Enlightenment piece that carries the intellectual seeds of a parliament of world's religions, not unlike the one that would gather only eight decades later in America. As such, it is a contribution to intellectual history and underscores the relationship of history and literature.[7] Yet, had it not been for a small group of curious students, the *Morgenblatt* essay might never have been written.

In November 1815 six university students in Königsberg wrote Goethe and enquired about *Die Geheimnisse,* which he had, coincidentally, only several months earlier discussed with Sulpiz Boiserée, an art collector who sympathised with the German Romantics.[8] The students, who had formed a reading circle, requested that Goethe sketch what his intentions would have been had he completed the epic.[9] He pub-

lished his answer to the students's query in the essay *Die Geheimnisse.
Fragment von Goethe* (The Mysteries. Fragment by Goethe), which appeared in the 27 April 1816 issue of the *Morgenblatt*. Goethe's article
was published during a period when the religious landscape in Germany
had changed significantly. 1816 was a watershed year for Goethe's Enlightenment ideas on religion, as he fastidiously refined his essay, the
Sankt-Rochus-Fest zu Bingen, and formulated a written opinion on the
much-anticipated 1817 Reformation festival, which will be discussed in
the following chapter. Additionally, Goethe announced his forthcoming book of poetry, *West-östlicher Divan*, a collection that includes a
lengthy prose appendix in which he reflects on middle-eastern cultures
and Islam.

In a letter dated 14 April 1816, Goethe confided to his friend Carl
Friedrich Zelter his general mood since the end of the French occupation. He anticipated the delight he will take in revising and publishing
many essays, especially since the horrors of the war appear to be over.[10]
The newly-won freedom and restored peace refreshed Goethe's artistic
desire. He found that for many, especially young people, his writings
were viewed as an aesthetic-ethical compass in the wake of the terror
and confusion of the Napoleonic wars. Two weeks later he wrote in a
preface of sorts to the *Morgenblatt* essay:

> Meine werthen Landsleute, besonders die jüngeren, erwiesen mir von
> jeher viel Vertrauen, welches sich noch zu vermehren scheint, gegen-
> wärtig, so nach Befreyung von äußerem Druck und wieder hergestell-
> ter innerer Ruhe ein jedes aufrichtige Streben nach dem Guten und
> Schönen sich aufs Neue begünstigt fühlt.[11]

> [My worthy countrymen, especially the younger ones, have for a long
> while shown me much trust, which seems to be increasing at present.
> Each and every sincere striving for the good and beautiful is encour-
> aged anew, especially after liberation from external pressures and res-
> toration of inner peace.]

Socio-political stability had rejuvenated Goethe's creativity and made
him more aware of his responsibility towards those in the devastated
German lands who were searching for spiritual and aesthetic renewal.
In this light it seems likely that he placed great importance on the students's question about *Die Geheimnisse*, one of his more oblique works.
It is telling that the students wanted to learn about a piece that reached
back more than thirty years, into the eighteenth century and to the
time before the French Revolution and Romantic nationalism.

Goethe begins his essay by summarising *Die Geheimnisse*. The fragment features a tired and hungry monk, Brother Markus, who has lost his way in a mountainous region and seeks shelter for the night. Brother Markus follows a path through a rocky vale, which leads him to a green lea and a glorious edifice. He is welcomed, fed, offered a bed, and learns about those who dwell there: "zwölf Ritter, welche nach überstandenem sturmvollen Leben, wo Mühe, Leiden und Gefahr sich andrängten, endlich hier zu wohnen und Gott im Stillen zu dienen, Verpflichtung übernommen" [twelve knights who, after surviving stormy lives filled with difficulty, suffering, and danger, have committed themselves to live here and serve God in stillness].[12] The lost monk also learns that a thirteenth knight, their leader Humanus, is preparing to take leave of the others and has begun to recite his life's story. Eventually Brother Markus retires, but is suddenly awakened and glimpses three torch-bearing youths running through a garden. At this point the poem breaks off.

Goethe now continues where he left off over three decades before and blends his idea of how the epic would have continued in order to establish his overall intent with *Die Geheimnisse*. He reveals that he would have taken the reader through an "ideellen Montserrat" [ideal Montserrat].[13] This allusion to Montserrat, which is not mentioned in the fragment, can be traced to an 18 August 1800 letter from Wilhelm von Humboldt to Goethe. Humboldt recounts a visit he had made to a Benedictine monastery on the Montserrat near Barcelona and refers to *Die Geheimnisse*:

> Ihre *Geheimnisse* schwebten mir lebhaft vor dem Gedächtnis. Ich habe diese schöne Dichtung, in der eine so wunderbar hohe und menschliche Stimmung herrscht, immer außerordentlich geliebt, aber erst, seitdem ich diese Gegend besuchte, hat sie sich an etwas in meiner Erfahrung angeknüpft; sie ist mir nicht werter, aber sie ist mir näher und eigner geworden.[14]

> [Your *Mysteries* floated with life before my memory. I have always especially loved this epic, in which such a wonderfully high and humane mood reigns. But only since I visited this region has it linked itself to something from my experience. It is not any more valuable to me, but it is has become more intimately my own.]

Later in the letter Humboldt quotes directly from *Die Geheimnisse*.

On 3 August 1815 Sulpiz Boiserée noted Goethe's explanation of the epic to him: "*Die Geheimnisse* . . . habe er zu groß angefangen, wie so vieles. – Die 12 Ritter sollten die 12 Religionen (?) sein und alles sich nachher durcheinanderwirren, das Würkliche als Märchen und dies umgekehrt als die Wirklichkeit erscheinen." [*The Mysteries . . .* he had begun too large, like so much. – The 12 knights would have been the 12 religions (?) and all would have become mixed together, reality as fairy tale and inversely this as reality].[15] In the *Morgenblatt* essay Goethe clarifies what he means by the twelve knights:

> Einen jeden der Rittermönche würde man in seiner Wohnung besucht und durch Anschauung climatischer und nationaler Verschiedenheiten erfahren haben, daß die trefflichsten Männer von allen Enden der Erde sich hier versammlen mögen, wo jeder von ihnen Gott auf seine eigenste Weise im Stillen verehre.[16]

> [One would have visited each of the knight-monks in their living quarters and learned, through observation of climatic and national differences, that the finest men from all ends of the earth assemble here, where each worships God in his own most individual way and in stillness.]

By selecting the superlative, "eigenste," Goethe implies that the most individualistic modes of worship could and would co-exist in this building, a metaphor for a pluralistic polity. The notion that all worship God quietly not only sparks associations with Pietism, but also contains the kernel of the idea that one's worship of God would not infringe upon other members of society. This points forward to the limitation that John Stuart Mill placed on personal freedom in his treatise, *On Liberty* (1859), namely that its exercise should not harm anyone else.

The architectural imagery is also significant, for as Scott Abbott points out, "Goethe subscribed to the Enlightenment belief that environmental form shapes the individual. In fact, he ordered architectural symbols along ritual routes in several of his works 'to affect the succeeding states of mind' of a character."[17] As Brother Markus visited each knight's living quarters, the reader would gain impressions of each religion through the symbols in the rooms. And the notion that each knight occupies his own quarters — but that all dwell in the same building — implies that although individual worship, history, and tradition are preserved, all religions are brought together and co-exist. This is a similar thought to one Goethe expressed in a letter dated 4 October 1782: "in unsers Vaters Apotheke sind viel Recepte" [in our Father's apothecary's shop are many prescriptions].[18] While the natural setting represents an ideal blend between nature and culture, by placing the twelve knights in a building Goethe rationalises to some degree the religions they stand for as they are given an external structuring principle. The walls between the rooms represent a suspension of belief through which, as Erich Trunz comments: "jeder bleibt für sich in seiner Eigenart, und doch streben alle in einem gleichen Sinne" [each retains his individuality and yet all strive in the same sense].[19] This is a theoretical leap that expands Enlightenment thought on religion. Lessing's *Nathan der Weise*, celebrated as a key text on religious toleration, portrays symbolically the common ground of divergent faiths. Nicholas Boyle, however, has shown that such a view is chimerical:

> The representatives of the three major religions, Judaism, Christianity, and Islam, are not here shown to tolerate one another's differences, for it is only temporary misunderstanding that prevents them from recognizing that they all think alike: they are shown rather to be agreed in a fourth, secret, religion of agnostic humanism.[20]

In Goethe's vision the three major religions are replaced by an astounding twelve and the plural title, *Die Geheimnisse*, underscores diversity. There are many mysteries, each with a truth claim, and each choosing concordant co-existence. As Goethe once commented in a letter a decade after he had written the *Morgenblatt* essay: "Glücklicherweise bleibt uns zuletzt die Überzeugung, daß gar vieles nebeneinander bestehen kann und muß, was sich gerne wechselseitig verdrängen möchte: der Weltgeist ist toleranter als man denkt" [Fortunately, we are left with the conviction that many things that would like to exclude each other can and must co-exist: the World Spirit is more tolerant than one thinks].[21]

Goethe validates the good and beautiful in each religion and yet holds in abeyance any judgement on ultimate truth. Thus, in an age of increased Romantic yearning for a unified Christian Europe along medieval lines, Goethe proffers an Enlightenment model by suggesting the recognition of religious diversity. The 1816 conception of *Die Geheimnisse* stands as his pluralistic vision of the possibility of religious harmony.

The reader would have developed appreciation for the twelve religions because each would have been encountered through the eyes of the pilgrim, Brother Markus:

> Der mit Bruder Markus herumwandelnde Leser oder Zuhörer wäre gewahr geworden, daß die verschiedensten Denk- und Empfindungsweisen, welche in dem Menschen durch Atmosphäre, Landstrich, Völkerschaft, Bedürfniß, Gewohnheit entwickelt oder ihm eingedrückt werden, sich hier, am Orte, in ausgezeichneten Individuen darzustellen und die Begier nach höchster Ausbildung, obgleich einzeln un-

vollkommen, durch Zusammenleben würdig auszusprechen berufen seyen.[22]

[The reader or hearer would have become aware of the most varied ways of experiencing the world that develop in or are impressed upon humankind through atmosphere, geography, ethnicity, need, and habit. This would be represented here in this place through excellent individuals who desire the highest training and education and, although singly imperfect, through community life are worthy and called to express this.]

Here Goethe catalogues something more than catalysts to difference, as Herder had before done, and raises the idea of "Zusammenleben" [community life]. He is not recommending a melting pot in which difference disappears, but suggests that through the process of learning to live together, uniqueness and individuality are preserved as each religious community cultivates its own identity in a civil society. Yet how is it possible to learn to live together peacefully amidst such diversity without the at least equal possibility of learning to despise one another? Goethe continues: "Damit dieses aber möglich werde, haben sie sich um einen Mann versammelt der den Namen *Humanus* führt, wozu sie sich nicht entschlossen hätten, ohne sämtlich eine Aehnlichkeit, eine Annäherung zu ihm zu fühlen" [So that this may be possible, they have gathered themselves around a man called *Humanus,* which they would not have decided to do had they not all felt a similarity and affinity with him].[23] Just as the knights represent different religions in their ideal forms, so too is Humanus an ideal representative figure; Goethe calls him a "Vermittler" [mediator], or in other words an embodiment of a humane relational ethos.[24]

The reader learns not only that Humanus will soon go away, but also why he will do so, and what form the recitation of his life will take. Each of the twelve knights would have been able in turn to tell a part of Humanus's history because each has come into contact with him at a different time. For each religion, continues Goethe, the point of contact and unification with this mediator is a high point in their history.[25] This intimates that religion ought to be mediated by the humane. One's relationship to the Divine is, for Goethe, intertwined with one's relationship to other human beings, and these two relationships are not mutually exclusive, but mutually enhancing. Catholics, Protestants, Jews, Muslims, and so on are never more beautifully Christian or Jewish or Muslim, nor more beautifully humane, than when their actions toward their fellow men are not only mediated and informed by their perceived individual stewardships to their Supreme Beings (vertical accountability), but also are mediated and informed by a humane spirit (horizontal accountability). Goethe's model does not abolish religious identity or even religious idiosyncrasy, but preserves and honours their highest manifestations, "so daß man jede Anerkennung Gottes und der Tugend, sie zeige sich auch in noch so wunderbarer Gestalt, doch immer aller Ehren, aller Liebe würdig müsste gefunden haben" [so that one would have found each manifestation of God and virtue, no matter how marvellously expressed, to be worthy of all honour and love].[26]

Humanus, after long community life, is ready to depart since each religion embodies what he represents, a humane spirit.[27] If all of this seems optimistic — and seeing the good in things is a characteristic of much Enlightenment thought — it is not because Goethe was naive to religious history; indeed, he writes that religions become hated through abuse and deception.[28] Up to this point in the *Morgenblatt* essay Goethe has written about the reader or listener, but now he uses the word "Theilnehmer" [participant], a significant change:

> Wenn nun nach diesem Entwurf der Hörer, der Theilnehmer durch alle Länder und Zeiten im Geiste geführt, überall das Erfreulichste, was die Liebe Gottes und der Menschen, unter so mancherley Gestalten, hervorbringt, erfahren, so sollte daraus die angenehmste Empfindung entspringen.[29]

> [When, according to this outline, the listener, the participant was led in spirit through all lands and times and experienced the most joyous of what the love of God among men in so many forms brings forth, the most pleasant feeling and perception would arise.]

Temporality and geography are displaced as the participant witnesses the love of God manifest among the children of men. Goethe hoped that the recognition that all forms of worship are, at their best, manifestations of divine and human love would motivate a deep gratitude for the diversity of life itself and encourage the listener to participate in creating a future history of religious harmony.

Goethe means nothing less than to take part in and make this future history: "Damit aber ein so schöner Bund nicht ohne Haupt und Mittelsperson bleibe, wird durch wunderbare Schickung und Offenbarung der arme Pilgrim Bruder Markus in die hohe Stelle eingesetzt" [So that such a beautiful society is not left without a head and intermediary, the poor pilgrim, Brother Markus, will be ordained in the high office through miraculous fate and revelation].[30] The reader, who is led to identify with Markus, is offered the opportunity to help create the envisioned future history by being humane, by living as a mediating agent within a world of cultural and religious diversity. The job description for Humanus's vacant position is represented through Brother Markus's qualifications. He is described as a humble and devoted man who engages in good causes and harbours no desire to attain the unattainable.[31] Assuming Humanus's mantle does not submerge one's own religion or distinctive culture and tradition; rather they are enhanced.

Die Geheimnisse as future history? Goethe certainly thought so: "Wäre dieses Gedicht vor dreißig Jahren, wo es ersonnen und angefangen worden, vollendet erschienen, so wäre es der Zeit einigermaßen vorgeeilt" [If this poem had appeared fully finished thirty years ago when it was conceived and begun, it would have been somewhat ahead of its time].[32] And thirty years later in 1816, after the devastation of Napoleon's rampaging, Goethe believed that his piece could assist and fortify those, regardless of religion, who were seeking to rebuild their homes, restore their houses of worship, and rekindle their spirits despite the devastation and ravages of war:

> Auch gegenwärtig, obgleich seit jener Epoche die Ideen sich erweitert, die Gefühle gereinigt, die Ansichten aufgeklärt haben, würde man das nun allgemein Anerkannte im poetischen Kleide vielleicht gerne sehen, und sich daran in den Gesinnungen befestigen, in welchen ganz allein der Mensch, auf seinem eigenen Montserrat, Glück und Ruhe finden kann.[33]

> [Also for the present, although since that epoch ideas have been broadened, feelings purified, and views enlightened, one would perhaps appreciate seeing in poetic dress what is now generally recognized, thus fortifying one's beliefs, which are the only things in which man, on his own Montserrat, can find happiness and peace.]

The Montserrat image became a life-long metaphor for Goethe. In the summer of 1828, amidst a period of grief and introspection, he retreated pilgrim-like to the beautiful environs of the Dornburg Renaissance castle near Weimar. On August 18 he wrote to his friend Knebel that he was at "my Montserrat." That he felt well, even spiritual, Goethe records in his journal entry for the same day: "Vor Sonnenaufgang aufgestanden. Vollkommene Klarheit des Thales. Der Ausdruck des Dichters: heilige Frühe ward empfunden" [Arose before sunrise. Perfect clarity of the valley. The expression of the poet: Holy dawn was perceived].[34]

Goethe's *Morgenblatt* essay on *Die Geheimnisse,* concerning as it does a diverse religious community dwelling peacefully on a mountaintop, contains his Enlightenment idea of a setting where exemplary members of the world's religions could dwell together without animosity. Perhaps it would not have come as a surprise to Goethe that a little over six decades after his death the First Parliament of the World's Religions — a place where members of different faiths could converse in a civilised manner with each other about their beliefs — would convene in Chicago. He read about the beginnings of such possibilities in his lifetime, and wrote admiringly that he had heard that in New York there were ninety differing Christian denominations.[35] That such things were possible in Goethe's visionary blueprint of the *Die Geheimnisse* or in far-away America was one thing. What about closer to home, in Germany? He explores this thought in another 1816 piece, an essay on the tercentenary celebrations of the Reformation festival.

Notes

[1] Richard H. Seager, *The World's Parliament of Religions: The East/West Encounter, Chicago, 1893* (Bloomington: Indiana UP, 1995).

[2] Vivian Green, *The European Reformation* (Phoenix Mill: Sutton, 1998), 1.

[3] Carter Lindberg, ed. *The European Reformations Sourcebook* (Oxford: Blackwell, 2000), 124.

[4] Maclear, *Church and State in the Modern Age*, 7.

[5] Hans-Dietrich Dahnke, "Die Geheimnisse" in *Goethe-Handbuch*, 4 vols., ed. by Bernd Witte et al. (Stuttgart: Metzler, 1996–1998); vol. 1, ed. by Regine Otto and Bernd Witte (1996), 546–52, (549). Herder includes a line from *Die Geheimnisse* in book 16 of his *Ideen zur Philosophie der Geschichte der Menschheit* (Ideas on the Philosophy of the History of Humanity, 1784–1791).

[6] Wolfgang Dietrich, "Die Geheimnisse, Achilles, Das Tagebuch" in *Goethes Erzählwerk*, ed. by Paul Michael Lützeler and James E. McLeod (Stuttgart: Reclam, 1985), 268–90, (271).

[7] Russel B. Nye, "History and Literature: Branches of the Same Tree" in *Essays on History and Literature*, ed. Robert H. Bremner (Columbus, OH: Ohio State UP, 1966), 123–59 (123–25).

[8] FA 20, 1475.

[9] FA 20, 1473–475. The entire letter of the students is reproduced in this edition.

[10] WA IV/26, 337. Cf. Werner Krauss, "Goethe und die Französische Revolution." *Goethe Jahrbuch* 94 (1977): 127–36.

[11] FA 20, 599.

[12] FA 20, 600.

[13] FA 20, 601.

[14] Wilhelm von Humboldt, *Gesammelte Schriften*, ed. by Albert Leitzmann, Königliche Preussische Akademie der Wissenschaften (Berlin: Behr, 1903–1936; repr. Berlin: De Gruyter, 1968), vol. 3, 1799–1818, 30–59, (33).

[15] FA 20, 1475.

[16] FA 20, 601.

[17] Scott Abbott, *Fictions of Freemasonry and the German Novel* (Detroit: Wayne State UP, 1991), 67.

[18] Letter to Lavater: WA IV/6, 66. Cf. John 14:2

[19] HA 2, 709.

[20] Nicholas Boyle, *Goethe: The Poet and the Age*, vol. 1, *The Poetry of Desire (1749–1790)*, 33. Cf. Ritchie Robertson, "'Dies hohe Lied der Duldung?' The Ambiguities of Toleration in Lessing's *Die Juden* and *Nathan der Weise.*" *Modern Language Review* 93 (1998): 105–20.

[21] Letter to Carl Friedrich Reinhard, 12 May 1826: WA IV/41, 30.

[22] FA 20, 601.

[23] Ibid.

[24] Ibid.

[25] Ibid.

[26] FA 20, 601–602.

[27] FA 20, 602.

[28] Ibid.

[29] Ibid.

[30] Ibid.

[31] Ibid.

[32] Ibid.

[33] Ibid.

[34] 18 August 1828: WA IV/44, 282 and WA III/11, 264.

[35] *Sprüche*: FA 13, 72.

6: Goethe's *Weltfest*

MOST GERMAN LANDS WERE DIVIDED along strict confessional lines, according to the laws of the Empire, until it was dissolved in 1806. Following the Wars of Liberation there was a great need to find new ways to organise religion in Germany. The issue was much in Goethe's thoughts: only one day after the Saint Roch festival, on 17 August 1814, he had already drawn up an outline of that adventure, which had so impressed him.[1] Two years later he was still intensely involved with that event, as he planned to publish the essay and in a letter to Pauline Servière, dated 1 February 1816, he recalled an earlier vow that he had solemnly taken to honour Saint Roch.[2]

From August through December 1816 Goethe revised his *Sankt-Rochus-Fest zu Bingen,* and wrote to his friend, the composer Carl Friedrich Zelter, who had accompanied him two years earlier on the Rhine excursion, remindinig Zelter about the trip.[3] Zelter responded that the day in Bingen was like a beautiful vision, and recalled how Goethe had been touched by the experience.[4]

On 7 November 1816 Goethe informed Zelter that he was going to publish the *Sankt-Rochus-Fest zu Bingen* with another essay to be written in collaboration with Johann Heinrich Meyer. This would be a polemical piece directed against religious nationalism in art, *Neu-deutsch religios-patriotische Kunst* (New German Religious-Patriotic Art, 1817). Goethe added that during the Saint Roch festival trip and a previous Rhine journey he had advocated love, or at least tolerance: "ich habe ja nur das Testament Johannis gepredigt: *Kindlein liebt euch,* und wenn das nicht gehen will: *laßt wenigstens einander gelten*" [I only preached the gospel of John: *children love one another*, and if that does not work: *at least let each other be*].[5]

It was during this fruitful letter exchange of 1816, while he reflected on and wrote about the Saint Roch festival and was at the same time concerned about rising jingoism, that Goethe pondered the anticipated festivities surrounding the tercentenary of the Reformation. A letter from Zelter spurred his thoughts about the upcoming celebrations, for the composer asked his opinion as to whether the subject would be suitable for a musical setting.[6] In his response — it is one of his lengthiest letters to Zelter that year — Goethe draws up an outline

for a Reformation cantata and notes that the *Weimarische Kunstfreunde*
[Weimar Friends of Art] are planning to construct a Luther monument.[7]

Goethe mused that the Reformation provides an occasion not only
for musical composition, but also for poetic treatment. It would appear
that Zelter had inadvertently asked Goethe a question on a subject he
had not only been writing about in connection with his multiple pre-
publication drafts on the celebration of the Saint Roch festival, but had
also been reading about that very summer, namely, Luther's writings.[8]
This helps to explain Goethe's immediate and lengthy response of November 14, including the incisive interpretation of Lutheranism it contains and the texts that he recommended that Zelter read in order to
compose a formidable oratorio — "im Sinne des Händelschen Messias"
[in the spirit of Händel's *Messiah*].[9] The work was never realised, although Goethe did compose a few lines for it.[10]

Nevertheless, the exchange crystallised Goethe's thoughts on how
such a festival ought to be celebrated. In the November 14 letter he
makes the comment that Lutheranism can never be united with the Papacy.[11] Towards the end of the letter, however, he feels it is time to
consider Catholicism, and he relates a standard Protestant view of
Church history by asserting the loss of Catholicism's original purity.[12]
Goethe opines that Luther's achievements ought to be recognised with
the right attitude. He specifies: "Dieses Fest wäre so zu begehen, daß
es jeder wohldenkende Katholik mitfeierte. Doch davon ein andermal"
[This festival ought to be celebrated such that every well-thinking
Catholic would celebrate too. But more on that another time].[13]
Goethe seems to be implying that Luther's achievements transcend
confessional boundaries. Despite the cliff-hanging ending, Goethe did
not address the subject again in his letters to Zelter.

He did, however, write an essay on the Reformation festival, probably conceived and written during the November 1816 exchange of letters with Zelter. In this posthumously published essay, *Zum
Reformationsfest* [For the Reformation Festival], Goethe writes that the
anniversary had already motivated many throughout the German lands
to make suggestions on how to celebrate.[14] Obviously it had set his
mind racing, for he sees that the Reformation festival has the potential
to create fresh religious rivalries: "Die Protestanten sehen dieser Epoche mit Freudigkeit entgegen; die Katholiken fürchten höhnenden
Übermut und befürchten neue Spaltung und Trennung" [The Protestants anticipate this epoch with joy; the Catholics fear jeering arrogance
as well as new division and separation].

Goethe contributes his own suggestion: that the date of the celebration be changed. He reasons that the Reformation festival is a
moveable feast anyway, since the various Protestant German principalities commemorate it on different days. Virtually any significant date
connected with Luther could serve as a milestone, but linking the festival to Luther's *Thesenanschlag* (31 October), the nailing of his ninety-
five theses to the church door in Wittenberg, means conflating religious
celebration with religious conflict: "Luther hat an diesem Tage, gleich-
sam die unwiderrufliche Kriegserklärung gegen das Papstthum gethan"
[On this day Luther declared an irrevocable war on the Papacy].
Goethe therefore suggests considering alternative dates.[15] He is both-
ered that the symbolically significant date of the *Thesenanschlag* might
be perceived as inherently bellicose, thus dampening the general joy of
the festival and sparking further strife.

Goethe tried to relate Luther's act of reformation productively to
personal ethics. For him a salient meaning connected to the Reformation is that of self-reformation, as he indicates in a posthumously published book review of the second half of the second part of Johann
Traugott Leberecht Danz's *Lehrbuch der neueren christlichen Kirchengeschichte* (Textbook of Recent Christian Church History, 1818–1826).
Danz (1769–1851), a Professor of Theology at the University of Jena,
dedicated the book to "Goethe, dem edlen Freunde und Verehrer
Luthers" [Goethe, the noble friend and admirer of Luther].[16] The review contains a variation of an oft-quoted maxim of Goethe's about
self-reformation and protest. The maxim reads "Genau besehen haben
wir uns noch alle Tage zu reformieren und gegen andere zu protesti-
ren, wenn auch nicht in religiösem Sinne" [Seen precisely, we must reform ourselves and protest against others on all days, if not in the
religious sense].[17]

Goethe believed that a central element of the Reformation was
protest, a positive right and personal responsibility that he based on
freedom of thought. In an unsent letter to C. C. von Leonhard, written
when his attention was first drawn to the 1817 Reformation festival, he
reflects frankly on highly personal acts of protest: "Im nächsten Jahr
feiert die protestantische Kirche ihr Jubiläum. . . . Und so will ich dieses Jahr von meiner Seite das Fest feiern, daß ich wie Luther kein Blatt
vors Maul nehme" [In the next year the Protestant Church celebrates
her jubilee. . . . And so this year will I, on my side, celebrate a festival,
namely, that I will, like Luther, not mince words].[18] While this has reference to a debate in the natural sciences, Goethe posits that protest is
symbolic of the Reformation itself in a poem entitled "Dem 31. Okto-

ber 1817" in which he compares his own activities in art and science to those of Protestants who fear neither the Pope nor the Turks.[19]

Goethe's concerns in *Zum Reformationsfest* are societal. His specific recommendation is to change the date of the festival and merge it with the festival to commemorate another significant event of protest and resistance, namely, the Leipzig *Völkerschlacht* (Battle of the Nations), 16–19 October 1813, when an international coalition defeated Napoleon's armies. Goethe lists three reasons for such a merger. The first justifies the use of this term from corporate finance. Since the two festivals would be celebrated within two weeks of each other, they would detract from each other and drain the "Oekonomische Kräfte" [economic strength] of the German people.[20] Economic recovery from the long war years was a concern of Goethe's in other writings during this period, including the *Sankt-Rochus-Fest zu Bingen* and a review essay entitled *Der Pfingstmontag* (Whit Monday).[21]

Goethe's second reason for wanting to change the date of the Reformation festival, a reason he deems a higher consideration than financial exhaustion, is the perception that "das Gefühl erschöpft sich auch" [emotions are also exhausted], in other words how can individuals be exultant on two celebrations spaced so closely together.[22] There is a lexical echo here as *erschöpfen* can refer to both economic and emotional exhaustion.

The third reason for merging the two festivals transcends local, regional, and even national considerations: it is Goethe's vision of unity. Celebrating the Reformation festival on the eighteenth of October would include most Germans, and parochial concerns, although important, would be overshadowed by universal possibilities: "Es wird von allen Glaubensgenossen gefeiert, und ist in diesem Sinne noch mehr als Nationalfest; ein Fest der reinsten Humanität" [It will be celebrated by all believers and is in this sense even more than a national festival; a festival of purest humanity]. This highlights again Goethe's primary motivation: overcoming division and separations, not just among Catholics and Protestants within the German principalities, but among all religions, for the international fight for freedom was also interdenominational. Goethe puts forward the cosmopolitan idea that all may celebrate: "Niemand fragt, von welcher Konfession der Mann des Landsturms sei, alle ziehen vereinigt zur Kirche, und werden von demselben Gottesdienste erbaut" [Nobody asks what is the confession of the man in the territorial reserve, all go unified to church and are edified by the same religious service].[23] Thus both Catholics and Protestants could celebrate if the eighteenth of October was chosen for the

Reformation tercentenary, as it would represent "the freedom of the nation from foreign domination and the freedom of thought from doctrinaire restraints."[24]

Goethe uses terminology his readers would have understood to describe the envisioned festival when he employs vocabulary such as "Kirche" [church] and "Gottesdienst" [religious service]. Nevertheless, he wants to go well beyond a specifically Christian festival, for he proposes not only a celebration that would include traditional religions, but also all others that could be represented in such a feast of humanity. The word Goethe chooses to signify this broad category is "Heiden" [heathen], yet he does not use this pejoratively; rather he gives it equal footing with world-wide religions: "Alle erheben den Geist . . . nicht etwa nur Christen sondern auch Juden, Mahometanern und Heiden" [The Spirit lifts all . . . not only the Christians, but also the Jews, Muslims, and heathens].[25] As Goethe does not expand on any previously known festival model, he has therefore to create the idea in language. He coins a neologism that contains the seeds that could outgrow traditional, religious festivals, by reaching out to and embracing all of humanity in a universal celebration: a "Weltfest" [world festival]:

> Man denke sich nun den Geist, von diesem großen Weltfeste, zurück auf ein speciales Kirchenfest gelenkt an welchem ein reines Gemüth, oft keine vollkommene Freude haben kann, weil man an Zwiespalt und Unfrieden ein ungeheures Unglück einiger Jahrhunderte erinnert wird, ja was noch schlimmer ist, daß er sich sagen muß, daß er sich von denjenigen, mit denen er sich vor vierzehn Tagen, aufs innigste und kräftigste verbunden gefühlt, trennen und sie durch diese Trennung kränken muß. Und gerade die Freude einer liebevollen Eintracht wird man . . . vermissen.[26]

> [Imagine the spirit of this great world festival turned back upon a specific church festival in which a person of pure disposition often cannot have a fullness of joy because he is reminded of conflict and discord, a monstrous disaster of some few centuries. And what is worse, that he must tell himself that he must separate himself from those with whom he celebrated fourteen days previously and to whom he felt deepest and strongest alliance and now through this separation offend them. And exactly the pleasure of a loving harmony one will . . . miss.]

This practical aim, of peace and harmony in society, is brought out in the conclusion of the essay, as he warns that Catholics will hide away in Protestant states and that in Catholic areas the Protestants will celebrate privately.[27] It is a bitter irony that Goethe's coinage is applied to the very opposite of his conception in the final sentence of Thomas

Mann's *Der Zauberberg* (The Magic Mountain, 1924), when it is suggested that the nations succumb to a "Weltfest des Todes" [world festival of death] in the First World War.[28]

Religious unity was a major political issue at the time Goethe was
writing *Zum Reformationsfest*. In 1817 Friedrich Wilhelm III of Prussia
utilised the Reformation tercentenary to issue a "religious but non-
dogmatic" call for the union of the Lutheran and Reformed Churches:
"The time was considered propitious. The Enlightenment was thought
to have minimised doctrinal differences between Lutheran and Reformed, Pietism had stressed their common Christian experience, and
resurgent nationalism had provided a favorable emotional climate."[29]
And on 31 October 1817, "twenty Berlin ministers attended a communion service, in which rites and formulas were used which left it to
the communicant to interpret the Lord's Supper in either Lutheran or
Calvinist manner. King and court held a similar service in Potsdam."[30]
Although in Baden, Nassau, and the Bavarian Palatinate a union was
brought about with local ecclesiastical co-operation, Friedrich Wilhelm
III nevertheless imposed his own order of worship.[31] This *Agende*, as it
was called in 1822, was a significant change in religious policy, for the
new church was closely allied with the state.

The inclusive festival atmosphere of Goethe's envisioned celebration
is captured by his description of loving Catholic and Protestant co-
operation in the *Sankt-Rochus-Fest zu Bingen*. The *Morgenblatt* essay
on *Die Geheimnisse* expands the number of religions in a fictional narrative, but *Zum Reformationsfest* provides a concrete proposal for
achieving harmony regardless of denomination. 1816 was a remarkable
year indeed in Goethe's writings, and the ones discussed above reflect
how much he wanted to contribute to the new peace and help rebuild
German society.

But there was more, and Goethe was going further: on 24 February
1816 subscribers to the *Morgenblatt* would have come across an exotic
item on oriental poets, places, and cultures, in an advertisement signed
by Goethe no less. It announced a major new lyrical work, his *West-
östlicher Divan*.

Notes

[1] WA III/5, 126.

[2] WA IV/26, 247.

[3] 9 August 1816: MA 20.1, 447.

[4] 22 August 1816: MA 20.1, 451.

[5] MA 20.1, 468.

[6] 4–5 November 1816: MA 20.1, 466.

[7] 14 November 1816: MA 20.1, 474–78.

[8] WA III/5, 265–66.

[9] MA 20.1, 475.

[10] WA I/16, 577–78.

[11] MA 20.1, 475.

[12] MA 20.1, 477.

[13] Ibid. Cf. Jörg Baur, "Martin Luther im Urteil Goethes," *Goethe Jahrbuch* 114 (1997): 11–22.

[14] FA 20, 603. Goethe did not give this essay a title; *Zum Reformationsfest* is the title in the FA. The essay was first published in 1895.

[15] FA 20, 603. For example, Luther's birthday (10 November), his death day (18 February) or the day of the *Confessio Augustana* (25 June). In the Saxony-Thuringia region October 31 had been the celebration day since 1667 (FA 20, 1484).

[16] As quoted by John in MA 13.1, 918. This essay was first published in 1903.

[17] FA, 13, 161.

[18] 7 November 1816: WA IV/27, 421.

[19] FA 20, 10. The poem was first published in KuA (II/1, 1818).

[20] FA 20, 603. Approximately 450 students from assorted student duelling societies (about half from Jena) celebrated the two festivals on 18 October 1817 in the Wartburg. After the festival had officially finished, a smaller group of students burned writings and symbols they believed were reactionary (Irmela Schneider: MA 13.1, 583–84).

[21] FA 20, 440. Goethe's review was first published in KuA (II/2, 1820).

[22] FA 20, 603–604.

[23] FA 20, 604.

[24] James J. Sheehan, *German History 1770–1866* (Oxford: Clarendon Press, 1993), 406.

[25] FA 20, 604. These (for the time) all-embracing religious categories reflect typical Enlightenment groupings. Cf. Stephan-Kopitzsch, *Aufklärungszeitschriften*, 58–59.

[26] FA 20, 604.

[27] FA 20, 604.

[28] Thomas Mann, *Gesammelte Werke*, 12 vols. (Oldenburg: Fischer, 1960), vol. 3, *Der Zauberberg*, 994.

[29] Maclear, *Church and State*, 185.

[30] Hajo Holborn, *A History of Modern Germany 1648–1840* (Princeton: Princeton UP, 1982), 488.

[31] Holborn, *A History of Modern Germany 1648–1840*, 489.

7: The Foreign and the Familiar in the *West-östlicher Divan*

IN A MAY 1815 LETTER, Goethe made an author's wish: that his latest book would reach a wide audience. His intention was to bind serenely the customs and ways of thinking of West and East, past and present, Persian and German.[1] This intention makes the *West-östlicher Divan* (West-Eastern Divan, 1819), as he would later name the work, an indispensable account of his thoughts on cultural mediation.[2] It must be stated before continuing along this line of reasoning that the *Divan* poetry grew from a context. To ignore this would be to miss defining features and specific characteristics of the parent material. This context was his 1814 and 1815 travels to the Rhineland in the autumn of his life to visit old friends and new acquaintances, to refresh his body at spas and his mind at art collections. He saw first-hand the devastation of war and the unquenchable will to rebuild. As a sixty-five-year-old man he expressed in poetry his love of life generally, as well as his deep feelings for a woman personally. The *Divan* is a collection of twelve books of poetry and each book has a German and Arabic title. The poetry is distorted and impoverished if one loses sight of Goethe's view of the Persian civilisation in which he immersed himself and with which the Napoleonic wars had brought him into contact. For example he saw a camel in Dresden and observed Muslims worshipping in Weimar — uncommon sights that impressed Goethe and heightened his interest in Persian culture.[3] Therefore the final (thirteenth) book of the *Divan*, the explanatory essay *Besserem Verständniss* (For Better Understanding) as it was originally named in the first edition, will be explored in the following chapter.[4]

The *Divan* (Arabic for collection) cannot be reduced to a set of intellectual positions, but it suggests several. The poems can be interpreted collectively as an effort to honour not only the life of a foreign poet (Hafiz), but also as an attempt to understand his world. Moreover, the *Divan* draws readers into an Enlightenment frame of reference, as, for example, society's tolerance of artists, and the social politics of personality, individuality, and freedom of thought are considered.[5] The *Divan* also throws light on two central ideas that arise elsewhere in

Goethe's writings, *Geltenlassen* and *Anerkennung* [acceptance and recognition].

The pre-publication poetry of the *Divan*

Goethe hoped that this work would attract his fellow Germans and that they would glimpse commonalities of the human experience in eastern and western cultures, and perhaps serve as a bridge between Islam and Christianity. His poetic self-confidence never wavered in the face of such an ambitious undertaking, yet he did not overestimate the public's desire for this encounter. He witnessed the limp reception of Hammer-Purgstall's translation of Hafiz and ascribed it to the great remove of the subject matter.[6] This betrays Goethe's belief that he would be able to communicate poetically Hafiz's circumstances, convictions, and literary idiom.

Less than a year after his first mention of the work in his correspondence, Goethe's private resolve became a public matter in the 24 February 1816 *Morgenblatt,* where he announced his forthcoming collection. Goethe included the poem "Hegire" [Arabic for flight] because he felt it gives a sense of the entire direction of the collection:

> Nord und West und Süd zersplittern,
> Throne bersten, Reiche zittern,
> Flüchte du! im reinen Osten
> Patriarchenluft zu kosten.
> Unter Lieben, Trinken, Singen,
> Soll dich Chisers Quell verjüngen.[7]

[North and West and South shatter; thrones explode, empires quake; seek refuge in the pure East to taste the air of patriarchs. With love, drinking, and song, Chiser's source will make you young.]

The imperative tone and words, an urgent call, would be understood in the socio-political context of the day. Napoleon's march through Europe — his latest (and final) dispatch had only recently occurred through Blücher and Wellington — left smashed nations in its wake, including the 1806 collapse of the Empire. During Goethe's two previous Rhine journeys in 1814 and 1815 he had been an eyewitness to the large-scale destruction and misery caused by the protracted war. Thus, even as his court position at Weimar made him aware of the European ramifications of the Congress of Vienna, he was not unaware of the individual men, women, and children who were picking up the pieces of their lives and homes (and churches, like Saint Roch). The announce-ment of the forthcoming *Divan* can be interpreted as advertising a tonic that will help rejuvenate war-weary readers, much as the new world of Persia and the personal experiences associated with the Rhine journey revitalised Goethe.

Goethe's ability to fuse poetically his personal experiences with world events is exemplified in the *Divan*. Many of the poems, some critics argue the core, derive explicitly from his deep friendship with the thirty-year-old Marianne Willemer,[8] yet also woven into the poems is an exploration of Persian poets and Middle East history and religion, which in turn allows Goethe to reflect on his contemporary society. Thus interpersonal communion evolves into intercultural communica-tion and this is nowhere more evident than in the sequence of two central *Divan* books. In *Buch Suleika* [Book of Suleika] the mutual feelings of Marianne and Goethe are called a "Duodrama." Yet, this book is placed just after *Buch des Timur* [Book of Timur, i.e. the con-queror Tamburlaine] in which are mirrored "Weltbegebenheiten" [world events]. Goethe wants his society to see its own fate in the "Wiederschein" [reflection] of these events, for scenes played out on the world stage and in private *Duodramen* co-exist.[9] The artistic mirror he holds up shows the people of his day and present readers that past ages and distant cultures faced similar circumstances on both micro-cosmic and macrocosmic levels.

Referring to himself in the *Morgenblatt* announcement in the third person, Goethe explains that the poet views himself as a "Reisender" [traveller] — the word denotes destination and purpose — who has just arrived in the Orient and is enthused to learn about the customs, con-ventions, objects, religious attitudes, and opinions of the region. He desires to empathise with the people and therefore suggests that he could even be a Muslim himself. This act of empathy, however, does not pretend to be one of perfect understanding, but an idiosyncratic identification as revealed by Goethe's discussion of the order and title of the first two books of his poetry collection. The first is called *Mo-ganiname* or *Buch des Dichters* [Book of the Poet]; when the *Divan* was first published in 1819 he would translate it as *Buch des Sängers* [Book of the Singer]. The second is named *Hafisname* and was trans-lated as *Das Buch Hafis* [Book of Hafiz]. Goethe, the travelling poet, was attracted to Persian poetry and songs and identifies strongly with the medieval Persian poet Hafiz, for despite the temporal and cultural remove, his poetry has the power to refresh and encourage "ein deutsches Herz" [a German heart].[10]

Although the German poet can observe, rejoice in, and aspire to empathise with the Persian predecessor, he does not desire to be, nor can he be, Hafiz. The Persian and German are compatible, but neither one subsumes the other. The *Divan* is written unabashedly for a German readership, and although the German poet may see himself as a "Zwilling" [twin] of the Persian poet, yet they are distinct individuals.[11] Past and present are shown to be similar, not the same, and whereas Islam and Christianity may be linked at certain points, yet they are also mutually exclusive.[12]

A month later Goethe released more poems for pre-*Divan* publication in the *Morgenblatt* (22 March 1816). "Talismane," a set of loosely connected mini-poems, opens similarly to "Hegire," with a prophet's-eye view:[13]

> Gottes ist der Orient,
> Gottes ist der Occident;
> Nord' und südliches Gelände
> Ruht im Frieden seiner Hände.

[God's is the Orient, God's is the Occident; northern and southern lands rest in peace in His hands.]

This vision originates in Qur'an Sura 2:115 and suggests spiritual assurance despite tribulations;[14] however, it also alludes to the contemporary post-Napoleonic situation. It can be read as a poetic vision of European peace to the east and west of the Rhine and is linked to the idea of justice, as intimated in the next stanza:

> Er, der einzige Gerechte,
> Will für Jedermann das Rechte.
> Sey, von seinen hundert Namen,
> Dieser hochgelobet! Amen.

[He, the only Just One, wants justice for every man. Of His one hundred names, let this one be praised! Amen.]

The theme of justice is carried into the following stanza as the mortal poet prays to be just in deed and in word (poetry). In the fourth stanza the poetic argument seems to be that the physical, even something as lowly as the dust, can be the basis for something higher:

> Ob ich Irdsches denk' und sinne,
> Das gereicht zu höherem Gewinne.

Mit dem Staube nicht der Geist zerstoben
Dringet, in sich selbst gedrängt, nach oben.

[Though I think on earthly things, these lead on to higher gain. Not with the dust is the Spirit blown, driven it is, pushed from within, upwards.]

A kind of concentration occurs in the poem that links with the metaphorical pressing of individuals by the Divine in the next one. The mortal condition is not bemoaned, rather the polarities of life are acknowledged:

Im Atemholen sind zweyerley Gnaden:
Die Luft einziehn, sich ihrer entladen.
Jenes bedrängt, dieses erfrischt;
So wunderbar ist das Leben gemischt.
Du, danke Gott, wenn er dich presst,
Und dank' ihm, wenn er dich wieder entlässt.

[In breathing are two graces: to breathe air in, and this release. One assails, one refreshes; so marvellously is life mixed. Give thanks to God when He squeezes you and thank Him when He releases you.]

The poem that follows this, published as a separate and preceding poem in the 1819 *Divan*, is named "Freysinn" and has strong connotations with the liberal idea of free thought. The acceptance of life's mercies and diversities in the previous poem can be connected to the poet's proclamation of his individuality as he uses *geltenlassen,* a word he has employed in other works, and a key to his understanding of tolerance:

Lasst mich nur auf meinem Sattel gelten!
Bleibt in euren Hütten, euren Zelten!
Und ich reite froh in alle Ferne,
Ueber meiner Mütze nur die Sterne.

[Let me only on my saddle be! Remain in your huts, your tents! And I gallop gaily into the distance, over my cap only the stars.]

Goethe's distinctive desire to guide his own life would arise later in a conversation with Eckermann, when he explained that in religion, science, and politics he had had the courage to say what he felt.[15] He chided those who rely constantly on the authority of others by spouting the phrase: "Autos epha!" (Greek for "he said it").[16] The poet claimed the freedom to experience life in all its variety and acknowledged no earthly authority over his mind and imagination. This drive toward individuality and unhampered exploration is expanded in the next poem, "Vier Gnaden" [Four Graces]:[17]

> Daß Araber an ihrem Theil
> Die Weite froh durchziehen,
> Hat Allah zu gemeinem Heil
> Der Gnaden vier verliehen.

[That Arabs should gaily roam through distant parts, has Allah for general benefit granted four graces.]

The next verses name these four graces as a turban, a tent, a sword, and a song. The turban, when compared to all "Kaiserkronen" [imperial crowns] is more useful for travelling, and has, perhaps, fewer inbuilt disadvantages, as the proverb goes: "Uneasy lies the head that wears a crown."[18] The tent, on the other hand, has natural advantages for someone traversing desert places. Of course, the sword can be read as the actual sword of an intrepid traveller as against the walls of timorous fortress-dwellers. But in the context of freedom and self-assertion, the sword signifies a poet's weapon — his pen — which suggests he prefers engaging with ideas openly rather than hiding behind what the poem later calls "hohe Mauern" [high walls], which can be seen as conformism.

Finally, the fourth blessing is a "Liedchen, das gefällt und nützt" [Song that pleases and benefits]. The pleasure and practical function of poetry are on offer in the *Divan*. The poet refers to himself as a market trader and calls attention to his wares:

> Und Blum' und Früchte weiß ich euch
> Gar zierlich aufzutischen;
> Wollt ihr Moralien zugleich,
> Ich geb' sie von den frischen.[19]

[And flowers and fruits I know how to set charmingly before you; if you want moralities as well, I offer fresh ones.]

Despite the prominence of individuality, these four graces serve ultimately the general well-being. The common good, an ethical notion, is an important check on the individuality highlighted in this poem. It could be that the glorification of a near nomadic existence (the tent) may leave one marginalised; the trumpeted self-reliance (the sword) may lead to arrogance; and artistic licence (song) may slide into self-indulgence. Recognising one's membership in a community provides a limit on these potential extremes. The tone and words at the end of the stanza imply that the poet can, if the listeners want, serve up frivolous moral homilies as if they were foodstuffs.

Goethe fused two pre-publication *Divan* poems for a Berlin publisher in *Gaben der Milde* (Gifts of Mildness, 1817), a volume created to raise money for a group that always seems to be forgotten, the "hülflose Krieger" [helpless veterans].[20] The first stanza lists four things that the poet describes as delightful: the look of a beckoning girl; the sight of a drinker before he drinks; the greeting of a lord who could command; and the autumnal sunshine. Finally, a needy hand receiving a small gift is described and this is held to be lovelier than all of the preceding images:

> Lieblicher als alles dieses habe
> Stets vor Augen: wie sich kleiner Gabe
> Dürft'ge Hand so hübsch entgegen dränget,
> Zierlich dankbar, was du reichst, empfänget.
> Welch ein Blick! ein Gruß! ein sprechend Streben!
> Schau es recht und du wirst immer geben.[21]

[More delightful than all of these have always before your eyes: how a needy hand presses so nicely toward a small gift, that delicately grateful, receives what you give. What a look! A greeting! An eloquent striving! Look at it justly and you will always give.]

A moral conclusion is reached in the final stanza:

> Was in vielen Büchern steht
> Ist dir aus der Brust geschrieben:
> Jeden, dem du selber giebst,
> Wirst du wie dich selber lieben.
> Reiche froh den Pfennig hin,
> Häufe nicht ein Gold-Vermächtniß,
> Eile freudig vorzuziehn
> Gegenwart vor dem Gedächtniß.[22]

[That which is written in many books is written on your heart: each, to whom you give, you will love as yourself. Give gladly your penny — do not hoard a legacy of gold — rush joyfully to prefer the present before the past.]

An act of service is a form of communication and speaks from the heart. Individuals are bound together as hand reaches out to hand in giving and receiving. Similar sentiments are expressed in "Was willst du untersuchen. . ." a poem in *Buch der Sprüche* (Book of Proverbs): "Was willst du untersuchen / Wohin die Milde fließt. / In's Wasser wirf deine Kuchen, / Wer weiß wer sie genießt." [Why will you investigate where mildness flows. Throw your cake into the water — who knows who will enjoy it.][23] It is interesting that in the 1819 *Divan* the poem published in *Gaben der Milde* begins, "Und was im Pend-Nameh steht. . ." [And that which is written in the Book of Counsel].[24] Goethe, in the 1817 version, tactically removed the specific Arabic title in order to universalise the moral application of the poem. This is the same fundamental strategy he uses in *Zum Reformationsfest,* as he universalises the upcoming Protestant festival into a *Weltfest.*

1818 brought yet another pre-publication release of *Divan* poems in Zelter's book of song accompaniments, *Liedertafel.* In one of the poems, entitled "Liederstoff" (Song Material; in the 1819 publication of the *Divan* it would be named "Elemente"), a technique typical of the poetry of the *Divan* is employed, that of question and answer. The question is how many elements are required to write a song that appeals to both the layman and the master. The answer is that four elements are necessary to write such poetry: love, wine, war, and hate.[25] Love and hate co-exist, and just as the poet finds the receiving hand lovely in the previous poem, he finds certain things despicable, and maintains that the poet must hate the ugly and tetchy.

Crabb Robinson, an English lawyer who resided in Jena for several years, reported that he conversed with Goethe in 1804 on the topic of Eastern literature, and noted that Goethe glibly voiced an aversion to the "Easterns," and a hate of the Egyptians: "And I am glad that I have something to hate — That is absolutely necessary, otherwise one is in danger of falling into the dull liberal habit of finding all things tolerable & good in their place — And that is the Ruin of all good Sentiments."[26] The critique of mere indifference masquerading as tolerance, and of seeing things as indiscriminate and indistinguishable, illustrates Goethe's view that a poet be able to feel and discriminate between love and hate, good and evil, wisdom and folly, joy and sorrow, pleasure and pain.

In a later poem in *Buch des Unmuths* [Book of Ill Humour], "Wanderers Gemüthsruhe" [The Wanderer's Peace of Heart], the mood is less truculent, as if the poet resigns himself to the thought that complaining about what is badly done would be a waste of time and effort, since this is the way things always are.[27] Nevertheless, discernment is the poet's hallmark in the *Divan*, as he criticises laziness, stupidity, priests, tyranny, even a rude waiter,[28] and praises love, poetry, the Islamic vision of paradise, Adam and Eve, and wine. These poems, of course, go beyond being little moral statements, but they do express individuality, freedom of thought, a universalising of the good, and a critique of indifference and shoddiness.

The first edition of the *Divan*

Goethe published his collection of poetry and prose in 1819 under the title:

West-Oestlicher Divan
Ad-diwan as-sarqi li'l-mu'allif al-garbi [29]

The German-Arabic double title is itself a gesture to the cross-cultural pollination that the *Divan* represents. It is also a linguistic emblem that repeats itself through all twelve books of the *Divan*, as each one is headed with an Arabic title, then an equivalent one in German. The reader is reminded with each new book that a western author has drawn on eastern materials, especially as the Arabic titles are presented first. The spliced and altered pre-*Divan* publication poems, and the few Goethe added in his *Neuer Divan* (New Divan, 1827), indicate that the collection is loosely organised. Themes are introduced and recur in multiple poems and parts of poems, so that the first poem of the *Buch der Sprüche* could serve as an introduction to the entire *Divan*: "Talismane werd' ich in dem Buch zerstreuen, / Das bewirkt ein Gleichgewicht. / Wer mit gläubiger Nadel sticht / Ueberall soll gutes Wort ihn freuen." [I will strew talismans in the book — that makes for a balance. Whoever pricks with a pious needle, everywhere shall a good word gladden him.][30]

Moganni Nameh/Buch des Sängers [Book of the Singer], the first book of the *Divan*, contains five poems that were published in some form earlier, namely, "Hegire," "Freysinn," "Talismane," "Vier Gnaden," and "Elemente." In "Derb und Tüchtig" [Coarse and Capable] the poet argues that "Dichten ist ein Uebermuth" [Writing poetry is an act of high spirits], and he refuses to be chastised for it. He does not despise modesty, but is repulsed by those critics whom he labels "Mönchlein" [little monks] who judge his writing without understanding. The poem concludes: "Denn wer einmal uns versteht / Wird uns auch verzeihn." [For he who once understands us will also pardon us.][31] This final couplet is a variation of an oft-postulated solution to interpersonal and intercultural problems — the relationship between understanding and pardoning — as attributed to Madame de Staël: "tout comprendre c'est tout pardonner" [to understand all is to pardon all].

The poet acknowledges implicitly the proverbial dangers of over-confidence and suggests that those who understand poets would forgive it. In a later poem he argues that "Ueberall will jeder obenauf seyn, / Wie's eben in der Welt so geht." [Everywhere every one wants to be on top; that's the way the world goes.][32] Self-assertion is described as natural. In a conversation with Eckermann about the *Divan* on 4 January 1824, Goethe gave important biographical keys to what he means by poetic self-confidence:

Man war im Grunde nie mit mir zufrieden und wollte mich immer anders, als es Gott gefallen hatte, mich zu machen. Auch war man selten mit dem zufrieden, was ich hervorbrachte. Wenn ich mich Jahr und Tag mit ganzer Seele abgemüht hatte, der Welt mit einem neuen Werke etwas zu Liebe zu tun, so verlangte sie, daß ich mich noch obendrein bei ihr bedanken sollte, daß sie es nur erträglich fand. – Lobte man mich, so sollte ich das nicht in freudigem Selbstgefühl als einen schuldigen Tribut hinnehmen, sondern man erwartete von mir irgend eine ablehnende bescheidene Phrase, worin ich demütig den völligen Unwert meiner Person und meines Werkes an den Tag lege. Das aber widerstrebte meiner Natur und ich hätte müssen ein elender Lump sein, wenn ich so hätte heucheln und lügen wollen. Da ich nun aber stark genug war, mich in ganzer Wahrheit so zu zeigen, wie ich fühlte, so galt ich für stolz, und gelte noch so bis auf den heutigen Tag.[33]

[People were never really satisfied with me and wanted me to be other than it had pleased God to make me. People were also seldom satisfied with what I produced. When I worked with all my soul yearly and daily to please the world, the world demanded that I needed to, on top of all, be thankful that my work was found merely bearable. – If I was praised, I was not supposed to accept joyfully that people owed me such tribute, rather I was expected to give some self-effacing, modest phrase in which I was to expose the complete unworthiness of my person and work. That went against my nature and I would have had to be a miserable scoundrel if I had so lied and been hypocritical. Because I was strong enough to show how I felt with complete truth, I was known as proud and am held to be so up until the present day.]

Indeed, critics continue to accuse Goethe of having an "appalling self-confidence."[34]

The case for tolerating poets is made in the poem "Medschnun heißt. . ." [Medschnun means. . .]: "Wenn die Brust, die redlich volle, / Sich entladet euch zu retten, / Ruft ihr nicht: das ist der Tolle! / Holet Stricke, schaffet Ketten!"[35] [When the breast, full of honesty, erupts to save you, do not shout: there is the madman! Fetch the cords and the chains!] Poets are presented as seers, sensitive to the signs of the times, and endeavouring to warn others. They should not be persecuted for seeing things differently to the rest of society.

Following directly on from "Derb und Tüchtig" is "Allleben" [Universal Life].[36] Goethe composed the lyric poem during a stormy night journey from Frankfurt to Wiesbaden. It is also a masterly intertextual competition with Hafiz, who also wrote poetry about love as well as plain things, like dust.[37] The poem "Elemente" teaches that war, wine, love, and hate are the stuff of poetry, but in "Allleben" Goethe composes a poem about dust and how life springs from it, for the gates of love have long been shut to him. The poet cries out to nature — to the thunder storm — to help restore him: "Heile mich Gewitterregen, / Laß mich daß es grunelt riechen!" [Heal me rainstorm, let me smell the refreshed earth!] In the final two stanzas, life is indeed created from the dust (the earth) and the combination of three other elements, wind, rain, and fire (thunder and lightning):

> Wenn jetzt alle Donner rollen
> Und der ganze Himmel leuchtet,
> Wird der wilde Staub des Windes
> Nach dem Boden hingefeuchtet.
>
> Und sogleich entspringt ein Leben,
> Schwillt ein heilig, heimlich Wirken,
> Und es grunelt und es grünet
> In den irdischen Bezirken.

[If now all the thunders roll and illuminate the entire heavens, the wild dust of the wind will fall to earth saturated. And immediately a life springs up, a sacred, mysterious force expands and it breathes and it greens in the earthly spheres.]

Goethe exhibits a virtuoso command of his seemingly banal subject, for he is able to create from the dust a poem about the creation of life. "Allleben" flows thematically from the previous poem in a number of ways. The last stanza of "Derb und Tüchtig" speaks of the "Dichters Mühle," or the poet's mill, a kind of creative generator. Here, Goethe quietly displays his "Uebermuth," not only by challenging Hafiz directly, but by showing the reader how even the dust of the earth that one encounters each day, can be a profound subject.[38]

Human creative potential, no matter how plain or undistinguished, should never be underestimated or denied. A poem about the creation of a pearl unfolds along these lines in *Mathal-Nameh/Buch der Parabeln* [Book of Parables], and this theme is echoed again in another poem: "Gottes Größe [ist] im Kleinen zu lernen" [God's greatness is to be learned in the little things].[39]

Goethe acquaints the reader in *Hafis Nameh/Buch Hafis* [Book of Hafiz] with the eponymous Persian poet and expresses his admiration for him. It becomes clear that he identifies strongly with Hafiz and his circumstances. The first poem, "Beyname" [Surname], features a dialogue between a poet, presumably Goethe, and Hafiz. Such exchanges continue throughout the book, between different characters. The poet learns that Hafiz is so named because he treasures, honours, and preserves the Qur'an.[40] The poet responds that he too has been brought up on a holy book, the Bible. This reference is inserted to provide a context for the next poem, "Anklage" [Indictment], which can be read both as an accusation of heresy brought against Hafiz (for his poems appear to contradict the Qur'an) and an indictment of those who make such accusations, called devils. Pious Muslims, knowledgeable in the law, are asked to pass judgement or *Fetwa*.[41] In the first poem, entitled "Fetwa," Abusu'ud judges:

> Hafis Dichterzüge sie bezeichnen
> Ausgemachte Wahrheit unauslöschlich;
> Aber hie und da auch Kleinigkeiten
> Außerhalb der Gränze des Gesetzes.
> Willst du sicher gehn, so mußt du wissen
> Schlangengift und Theriak zu sondern —   [42]

[The poetic strokes of Hafis express accepted, inextinguishable truth; but here and there minor points outside of the borders of the law. If you would walk safely, you must know how to part serpent's venom from its antidote —]

Here is a case of intracultural tolerance as a Muslim sits in judgement on a Muslim poet. The judgement suggests that the overall truths expressed in Hafiz's poems supercede minor infractions of the law. The

Enlightenment ethos of the judge in the poem is highlighted dramatically, as he places the burden of responsibility on the accuser (and by extension, on the critic and reader) who must learn to distinguish between poison and medicine. There is a resemblance to Lessing's judge in *Nathan der Weise*, who does not identify the one true ring, but leaves it to the sons to discover through their good works.[43] By refusing to tell the accusers (readers) what they can learn and should know for themselves, one can hear echoes of Kant: "Habe ich ein Buch, das für mich Verstand hat, einen Seelsorger, der für mich Gewissen hat, einen Arzt, der für mich Diät beurteilt, u.s.w.: so brauche ich mich ja nicht selbst zu bemühen. Ich habe nicht nötig zu denken" [If I have a book that has understanding for me, a pastor that has conscience for me, a doctor that judges my diet, etc. I do not need to make an effort. I do not need to think].[44] The Islamic judge goes on to suggest that the accusers do spontaneous good deeds and avoid those serious misdeeds that will truly endanger their souls. "Heiliger Ebusuud, du hast's getroffen!" [Saintly Abusu'ud, you have hit the mark!] exclaims the poet, twice, in the following poem, "Der Deutsche dankt" [The German gives thanks]. Significantly, this poem appears to correspond to Goethe's rubric, "Anerkennung," in his 1815 "Wiesbadner Register," a manuscript that contains early versions of the order and titles of the poems in the *Divan*.

Goethe's *Anerkennung* — his recognition, acceptance, praise, and respect — for Abusu'ud's wisdom is contained in the wish: "Solche Heilige wünschet sich der Dichter" [Such saints the poet likes to see].[45] Katharina Mommsen observes that Goethe found in the world of Islam advocates for poets who protected them from overly narrow interpretations of the law.[46] Goethe was, of course, no stranger to intolerance: "Ich glaubte an Gott und die Natur, und an den Sieg des Edlen über das Schlechte; aber das war den frommen Seelen nicht genug, ich sollte auch glauben, daß Drei Eins sei und Eins Drei; das aber widerstrebte dem Wahrheitsgefühl meiner Seele" [I believed in God and Nature and the victory of the noble over the badly done; but that was not enough for righteous souls, I was supposed to believe that three was one and one three; that went against my soul's feeling of truth].[47] Hence the example of tolerance shown for Hafiz's individuality, even poetic exceptionality, by the judge may have held a personal significance for the German poet. Goethe realised that he, too, was responsible for his own writing, just as his accusers were responsible for their own reading, as shown in the next poem, also called "Fetwa."

This second *Fetwa* features another judgement on literature, and in this particular court of poetic justice the poet is saved, exceptionally, from an *auto-da-fe*. The unnamed *Mufti* (judge) pronounces that all who speak and believe like the poet Misri will be, like his poems, burned. But the judge saves Misri himself from the flames. He declares that the poet is responsible for his gift and accountable to Allah for its use.[48]

Goethe, however, advocates a more embracing tolerance than outlined by these two *Fetwas*. In "Offenbar Geheimnis" [Open Secret] the learned are castigated for accusing Hafiz of mysticism:

> Du aber bist mystisch rein
> Weil sie dich nicht verstehn,
> Der du, ohne fromm zu seyn, selig bist!
> Das wollen sie dir nicht zugestehn.[49]

[You are however free of mysticism because they do not understand you who, without being pious, are blessed! They do not want to allow you this.]

Hafiz's poetry is put forward as embodying a kind of *Weltfrömmigkeit* [secular piety] that the narrow-minded refuse to recognise. In the poem "Wink" [Hint], the final one in the *Buch Hafis*, the poetic words, like an allegory, at once cover and disclose the presence of the maid:

> Und doch haben sie Recht die ich schelte:
> Denn daß ein Wort nicht einfach gelte
> Das müßte sich wohl von selbst verstehn.
> Das Wort ist ein Fächer! Zwischen den Stäben
> Blicken ein Paar schöne Augen hervor.
> Der Fächer ist nur ein lieblicher Flor,
> Er verdeckt mir zwar das Gesicht;
> Aber das Mädchen verbirgt er nicht,
> Weil das schönste was sie besitzt
> Das Auge, mir in's Auge blitzt.[50]

[And yet they are right whom I criticise for that a word is not simply a word ought to go without saying. A word is a fan! Between the blades a pair of beautiful eyes looks out. The fan is only a lovely veil. It does indeed cover the face — but the maid it does not hide — since the chief beauty she possesses, the eye, flashes in my eye.]

The images and the signs, as implied by the title, are in a state of play. The argument to view poetry as if in a state of flux suggests "that artistic works and the artist's activity have a special status. We still hear the cry 'tolerance'; but we already hear the cry 'Spiel.'"[51] The status of the poet, a notion dramatised by Goethe in *Tasso* (1790), is raised again in *Besserem Verständniss*.

Usch Nameh/Buch der Liebe [Book of Love] and *Tefkir Nameh/Buch der Betrachtungen* [Book of Reflections] are the next books in the *Divan*, but *Rendsch Nameh/Buch des Unmuths* [Book of Ill Humour] is where ideas about tolerance and recognition flicker brightest within certain poems. In "Keinen Reimer wird man finden . . ." [No rhymer will one find . . .][52] the speaker asks one of the central questions of the book: "Lebt man denn wenn andre leben?" [Does one live when others live?] He opines that "rhymers" and "fiddlers" like their own works best and wonders if it is possible to honour others without demeaning oneself. He also mocks the inability of some to tell "Mäusedreck von Koriandern" [Mouse droppings from coriander seed].

The poet then compares new brooms and old ones. The old brooms hate the energetic new ones and refuse to acknowledge them, and the new brooms will not accept [nicht gelten lassen] that which came before. This highlights society's need for continuity in time, its ability to keep what is good in the old ways even while reforming and innovating. In the penultimate verse, the metaphor of the brooms is applied to nations. The question whether "one lives when another lives" is examined on the international level:

> Und wo sich die Völker trennen,
> Gegenseitig im Verachten,
> Keins von beyden wird bekennen
> Daß sie nach demselben trachten.

[And where the nations part, each despising the other, neither of the two will confess that they are pursuing the same thing.]

The poem concludes by suggesting that egoism is often most manifest in those who decry it, especially when someone else succeeds.

International relations were on Goethe's mind at various stages when he wrote the *Divan*. By 1814 Napoleon's armies were in retreat and Mme de Staël's *De l'Allemagne* (On Germany, 1810) had been published. On 7 February 1814 Goethe wrote to Sara von Grotthus, a Jewish friend he had known for twenty years, and expressed his feelings about the German tendency to disintegrate when freed from "fremden

Druck" [foreign oppression].[53] Another letter to Grotthus that month contains a prescription for improved relations between Germans after the "ausländische Sclaverey" [foreign slavery], in that they begin to recognise each other's merits [sich anzuerkennen] in order to overcome partisanship.[54]

In the "Fetwa" poems, Goethe defends indirectly his desire for the personal recognition of artistic individuality and talent and for the rights these entail. He asserts that this should be forthcoming to artists of merit, preferably while they are still living. *Anerkennung* in interpersonal relationships was also important to him. Here, however, Goethe hopes that mutual recognition in the relations between Germans, especially in the arts and sciences, could inspire mutual co-operation and overcome intra-German rivalry. The recent subjugation by the French is an antipode to mutual *Anerkennung*.

Goethe was not overly optimistic about all of this. The next poem provides insight into why he would be somewhat reserved about overcoming animosities: "Befindet sich einer heiter und gut, / Gleich will ihn der Nachbar peinigen" [If someone finds himself serene and good, his neighbour wants to torment him immediately].[55] Being a good neighbor encompasses Goethe's attitude of acceptance. This description is declared to be an attribute of the Divine: "Wenn Gott so schlechter Nachbar wäre / Als ich bin und als du bist, / Wir hätten beyde wenig Ehre; / Der läßt einen jeden wie er ist" [If God was as bad a neighbour as I am and you are, we would both have little honour; He lets each be as he is].[56]

But fences, borders, and boundaries are permissible, as implied in "Wenn du auf dem Guten ruhst . . ." [When on the Good you rest . . .]:[57]

> Wenn du auf dem Guten ruhst,
> Nimmer werd' ich's tadeln,
> Wenn du gar das Gute thust,
> Sieh das soll dich adeln;
> Hast du aber deinen Zaun
> Um dein Gut gezogen,
> Leb ich frey und lebe traun
> Keineswegs betrogen.

[When on the Good you rest, I will never blame you if you do good that will ennoble you. But if you have put your fence around your property, I live free and trust I live undeceived.]

Even on a personal level the poet does not feel cheated because of another's desire for privacy, but rather relishes his own independence and individuality, without necessarily excluding the option of working together:

> Denn die Menschen sie sind gut,
> Würden besser bleiben,
> Sollte nicht wie's einer thut
> Auch der Andre treiben.
> Auf dem Weg da ists ein Wort,
> Niemand wird's verdammen:
> Wollen wir an Einen Ort,
> Nun! wir gehn zusammen.

[For people they are good and they would remain better if the one did not do what the other does. On the way there is a word, none will condemn it: if we want to get to one place, well then! Let us go together.]

Birus sees Goethe drawing on the Enlightenment's belief in the goodness of man, but not man's perfectibility through "Gleichmacherei" [egalitarianism].[58] The poem also puts forward the idea that cooperation and sharing, if a similar goal has been agreed upon (notice the capitalised "Einen Ort" which makes it mean "one," not "a" place), are completely acceptable. But the poet also realises in the next stanza that love, money, wine, and honour easily divide people.

Respect for individuality is a theme that continues in the *Buch des Unmuths* in the poem "Hab ich euch denn je gerathen . . ." [Have I ever counselled you . . .][59] Goethe asks whether he has ever told others how to conduct a war or conclude a peace; he describes watching without interfering as fishermen cast their nets; and he does not recall ever needing to tell a carpenter how to measure. The poet claims that he has also been industrious with what Nature has given him and in the final stanza challenges those who would interfere in his work:

> Fühlt ihr euch dergleichen Stärke,
> Nun, so fördert eure Sachen;
> Seht ihr aber meine Werke,
> Lernet erst: so wollt' er's machen.

[If you feel such strength, then tend to your own affairs; but should you see my works, learn first: he wanted to make it this way.]

Later, in *Saki Nameh/Das Schenkenbuch* [Book of the Cup Bearer], he defies any limits on his thoughts: "Niemand setzt mir Schranken, / Ich hab' so meine eigne Gedanken" [No-one sets me bounds, thus I have my own thoughts].[60] Thinking for oneself is another Enlightenment clue that can be traced in the *Divan*.

The penultimate poem of the *Buch des Unmuths*, "Und wer franzet oder brittet . . ." [And anyone who goes in for things French or British . . .] is aimed at European nationalism and its roots in self-interest and egoism. The poet diagnoses why this nationalism exists: "Denn es ist kein Anerkennen" [Because there is no recognition].[61] Bürgel interprets this as Goethe's political commentary on the "Zersplitterung des Abendlandes" [splintering of the Occident].[62] The lack of *Anerkennung* leads the poet to a bleak conclusion: if European life continues without it, "das Rechte" [the just] would be squeezed out by "das Schlechte" [the wicked].

Goethe saw the constancy of human nature as producing patterns in history. He demonstrates one such pattern in the epic-poetic *Buch des Timur*. After hearing Goethe read the *Divan* poem "Der Winter und Timur" [The Winter and Timur], Sulpiz Boisserée noted in his journal on 8 August 1815: "Timurs Winter-Feldzug — Parallel-Stück zu Napoleons Moskowitischem Feldzug" [Timur's winter campaign — parallel piece to Napoleon's Russian's campaign].[63] Goethe used the history of Tamburlaine (1336–1405), ruler of Central Asia and conqueror who died in a winter campaign in China, to mirror Napoleon's doomed invasion of Russia. In *Buch des Timur* the "Tyrann des Unrechts" [tyrant of injustice], and by extension all tyrants, are criticised and compared to Mars.[64]

The poet-prophet's task is nearly done,[65] for he has shown that throughout history there has been little recognition between peoples. Goethe has thus brought together not only East and West, but past and present as well. The reader, as a steward, is charged in the last stanza of "Und wer franzet oder brittet . . ." to render an acount of human nature, beginning with the *Odyssey* and the *Iliad*, and heed his warning about the lack of *Anerkennung*:

> Wer nicht von dreytausend Jahren
> Sich weiß Rechenschaft zu geben,
> Bleib im Dunkeln unerfahren,
> Mag von Tag zu Tage leben.

[He who cannot give account of three thousand years, let him remain in the Dark, inexperienced; let him live from day to day.]

The poet has attempted to illuminate the past and throw a little light ahead; if the reader will not see it, he remains uninformed. The beginning of any enlightenment and cultural progress rests on tolerance and recognition:

Für den Divandichter steht das *Geltenlassen* am Anfang jeder Kultur, die erst dann zu sich selbst kommt, wenn sie sich zum *Anerkennen* steigert. Im Anerkennen sah Goethe das Siegel des souveränen Geistes. Wie beim Individuum, so drückt sich auch bei Nationen ein gesundes Selbstbewußtsein nicht zuletzt in der Fähigkeit aus, den Wert des andern, des Fremden gelten zu lassen und anzuerkennen.[66]

[For the poet of the *Divan*, *Geltenlassen* stands at the beginning of each culture, which only then comes to itself when it rises to *Anerkennen*. In recognition Goethe saw the seal of the sovereign spirit. A healthy self-confidence is expressed as in individuals so too in nations not least in the ability to allow and recognise the worth of the other, the foreign.]

Goethe never claimed that he achieved anything near perfect understanding of the foreign world he delved into late in life; he professed merely, and significantly, better understanding.

Notes

[1] Letter to Cotta (unsent), 16 May 1815: WA IV/25, 414. Goethe was writing poems for *West-östlicher Divan* and exploring Persian culture from at least 1814. Cf. *Nachlass-Stücke* [pieces not used in the *Divan*] in FA 3/1, 585–636.

[2] Katharina Mommsen reminds readers that most chapters in the explanatory essay Goethe appended to the *Divan, Besserem Verständniss* (For Better Understanding) are about politics. She also argues that the *Divan* can be interpreted as a political work in that it asks readers about their humanity. Katharina Mommsen, "'West-östlicher Divan' und 'Chinesisch-deutsche Jahres- und Tageszeiten,'" *Goethe Jahrbuch* 108 (1991): 169–78, (174).

[3] He wrote to his wife, Christiane, about the camel on 25 April 1813 (WA IV/23, 330). Goethe also witnessed a Muslim worship service of the Bashkir Host (held in a Protestant school), who were serving in the Russian army (Letter to Trebra, 5 January 1814: WA III/5, 348–49).

[4] This mix of poetry and prose is not uncommon in European and non-European traditions. Konrad Burdach, *Die älteste Gestalt des West-östlichen Divans*, Sitzungsbericht der königlich preussischen Akademie der Wissenschaften 27 (Berlin: Reichsdruckerei, 1904), 41–43.

[5] Kant appears in the *Divan Nachlass-Stücke* in a poem to one of Goethe's favourite wines, the 1811 ("Eilfer"). He, along with another figure associated with the Enlightenment, Friedrich II, are cited as figures of excellence, comparable to the 1811: FA 3/1, 597.

[6] Letter to Cotta, 16 May 1815: WA IV/25, 415. Joseph Freiherr von Hammer-Purgstall (1774–1856) was an Orientalist and Austrian diplomat.

[7] FA 3/1, 549.

[8] Marianne (1784 Linz – 1860 Frankfurt am Main), a dancer, was married to a friend of Goethe's. Cf. H. A. Korff, *Die Liebesgedichte des West-östlichen Divans* (Zurich: Hirzel, 1949). For other interpretations of individual poems see: *Interpretationen zum West-östlichen Divan Goethes*, ed. by Edgar Lohner, Wege der Forschung 288 (Darmstadt: Wissenschaftliche Buchgesellschaft, 1973).

[9] FA 3/1, 549–50.

[10] FA 3/1, 549. Cf. the poem "Nachbildung": FA 3/1, 32.

[11] In the poem "Unbegrenzt" [Limitless] in the *Buch Hafiz* Goethe calls himself Hafiz's twin: FA 3/1, 31.

[12] Cf. *Buch der Sprüche* [Book of Proverbs]: "Welch eine bunte Gemeinde! / An Gottes Tisch sitzen Freund und Feinde" [What a colourful community / Friends and enemies sit at God's table] (FA 3/1, 65).

[13] FA 3/1, 552–53.

[14] Birus: FA 3/2, 906.

[15] *Gespräche mit Eckermann*, 4 January 1824: FA 39, 530.

[16] "Ihr lieben Leute bleibt dabei . . ." [You Good people remain . . .] in *Buch der Sprüche* [Book of Proverbs]: FA 3/1, 65; Birus: FA 3/2, 1143.

[17] FA 3/1, 553–54. This poem was also published in the *Morgenblatt* (22 March 1816).

[18] Shakespeare, *Henry IV*, Part 2, III, i, line 30.

[19] FA 3/1, 554.

[20] "Hülflose Krieger" is from the full title of the poem: FA 3/2, 1715.

[21] FA 3/1, 564. Goethe published other *Divan* poems in *Taschenbuch für Damen auf das Jahr 1817* [Lady's Pocketbook for the Year 1817].

[22] FA 3/1, 564.

[23] FA 3/1, 64.

[24] This poem is featured in *Tefkir Nameh/Buch der Betrachtungen* [Book of Reflections]: FA 3/1, 45. Giving alms is a central tenet of Islam (Birus: FA 3/2, 1065).

[25] FA 3/1, 566. Cf. Gisela Henckmann, *Gespräch und Geselligkeit in Goethes "West-östlichem Divan,"* Studien zur Poetik und Geschichte der Literatur 42 (Stuttgart: Kohlhammer, 1975).

[26] 3 June 1804: *Crabb Robinson in Germany 1800–1805: Extracts from his Correspondence,* ed by Edith J. Morley (London: H. Milford, Oxford UP, 1929), 147–48.

[27] FA 3/1, 58.

[28] "Fünf Andere" [Five Others] in *Buch der Betrachtungen* (FA 3/1, 44); "Dümmer ist nichts zu ertragen . . ." [There is nothing more stupid . . ."] in *Buch der Sprüche* (FA 3/1, 62); "Was hilft's dem Pfaffen-Orden . . ." [What help are priests . . .] in *Buch der Sprüche* (FA 3/1, 63); "Der Winter und Timur" [Winter and Tamburlaine] in *Buch des Timur* (FA 3/1, 70); "Dem Kellner" [For the Waiter] in *Das Schenkenbuch* (FA 3/1, 106).

[29] Translation of the Arabic: "The eastern Diwan of the western author" (Birus: FA 3/2, 876).

[30] FA 3/1, 62. Goethe explains this image in *Besserem Verständniss* as the oracular tradition of sticking a needle in an important book and revering the words it sticks (FA 3/1, 208).

[31] FA 3/1, 23.

[32] *Buch der Sprüche*: FA 3/1, 63.

[33] FA 39, 530.

[34] Harold Bloom, *The Anxiety of Influence: A Theory of Poetry* (London: Oxford UP, 1973), 52.

[35] FA 3/1, 57.

[36] FA 3/1, 23–24.

[37] Birus: FA 3/2, 959–60.

[38] Cf. Genesis 3:19: "In the sweat of thy face shalt thou eat bread, till thou return unto the ground; for out of it wast thou taken: for dust thou art, and unto dust shalt thou return."

[39] From "Ich sah, mit Staunen und Vergnügen . . ." [I saw with amazement and pleasure . . .]: FA 3/1, 117. The pearl poem is "Vom Himmel sank, in

wilder Meere Schauer . . ." [From Heaven fell into the wild sea . . .]: FA 3/1, 116.

[40] FA 3/1, 28.

[41] FA 3/1, 29.

[42] FA 3/1, 29–30. "Fetwa" means judgement in Arabic. Abusu'ud was a high spiritual authority in sixteenth-century Constantinople. Goethe bases his poem on a historical judgement (Birus: FA 3/2, 944).

[43] Katharina Mommsen makes an important distinction between the tolerance of Goethe and that of Lessing, for in the *Divan* she sees an expanded acceptance of religions ("West-östlicher Divan," 176).

[44] Kant, *Was ist Aufklärung?*, 53.

[45] FA 3/1, 30.

[46] Katharina Mommsen, *Goethe und die arabische Welt* (Frankfurt am Main: Insel, 1988), 472.

[47] *Gespräche mit Eckermann*, 4 January 1824: FA 39, 530.

[48] FA 3/1, 30–31.

[49] FA 3/1, 32–33.

[50] FA 3/1, 33.

[51] Reed, *The Classical Centre*, 93. Cf. Bürgel, who connects *Spiel* with *Toleranz*: Johann Christoph Bürgel, *Drei Hafis-Studien: Goethe und Hafis, Verstand und Liebe bei Hafis, Zwölf Ghaselen,* übertragen und interpretiert [by Johann Christoph Bürgel], Europäische Hochschulschriften, Reihe 1, Deutsche Literatur und Germanistik 113 (Bern: Lang, 1975), 29.

[52] FA 3/1, 53.

[53] WA IV/24, 134.

[54] 17 February 1814: WA IV/24, 161.

[55] FA 3/1, 53.

[56] *Buch der Sprüche*: FA 3/1, 62.

[57] FA 3/1, 55.

[58] Birus: FA 3/2, 1104.

[59] FA 3/1, 57.

[60] *Das Schenkenbuch*, "Sitz' ich allein . . ." [When I sit alone . . .]: FA 3/1, 104.

[61] FA 3/1, 59.

[62] Bürgel, *Drei Hafis-Studien*, 39.

[63] As quoted in Birus, FA 3/2, 1161.

[64] FA 3/1, 70.

[65] In the poem "Als ich auf dem Euphrat schiffte . . ." [As I travel by ship on the Euphrates . . .] in the *Buch Suleika* [Book of Suleika], Suleika challenges Hatem (Goethe) with the words "Sag Poete, sag Prophete!" [Tell, poet! Tell, prophet!]: FA 3/1, 77.

[66] Mommsen, "West-östlicher Divan," 175.

8: *Besserem Verständniss*

JOACHIM WACH'S MONUMENTAL three-volume study, *Das Verstehen* (Understanding), is an attempt to encapsulate Germany's nineteenth-century fascination with hermeneutics.[1] Wilhelm Dilthey is of course associated with the hermeneutics of that age. Goethe too, engaged with the subject of understanding in the thirteenth book of the *Divan*, a collection of essays, poems, and reflections published with the original 1819 edition and entitled simply, *Besserem Verständniss* (For Better Understanding). His concerns were pragmatic, for most readers would be unacquainted with the Middle East.[2] The motto poem that prefaces this large prose work suggests that *Verstehen* is an act of communication even within a culture, between author and reader as they enter into a relationship with each other:

> Wer das Dichten will verstehen
> Muß in's Land der Dichtung gehen;
> Wer den Dichter will verstehen
> Muß in Dichters Lande gehen.[3]

[Who would understand poetry must enter the land of poetry. Who would understand the poet must enter the poet's land.]

These lines represent a main theme in the *Divan*, the process of entering into the individual world of poets. Goethe, through the life of Hafiz, was able to reflect his own relationship to society and it is this relationship that prompts, in part at least, the massive *Besserem Verständniss*, which is easily double the length of the preceding twelve books of poetry combined.[4]

"Who would understand the poet"

In *Besserem Verständniss,* Goethe remembers himself as a young poet who desired his artistic works to be recognised, but found that his writings were not always well received. If society is to understand poets there must be communication. And here, as in his 1816 essay on *Die Geheimnisse*, Goethe expresses his gratification that through the institution of literature he has fostered and achieved inter-generational

communication. He also claims that art or "Dichters Lande" is its own
kingdom, governed by its own laws, and that it needs to be understood
on its own terms. Similarly, he alludes to the non-teleological nature of
poetry: "auch bleibt sie immer wahrhafter Ausdruck eines aufgeregten
erhöhten Geistes, ohne Ziel und Zweck" [it also remains a true expression of an excited and elevated intellect, without goal or purpose].[5]
Scattered throughout *Besserem Verständniss* are insights about writing
poetry that will be explored as they apply to intercultural understanding.

Another primary intention in *Besserem Verständniss* is to assist the
reader in visiting the "land of poetry." This conception combines three
elements, for not only does it refer to understanding the creative act of
poetry, but also Persian poets and their works, as well as Goethe's own
Divan poems. His prominent concern is to ensure that the *Divan* readers not be put off by foreign words, beliefs, and traditions.[6] Therefore
his project involves enlightening his fellow Germans, like others before
him — he mentions Herder and Eichhorn and compares them to a rising sun — about the literary treasures of the Middle East.[7] Goethe's acknowledgement of Herder is significant because doses of Herder's
thought are evident in his own practice, as will be shown.[8] Reflecting
on his own initial exploration of the Middle East, Goethe recalls that he
needed cultural context in order to feel "einheimischer" or more at
home in the foreign literature.[9] *Besserem Verständniss* would be an initiation of German readers designed to help them feel comfortable in
the *Divan* poetry by explaining many of its referents. Yet Persian poetry
was also to be displayed, especially as more translations were being
made available.[10] Goethe views himself as a cultural mediator, assisting
the German reception of his *Divan* and of Persian poetry. He realises
that since his poetry refers to the faith, customs, and literature of an
alien region, he must elucidate these within a wider cultural context.[11]

Goethe presents himself as a poet, and though he assumes other
guises, he remains a poet throughout *Besserem Verständniss*. In this
sense it remains secondary to the *Divan* poetry in creative content and
originality.[12] Unfortunately, a single strand of Goethe's intention, navi-
gating his readers through foreign words and objects in his *Divan* poems, has tended to limit the way some critics see *Besserem Verständniss*.
Normally, the *Divan* is read, whereas *Besserem Verständniss* is raided
occasionally for its gems. Reduced to a reference work forever subordi-
nated to the more delicate *Divan*, it is treated as a bulky index that
conveniently calibrates Goethe's relationship to Islam and the intellectual range of scholarly sources that informed him about this region of
the world.[13] Such an approach has its merits, of course, but *Besserem*

Verständniss contains much more than a description of the *Divan's* historical sources.[14] By focusing on the images in Goethe's text it will be possible to trace his thoughts on *Verstehen* and the emergence of new concepts along with those that have already been examined such as *Toleranz, Anerkennung,* and *Geltenlassen. Besserem Verständniss* links these in a way that makes it Goethe's most sustained effort to analyse and describe his approach to intercultural understanding.

Images

Goethe generates several descriptive images that reflect his roles in helping the reader achieve "better understanding." Konrad Burdach notes that these roles show the *Divan* to be an allegory and that it ought to be understood symbolically.[15] The roles themselves also highlight the processes that Goethe has undergone as a poet who attempts to understand foreign poetry, an exotic religion, and an alien culture. These specific tasks are also considered abstractly as Goethe reflects systematically on translation as an act of mediating between one culture and another.

The Gardener

The garden image is a recurring metaphor in the text. In the introduction Goethe implies that he is a gardener and the streams and other sources of water or "Quellen" — also meaning his historical sources — are the "erquickliches Naß" [quickening moisture] that he has channeled to his "Blumenbeete" [flower beds].[16] As in the *Sankt-Rochus-Fest zu Bingen,* where *erquicken* refers to the restorative rain as well as the rejuvenation of the Rhine region, moisture is here associated with the new blossoming of Goethe's lyric poetry. The flowers, his *Divan* poems, are nourished through the historical waters of his Middle East studies, yet their genesis is also personal and they contain their own organic history. The poet-gardener has selected and guided the sources, not they him.

The Traveller

The role of a traveller is the poet's favourite: "Am liebsten aber wünschte der Verfasser vorstehender Gedichte als ein Reisender angesehen zu werden" [Most of all, however, the writer of the above poetry would like to be seen as a traveller].[17] Throughout *Besserem Verständniss* readers are introduced to various travellers, from pilgrims and crusaders to explorers like Marco Polo and Pietro Della Valle down to Goethe's contemporaries. He values highly their travel descriptions and other writings they brought forth in the midst of great danger and adventure.[18]

Goethe explains that he strives to be a traveller who attempts to understand foreign ways, thoughts, and customs with sympathy.[19] "Gesinnungen zu theilen," another phrase Goethe uses, conveys the notion that the author will communicate the thoughts of those whom he has met, as well as his own. The poet-traveller furthermore desires to understand the customs of the region he visits. To perceive the moral order of a society is to do more than read about its religion, history, laws, and culture; it is more than knowing how to communicate through language, it is understanding what constitutes being an insider of the culture. He also explains that he will appropriate ("aneignen") the idioms of the foreign culture. *Aneignen*, in Goethe's usage, is an important, potentially misleading concept. "To appropriate" is an insufficient translation, especially as it has come to have negative overtones in some critical writing, and does not capture the organic connotations of "aneignen." Stephen Prickett, drawing on Paul Ricoeur, defines *Aneignen* as "meaning to make one's own what was initially 'alien,'" but not conveying pejorative undertones. Prickett continues: "It comes to prominence in the late eighteenth century from linguistic roots that are biological and organic rather than legal — to be associated more with the untranslatable romantic word *Bildung* (the Goethean idea of 'growth' or 'self-development') than it is with 'theft.'"[20] Goethe, particularly in his intense identification with Hafiz, was able to learn from and grow through the Persian poet and develop his own poetry further. *Besserem Verständniss* acknowledges this poetic symbiosis and presents Goethe's anthropological approach to understanding a foreign culture; he is not just passing through, but seeking to be a sympathetic traveller.

Crucially, however, Goethean hermeneutics does not aspire to the omniscience of Dilthey, who sought to understand historical subjects better than they understood themselves. Goethe makes a telling point about the limits of intercultural understanding, for he writes that he still retains his own "Accent" and remains a "Fremdling" [foreigner]. *Das Eigene* and *das Fremde* can learn from and approach each other and operate through the process of *Aneignen*, but only "bis auf einen gewissen Grad" [to a certain degree].[21] They cannot become each other: an accent of *das Eigene* is retained in *das Angeeignete*. *Divan* poetry is German poetry, not an attempt to be Persian, yet it is also a serious negotiation between the German and Persian cultures.[22]

Digression on Comparison

In *Besserem Verständniss* Goethe makes it clear that acceptance of difference does not presuppose that everything is equal or that evaluation
cannot occur, particularly in works of literature. Yet Goethe's judgement and aesthetic standards blend with his idea of *geltenlassen*, a move
that can be detected in the essay's critique of the English Orientalist Sir
William Jones (1746–1794).[23] He admired Jones as one of the eighteenth-century Englishmen who had enlightened him and others about
the Middle East.[24]

Goethe's admiration is not unbounded, however, and he reviews
critically Jones's method, which he calls "Vergleichung" or comparison. He first assures readers of his good will toward the poetry he has
heralded,[25] then warns those who possess a scholarly knowledge of the
region about doing "allen möglichen Schaden" [all kinds of damage]
to Middle East cultures by comparing one culture to another.[26] To illustrate the danger he cites the case of Jones.

In short, Goethe holds that Jones applied an unwittingly self-
defeating stratagem when he compared "oriental" to classical poets.
Jones needed this tactical ploy, Goethe suggests, to overcome the
prejudice of his countrymen who would not accept anything ("gelten
lassen") that was not connected in some way to Rome or Athens.[27] In
order to outflank this prejudice, the English philologist even went so
far as to allege detailed similarities between classical and Persian poetry.[28]

Goethe's own approach to non-canonical literature is "vergleiche sie
mit sich selbst . . . in ihrem eignen Kreise" [to compare it to itself . . .
in its own sphere] and forget about the Greeks and Romans.[29] Differences, *das Fremde* must be appreciated on their own terms; their
evaluation ought not to rest upon inapplicable stylistic conventions.
One could compare Goethe's approach to a naturalist's who discerns
ecological unity amidst nature's diversity, yet comprehends that distinct
domains exist. Nonetheless, appreciation of difference does not in itself,
even as a method, dominate or dilute individual tastes and preferences.
Goethe's own aesthetic predilections were akin to those in his description of "Alt-England," namely, classical. While Goethe respects Jones's
scholarship and passion for Persian poetry, he perceives a tactical error
that hindered its dissemination. He hopes to turn this insight to his
own advantage by employing new marketing skills.

Furthermore, Goethe holds that any comparison, for example, of
Firdusi — whom he credits with creating a literary mythic-historical

"National-Fundament" [national foundation] for Persia[30] — with Homer would show up the former.[31] Goethe is no less decided about comparisons with Germanic literature:

> Haben wir Deutsche nicht unsern herrlichen Niebelungen durch solche Vergleichung den größten Schaden gethan? So höchst erfreulich sie sind, wenn man sie sich in ihren Kreis recht einbürgert und alles vertraulich und dankbar aufnimmt, so wunderlich erscheinen sie, wenn man sie nach einem Maßstabe mißt, den man niemals bey ihnen anschlagen sollte.[32]

> [Have we Germans not done the greatest damage to our glorious Nibelungen through such comparison? Highly enjoyable as they are when one naturalises them in their own sphere, takes them with gratitude and trust, so strangely do they appear when one measures them against a criterion that one should not apply to them.]

Herder occupied a similar critical position, as Charles Taylor writes, for he "put forward the idea that each of us has an original way of being human. Each person has his or her own 'measure' as is his way of putting it. This idea has entered very deep into modern consciousness. It is also new. Before the late eighteenth century no one thought that the differences between human beings had this kind of moral significance."[33] In *Über die neuere deutsche Literatur* (On the New German Literature, 1766) Herder asks polemically: "Wie weit sind wir denn im Nachbilden der *Griechen?*" [How far along are we in imitating the *Greeks?*] After not very seriously suggesting that perhaps Bodmer is the German Homer, Gleim the German Anacreon or Karsch the German Sappho, and ultimately refusing to compare Bodmer and Homer, he turns to Homer and Klopstock. But he asks immediately, "Wo hat K[lopstock] ein Homer sein *wollen?*" [When did Klopstock *want* to be a Homer?] And he suggests that one ought to compare German literature with itself.[34]

Herder continues later in a vein similar to Goethe's regarding the violence that can be done to a foreign culture, as well as one's own, by comparisons: "Jetzt denke weiter! Kein größerer Schade kann einer Nation zugefuget werden, als wenn man ihr den *National-charakter,* die *Eigenheit ihres Geistes,*[35] und *ihrer Sprache* raubt."[36] [Now think further! No greater damage can be done to a nation than when one robs her of *national character*, the *peculiarity of her spirit*, and *her language*.] Isaiah Berlin summarises Herder's achievement: "The philosopher, poet, critic, pastor Johann Gottfried Herder was perhaps the first wholly articulate prophet of this attitude . . . every human society, every people, indeed every age and civilisation, possesses its own unique ideals, standards, way of living and thought and action."[37]

Cultural products are at home in diverse places and need to be evaluated according to their own standard. Goethe's word "einbürgern" (to naturalise), with its denotation of citizenship, is crucial in this context. He holds out the possibility of naturalising foreign literatures (as well as one's own)[38] through translation, thus making *Weltliteratur* an unprecedented possibility. The notion "in ihrem Kreis" [in its own sphere] reveals again Goethe's organic preferences. Cultural products are influenced by language, society, religion, and so on, and they are all works of the human imagination. A successful intercultural comparison would be one that highlights the similarities of the creative process and shows the common human condition.

The Trader

A further role flows from the poet's part as a sympathetic traveller, for he wants to attract others to the wares he brings back from his travels and therefore takes on "die Rolle eines Handelsmanns" [the role of a trader].[39] Goethe wanted his *Divan* poems to be a success. But he also knew that the exotic references might prove a barrier to the reception of his poetry — and they did. In a section entitled "Zweifel" [Doubt] he writes that Westerners find it difficult to comprehend foreign religions, fairy tales, fables, parables, anecdotes, and jokes, although they are not insurmountable hurdles. It is the intellectual (and physical) subjugation that he finds in some Persian writing that puts off Westerners.[40]

The issue of individual liberty is brought to the fore in a section on despotism. No matter how absolute the ruler, Goethe surmises that it is human nature to want to think for oneself: "da finden wir denn überall daß der Frey- und Eigensinn der Einzelnen sich gegen die Allgewalt des Einen ins Gleichgewicht stellt" [we find everywhere that freedom to think and individuality oppose the absolute power of the one].[41] Whether or not readers find despotism in Persian literature an obstacle is a moot point, but Goethe certainly found it difficult to accept, even amidst his unabashed advocacy of the literature, and this added to his concern about the reception of the *Divan*.

This concern led to the long months of preparatory work before the *Divan* was published and the lengthy insurance policy, *Besserem Verständniss,* attempts on Goethe's part to comfort and put at ease his readership so that his poetry will appeal. Like a merchant at a market place hawking his wares, Goethe draws attention to them by "ankündigende, beschreibende, ja lobpreisende Redensarten" [anticipatory, descriptive, even laudatory ways of speaking].[42]

Goethe merges the roles of traveller and trader, and commends their contributions to the public good by praising "Reisende Handelsleute" [travelling traders] and the knowledge and treasures they bring with them.[43] So, too, he has brought forth treasures in the *Divan* poetry and knowledge in *Besserem Verständniss*. Grasping Goethe's high regard for the roles of traveller and trader makes fathomable his otherwise bizarre praise for Jean Paul, whom he likened to a Bedouin. This is intended to describe him as one who gives the impression of knowing the world through trading and pilgrimages.[44]

The word *Handelsmann* has for Goethe an aesthetic resonance that is not captured by its translation as trader or merchant. In the section entitled "Verwahrung" [Protest], Goethe defends the notion of poetry against rhetoric. Tellingly, he intimates that words and phrases do not freely circulate like coins or monetary notes, but are part of an intellectual transaction.[45] Treating words like money can distort ideas. The role of *Handelsmann* reflects Goethe's work "im geistigen Handel und Wandel" [in intellectual change and exchange] whereby he seeks the equivalents of Persian poetry and thought in the German language. This is particularly the case, as we shall see, with translation, the delicate act of turning words, ideas, and meanings — the "heilige Zeugnisse" [holy testimonies] — over from one language and culture to another.

The Messenger

The roles of traveller, trader, and translator merge with that of messenger, one who works in political commerce. Goethe quotes the proverbs of the Persian Ambassador to St. Petersburg and London, Mizra Abu'l Hassan-Han,[46] with their exhortation to protect, befriend, and exercise justice regarding foreigners, travellers, and traders. This not only fits with the images generated in *Besserem Verständniss*, but can also be interpreted as a tip to Germans to be open- and fair-minded towards the *Divan*.

Near the end of *Besserem Verständniss*, under the heading "Endlicher Abschluss!," [Final Conclusion!] the reader is asked to judge whether this project has indeed fostered "Wohlwollen" [good will].[47] This echoes the introduction in which he admits his difficulty in representing the foreign, and asks the reader's pardon.[48] Again, as in the *Divan* itself, Goethe posits that understanding and forgiving are interrelated and that good will is an essential ingredient of cultural appreciation.

Goethe alludes to himself as an envoy in another clever double movement at the end of the *Divan*. Here he includes a poem in honour of the renowned French Orientalist Silvestre de Sacy, along with an Arabic translation of the same by Kosegarten:

> Unserem Meister, geh! verpfände
> Dich, o Büchlein, traulich-froh;
> Hier am Anfang, hier am Ende
> Oestlich, westlich A und Ω.[49]

[To our master go! Pledge yourself, o booklet, intimate-happy; here at the beginning, here at the end, easternly, westernly, A and Ω.]

The end of the *Divan* for a western reader is the beginning for a Middle Eastern reader, who would read a book in Arabic from the back cover from a Western perspective, hence Goethe's dual emphasis "Hier am Anfang, hier am Ende." But the final poem of the *Divan*, actually therefore the first, is a translation from Arabic into German.[50] The poem is by Sa'di, from his collection *Gulistan* (Garden of Roses), and thus mirrors Goethe's flowerbed image in the introduction. This image also initiates and concludes *Besserem Verständniss*, giving it an organic symmetry and recalling the poet's role as gardener. A bed of flowers, nature cultivated, stands for the poetry that became Goethe's *Divan*.

Goethe places the Arabic original above the German translation, which creates a parallel with the dual language title of the *Divan* and those of its individual books. This linguistic symmetry unifies the threads of co-existence and communication that run throughout the *Divan* and *Besserem Verständniss*. The theme of the poem is also significant, for it identifies the poet's first and final role:

> Wir haben nun den guten Rath gesprochen,
> Und manchen unsrer Tage dran gewandt;
> Mißtönt er etwa in des Menschen Ohr —
> Nun, Botenpflicht ist sprechen. Damit gut.[51]

[We have spoken good counsel, and spent much of the day; if it strikes a discordant note in the ear — well, the duty of the messenger is to speak. That's that.]

The poem paraphrases a Qur'an verse that commands obedience to God and his messenger.[52] The poet as messenger has fulfilled his "Botenpflicht" or obligation to speak, and the curt ending "Damit gut" implies a shift in responsibility from the messenger, who has done his part and done his best, to the reader. But Goethe achieves yet another significant structural symmetry in *Besserem Verständniss,* as its introductory sentences are a paraphrase of Ecclesiastes: it occupies an intermediary position between two holy books, the Qur'an and the Bible.[53] The introductory words announce that there is a time to speak and a time to be silent, and that the poet has decided to speak.[54] By using the word *Botenpflicht* Goethe again enhances the book's symmetry, for in the introduction he defines the poet's "Pflicht" [duty] is that of "Verständlichkeit" [clarity].[55] At the *Divan's* simultaneous conclusion and beginning, the poet-messenger's duty is to foster better understanding between Eastern and Western lands of poetry, as well as between the world of the poet and society at large.

Goethe has represented the Lord in the previous poem by utilising the Greek letters alpha and omega.[56] But in the context of *Botenpflicht* from the following poem, the Greek letters generate faint associations with Hermes, the messenger of the Olympians, whose duty it was to translate their words and deliver them to mortals. The word hermeneutics, as an act of encounter, translation, and understanding, has its roots in the name of this wing-footed messenger.

The messenger theme connects several central figures in *Besserem Verständniss.* Goethe owed much of his learning about the Orient to two men who were associated with the diplomatic corps of their states, and he generously thanks each in the section entitled "Lehrer" [Teachers]. Both of these men made German translations of Persian writings that Goethe read. Joseph von Hammer-Purgstall (1774–1856) studied the Middle East at the University of Vienna and was then assigned to the Imperial Embassy in Constantinople. Later, after serving as an assistant to Metternich, he worked as the Imperial Court Translator in Vienna.[57] Goethe utilised Hammer-Purgstall's translations and writings extensively.[58] Goethe also acknowledged the influence of Heinrich Friedrich von Diez, who served for a time as the Prussian envoy to Constantinople.[59]

Goethe further praises Adam Olearius (Oelschläger, c. 1599–1671), a trained theologian and philologist (and friend of Paul Fleming), who was sent as part of an official legation by Duke Friedrich III von Schleswig-Holstein-Gottorf to Russia and Persia. Through a translation by Olearius, Goethe was able to acquaint himself with the poetry of Sa'di.[60]

A fourth messenger figure exerted a strong influence on Goethe's learning about the Middle East: the aforementioned Hassan-Han, a "geborner Gesandter" [a born envoy]. Goethe sought to demonstrate that *Besserem Verständniss* contained difficult to obtain contemporary information by reproducing a full-length translation of a letter that Han delivered from the wife of the Persian Emperor to the Empress of Russia, the Empress Maria Fedorovna.[61] Upon closer reading, another more persuasive purpose for the letter's inclusion comes to mind. The letter and accompanying gifts are a microcosm of what Goethe was trying to do through the *Divan* and *Besserem Verständniss*, namely, serve as an introduction and invitation to further contact with the world beyond Europe. The wife of the Persian Emperor characterises the letter as a key that would open the doors of friendship. This important letter synthesises the images of poet, traveller, trader, translator, messenger, and gardener. It is the latter image that is thrown into the most vivid relief, as the letter metaphorically refers to Russia and Persia as gardens and encourages a relationship that will bring forth fresh rose blossoms. Moreover, the writer enjoins sincere unity and friendship in overcoming past differences. She proposes to build on the established contact (not unlike Iphigenie's suggestion to Thoas of establishing a convention of hospitality) by recommending that they continue to maintain contact. After offering the gifts from her country, the garden image recurs on a personal level as she refers to future letters as droplets that will refresh the garden of her heart.[62]

What the letter endeavours to accomplish politically, Goethe undertakes in poetry and prose. He has pointed his fellow Germans to the delights of Persia, to its literary landmarks and scriptural monuments. The unity and friendship wished for in the letter contrast with the divisions Goethe protests against in *Zum Reformationsfest*, and the letter's friendly tone towards an erstwhile enemy suggests healing relations between war-torn regions, as depicted in the *Sankt-Rochus-Fest zu Bingen*. Having written and worked through what Goethe calls the "bedenkliche Zeiten" [disturbing times] of the Napoleonic wars, he also savours the "Früchte des errungenen Friedens" [fruits of the achieved peace].[63] Among these fruits are his personal flowerbeds: the poetry of the *Divan* and the insights nurtured through the refreshing water of the sources he cites in *Besserem Verständniss*. Like the Persian Emperor's wife, he invites the reader: "nehmen [Sie] das Dargebotne unbefangen auf" [take what is offered with an open mind].[64]

After this letter, Goethe includes two Arabic poems, "Auf die Fahne" and "Auf das Ordensband," with the German translations by

Kosegarten facing each.[65] He calls these the "Schlußstein" [keystone] of a "Domgewölbe" [cathedral's vaulted arch] that he has built with many materials.[66] This keystone is the process of intercultural communication embodied in the poetry and prose in *Besserem Verständniss* and the *Divan*. "Auf die Fahne" [To the Flag], is an ode to the Emperor, Fetch Ali Schah. Its final lines describe the vital role of the envoy, Hassan-Han: "Aus Liebe ward nach London er gesandt / Und brachte Glück und Heil dem Christenherrn" [He was sent out of love to London and brought happiness and salutations to the Lord of Christians].[67] The second poem, "Auf das Ordensband" [To the Order's Ribbon], is another ode and encomium to the emperor, and indicates that the envoy Hassan-Han has been elevated into the royal "Order of the Sun." One reason why these poems could be called the "keystone" of *Besserem Verständniss* is that they, like the letter to the Russian Empress, express the idea of recognition. The Emperor of Persia and the King of England have the opportunity of recognising each other: "ein freundliches liebevolles Verhältniß zu England wird zuletzt ausgesprochen" [a friendly, kind relationship to England is finally expressed].[68] By extension Islam and Christianity have the chance to recognise each other. Likewise, as the relationship of the sun (emblematic of the Divine) is to the Persian Emperor, so too is the emperor's relationship to his envoy Hassan-Han, which Goethe interprets as meaning that the confidence of the English court could be placed in him as if the emperor himself were present.[69]

Digression on Tolerance

In the section entitled "Geschichte" [history] Goethe describes how intolerance of religious worship can lead to deep-rooted hatreds. Persepolis, in Persian Parsa, was founded by Darius I in 518 B.C. and in 330 B.C. razed by the Greeks as revenge for the destruction of the Athenian Acropolis in 480 B.C. Goethe attributes the destruction of the Acropolis to religious and cultural intolerance. The Persians, who worshipped elemental gods in the open world, found it despicable that the Greeks locked their gods in residences, and therefore destroyed their temple.[70]

Goethe compares Emperor Mahmud of Ghazna (999–1030) to Alexander the Great and Friedrich II.[71] All are conquering sons of conquering fathers and each used tolerance as a means to gain an advantage for the State (*raison d'état*). Friedrich surfaces again in the essay in association with another Muslim Emperor, Abbas I, who ruled between 1587–1628.[72] Tolerance is one of the salient features in

Goethe's commentary, as he mentions the emperor's "Freysinn in Religionssachen" [freedom of thought in matters of religion].

But he does not underestimate how easily tolerance may disappear from the socio-political sphere under an absolutist ruler, for he goes on to show how Emperor Abbas allowed the destruction of Armenian Christians and reigned as a tyrant.[73] As an exponent of evolutionary change, Goethe praises a limited monarchical government,[74] and interestingly Saxe-Weimar was among the first German principalities to create a new constitution after the Napoleonic wars (1816).[75]

Goethe's examples, however, not only allude to the eighteenth century (via Friedrich II) they reach into it as well. He cites the lives of two men who experienced Louis XIV's Revocation of the Edict of Nantes (1685), a *cause célèbre* of the Enlightenment discussion on tolerance. The revocation was enforced on pain of death: Protestant ministers had fifteen days either to convert or to leave France. All Protestant places of worship were to be destroyed immediately and the goods and properties of disenfranchised Protestants would be confiscated.[76] Jean Baptiste Tavernier (1605–1689), a goldsmith and jewelry merchant, undertook journeys to Russia, Persia, India, and Turkey, and later wrote about his voyages. On his return, Goethe notes, he felt uncomfortable as a Protestant in Paris and eventually moved to Switzerland.[77] His contemporary Jean Chardin (1643–1713), another merchant and traveller whose writings Goethe knew, was likewise persecuted in France for his religious convictions: "Die Verfolgungen, die er als Protestant erfuhr, trieben ihn von neuem auf Reisen; nach der Rückkehr nahm er seinen Aufenthalt in England" [The persectuions that he experienced as a Protestant drove him once again on journeys; after his return he resided in England].[78] Friedrich Wilhelm invited expelled Huguenots to Prussia and granted them religious tolerance on 8 November 1685 in the Edict of Potsdam.[79] Goethe's praise for the two men has another purpose, to inspire a cosmopolitan outlook and to cite registers of character that are worth emulating: "Verstand, Gleichmuth, Gewandtheit, Beharrlichkeit, einnehmendes Betragen und Standhaftigkeit" [reason, composure, skillfulness, endurance, winning behaviour, and steadfastness]. Goethe suggests that these qualities ought to accompany every man of the world on his personal "Lebensreise" [life's journey] and that the two men may be honoured as models.[80] Goethe's vision of a *Weltfest* is matched by his quiet exhibition of two men, each of whom he could call a *Weltmann*.[81] Furthermore, the topos *Lebensreise* links with the motif of the tolerant travellers whom Goethe describes. Travel can make one more understanding of foreign cultures and develop other qualities like those with which Goethe credits the two Huguenots, Chardin and Tavernier.

Thus Goethe brings his subtext on tolerance down to the century of his birth. In another sense, however, he has never left the eighteenth century, for his references to Islamic tolerance are linked with Friedrich II, the ruler whom Kant praises for his non-interference in religious matters.[82] Friedrich II's famous tolerance decree of 1740 was another step in the direction of freedom of belief. But Goethe brings matters up to the present by citing another envoy, his contemporary, the "bedächtiger Engländer" [thoughtful Englishman] Sir John Malcolm (1769–1833).[83] He quotes from a translation of Malcolm's *History of Persia* (1815) to illustrate absolutism in the Middle East, but the translation also reveals an Enlightenment attitude in Malcolm's description of the "usages and knowledge of a civilized age" that have softened absolute power in Europe into moderate governments.[84] Those "usages" are focused by Goethe's twin motto: *Kunst und Wissenschaft* [Art and Science]. He would pursue and share both until his death.

When Goethe elevates the two poems by Fetch Ali Chan to function as a "keystone," it is because they, along with the letter from the Persian Emperor's wife, signify an encounter and potential which are vital to the reader's future. Goethe hints at a future history by announcing a future *Divan*, which is published in 1827, a move that keeps the conversation between cultures open. This is Goethe's concrete proposal as a poet who speaks through the many masks of *Besserem Verständniss*, guises that personify and define his approach to better understanding.

Digression on Translation

The *Divan* collection is not only a personal, poetic response involving Goethe's encounter with Persian poetry, but it is also a part of another agenda, that of cross-cultural mediation, his "calling" in *Besserem Verständniss*:

> Möge das Bestreben unseres dießmaligen Berufes angenehm seyn! Wir dürfen es hoffen: denn in einer Zeit, wo so vieles aus dem Orient unserer Sprache treulich angeeignet wird, mag es verdienstlich erscheinen, wenn auch wir von unserer Seite die Aufmerksamkeit dorthin zu lenken suchen, woher so manches Große, Schöne und Gute seit Jahrtausenden zu uns gelangte, woher täglich mehr zu hoffen ist.[85]

> [May the striving of our current profession be pleasant! We are permitted to hope so: because in a time where so much from the Orient

is appropriated faithfully by our language, it would appear meritorious
if we from our side sought to direct attention there where so much
that is great, beautiful, and good has for millenia come to us, from
where daily more is to be hoped.]

Goethe refers to the poetic products of Persia that have been appropriated through translation, and he calls attention to the humane in that
culture. How one interprets foreign literary treasures, whether one
learns to value them as riches or not, is in large measure determined by
the kind of translation one uses. Galvanised by this point, Goethe di-
gresses into a discussion of translation, specifically the advantages and
disadvantages of three methods.[86]

The prose translation is the first method of translation as it allows
readers an initial prose exposure to foreign poetry (including one's own
older literature). Getting to know the foreign through translation, says
Goethe, "macht uns in unserm eigenen Sinne mit dem Auslande
bekannt" [makes us acquainted with foreign countries in our own
way]. However, there are drawbacks as the first stage of translation
empties foreign poetry of art by doing away with "allen Eigenthüm-
lichkeiten" [all peculiarities]. Nevertheless, Goethe believes that even in
this form the excellence of the work has the power to edify the reader,
and he cites Luther's Bible translation as an example.[87] The second
method is that of verse translation.[88] Perhaps Goethe's clearest example
of this method is his mention of H. H. Wilson's translation of Kali-
dasa's *Megha Duta* (Cloud Messenger) into what he calls a flattering
iambic pentameter — for English ears would be attuned to this.[89] Such
an approach is similar to Sir William Jones's stratagem of assimilating
Persian to Classical poetry.

The first two methods of translation ignore the poetic and rhetorical
conventions of the original text and let readers remain in their comfort
zones. The third and final method cleaves closely to the original, but in
reality becomes a hybrid, a text that exists somewhere between the
original and the new language, "ein Drittes" [a third] Goethe calls it.[90]
He praises the translations of Voß, but notes that the general public,
while not intransigent, needed time to adjust "bis man sich nach und
nach in die neue Art hinein hörte, hinein bequemte" [until people lis-
tened themselves into and became comfortable in the new way].[91] The
third method of translation makes fresh literary demands on readers
and requires a new way of hearing. A part of this difficulty lies in the
decision to trust the translator by surrendering one's own cultural expectations. The emergent *Drittes* can expand the language, literature,
and culture of the nation that attempts this method of translation —

even bring pleasure and illuminate the reader. Goethe encourages the reader to consider how enriched the German language has become since excellent translations of Shakespeare, Tasso, Ariosto, and Calderon appeared. He calls these authors "eingedeutschte Fremde" [Germanised foreigners].[92] This term recalls that of "einbürgern," the naturalisation of the foreign into one's own language community. The foreign original must determine what approach or combination of approaches would be best suited for translating it, since each of the three methods allows different aspects of the foreign text to be experienced.[93]

But translation, although immensely important for cultural reception, is insufficient. All translations, Goethe submits, distance one from the original, "so, daß wir nur ein allgemeines Bild ohne die begränzte Eigenthümlichkeit des Originals gewahr werden" [so that we have only a general picture without becoming aware of the limited peculiarity of the original].[94] For Goethe, the translator is the one who helps others along the way to the original.[95] Ever the shrewd trader, he would have readers take out the middle man as far as possible in order to gain more profit and engage with the text itself:

> Eine Uebersetzung die sich mit dem Original zu identificiren strebt nähert sich zuletzt der Interlinear-Version und erleichtert höchlich das Verständniß des Originals, hiedurch werden wir an den Grundtext hinangeführt, ja getrieben und so ist denn zuletzt der ganze Zirkel abgeschlossen, in welchem sich die Annäherung des Fremden und Einheimischen, des Bekannten und Unbekannten bewegt.[96]

> [A translation that identifies itself with the original is approaching an interlinear version and makes it much easier to understand the original, hereby we are led, even driven towards the original text, and so, finally, the entire circle is closed in which the nearing of the foreign and the native, the familiar and the unfamiliar occurs.]

This is the hermeneutic circle or the circle of understanding. The best that Goethe could provide in *Besserem Verständniss* was something akin to an interlinear version of Fetch Ali Chan's poems (Arabic original and German translation side-by-side). At the end (and the beginning) of the work, the two cultures are chiastically intertwined, as he places his original German poem above the Arabic translation, and then an Arabic original above the German translation. Even as the diplomat Hassan-Han filled the measure of his "Dienstweg" [duties], so too does Goethe complete his *Botenpflicht*.[97] The presence of the dual-language poems and the thrust of his digression on translation remind the reader that an original text exists.

In one way this is fully in the tradition of the Enlightenment: a recognition of our common humanity, which exists despite differences in religion, culture, language, and ethnicity. Yet it is also an undeniable recognition of the foreign as distinct, as ultimately untranslatable, and unique. The foreign is original, that is, stemming from its own origins. We must not attempt to naturalise ("einbürgern") or Germanicise ("eindeutschen") the foreign; we must eventually be, as Goethe puts it, "orientalisirt" [Orientalised], that is, we must go to the sources and face the foreign on its own terms and turf, and allow it, if not to transform us, at least to make demands upon us.[98] Hence Goethe admired Sir William Jones's philologic skills, as he was able to work in the original languages of texts and could therefore treasure in each nation the "Schöne und Gute" [beautiful and good].[99]

Despite Goethe's respect for Jones, he reviews again Jones's tactical error in promoting the cultural products of the Middle East via the Classical literatures. From the foregoing, it is understandable why Goethe frowned upon a comparison of foreign literature with one's own literature: the foreign is, in a sense, incommensurate. A comparative approach such as Jones's, though well-intentioned, places foreign poetry in a virtual no-win situation. How could poetry translated from its original language and forced into artificial metre compare with poetry that developed historically? This leads inevitably to the "Herabsetzung orientalischer Dichtkunst" [degradation of Oriental poetry] and ignites again Goethe's oft-repeated Herderian-historicist conclusion: "daß man jeden Dichter in seiner Sprache und im eigenthümlichen Bezirk seiner Zeit und Sitten aufsuchen, kennen und schätzen müsse" [that one must seek out, get to know, and treasure each poet in his language and peculiar district of time and customs].[100]

The manifold approaches to understanding are not exhausted in Goethe's essay, but he has, implicitly and explicitly, shown several. He is also aware that his approaches are skewed by his own attitudes. Thus, in a section appropriately entitled "Entschuldigung" [Apology] Goethe exposes his own prejudice and suggests that it is a general one: "Es läßt sich bemerken daß ein jeder den Weg, auf welchem er zu irgend einer Kenntniß und Einsicht gelangt, allen übrigen vorziehen und seine Nachfolger gern auf denselben einleiten und einweihen möchte" [It is noteworthy that each prefers the way that he came to some knowledge or insight above all others and would like to direct and initiate those that come after him on the same].[101] Poetic practice in the form of the *Divan* was Goethe's way to better understanding and to communication with another man who lived centuries before, thousands of miles distant, and who was brought up in a completely different language and society. He believed that poetry could bridge time, distance, religion, and culture. Thus he welcomed the growing desire of others to learn more languages, and sought to recognise the service of merchants and traders, travellers and translators, diplomats and scholars, as cultural mediators.[102] He saw this diligent multitude at work striving to reach out across continents, customs, histories, religions, languages, ethnicities, and establish, if not a *Weltfest*, at least a world that would perhaps be less racked by despotism and political as well as religious division and characterised by more "Menschen-Gefühl" [humane feeling].[103] So Goethe writes himself into this progress both as a participant, with the *Divan*, and as a witness, in *Besserem Verständniss*: "Wenn wir bedenken, welche Schritte Geist und Fleiß Hand in Hand gethan haben . . . so erfreut man sich, seit so vielen Jahren Zeuge dieses Fortschreitens zu seyn" [When we consider what steps intellect and diligence have taken hand in hand . . . one rejoices to have been a witness of this progress for so many years].[104] He calls on his fellow Germans to consider the lives of two persecuted French Protestants, to view them as examples of "men of the world" whom he holds up as models.[105] Furthermore, throughout the entire work runs the subtext of England as a land of Enlightenment. And the references to Friedrich II, in connection with tolerance are a further hint. His readers are called upon to have the courage to exercise reason and "commission themselves" to participate as cultural mediators.

Goethe's text is a key to his view of the Middle East, but more significantly, to his vision of poetry as the habitation of "reine Menschlichkeit, edle Sitte, Heiterkeit und Liebe" [pure humanity, noble morals, serenity, and love][106] and to his effort to elevate humans above social, religious, and political strife by providing an "Uebersicht des Weltwesens" [overview of the ways of the world].[107] *Besserem Verständniss* is Goethe's most sustained and concrete espousal of intercultural understanding and *Weltliteratur* and the basis upon which these ideas develop, spread, and establish themselves.

Notes

[1] Joachim Wach, *Das Verstehen: Grundzüge einer Geschichte der hermeneutischen Theorie im 19. Jahrhundert*, 3 vols. (Tübingen: Mohr, 1926–1933).

[2] "Einleitung" [Introduction]: FA 3/1, 138. In the 1827 *Divan* the title *Noten und Abhandlungen Besserem Verständniß des West-östlichen Divans* replaces the original, *Besserem Verständniss*.

[3] *Besserem Verständniss.* FA 3/1, 137.

[4] "Einleitung": FA 3/1, 138. Cf. Monika Lemmel, *Poetologie in Goethes west-östlichem Divan*, Reihe Siegen 73 (Heidelberg: Carl Winter, 1987), see: "Die Souveränität des Dichters," 210–17.

[5] "Verwahrung" [Protest]: FA 3/1, 205.

[6] "Einleitung": FA 3/1, 139. Goethe provides an index of foreign words and names.

[7] "Hebräer" [Hebrews]: FA 3/1, 140. Herder wrote essays on biblical and other ancient cultures in the 1770s, but one of the most influential was *Vom Geiste der Ebräischen Poesie* (On the Spirit of Hebrew Poetry; 1782–1783). University of Jena Professor Johann Gottfried Eichhorn (1752–1827) wrote *Einleitung in das Alte Testament* around the same time (Introduction to the Old Testament; 1780–1783). Note Goethe's use of a typical Enlightenment emblem, the sun.

[8] Cf. Burdach, *Die älteste Gestalt des West-östlichen Divans*, 1.

[9] *Tag- und Jahreshefte* (Annual Journal) 1818: FA 17, 290.

[10] From a conversation with Chancellor von Müller 2 February 1823, as quoted in Birus, FA 3/2, 1467.

[11] "Einleitung": FA 3/1, 139.

[12] Goethe admits tacking on the lengthy essay "Israel in der Wüste" [Israel in the Wilderness], a text he wrote years earlier ("Alt-Testamentliches" [Of the Old Testament]: FA 3/1, 229).

[13] "Einleitung": FA 3/1, 138. Wolfgang Lentz's study is schematic and links Goethe's essays by showing their interconnected thoughts. Wolfgang Lentz, *Goethe Noten und Abhandlungen zum West-östlichen Divan* (Hamburg: Augustin, 1958). Ursula Wertheim situates *Besserem Verständniss* among Goethe's prose works. Ursula Wertheim, *Von Tasso zu Hafis: Probleme von Lyrik und Prosa des "West-östlichen Divans"* (Berlin: Rütten & Loening, 1965).

[14] Joachim Wohlleben, "Des Divans Poesie und Prose: Ein Blick auf den 'West-östlichen Divan' im allgemeinen und die 'Noten und Abhandlungen' im besonderen," *Goethe Jahrbuch* 111 (1994): 111–23, (114).

[15] Konrad Burdach, *Die älteste Gestalt des West-östlichen Divans*, 40. He synthesises several roles that Goethe assumes and weaves them into the meaning of the *Divan*.

[16] "Einleitung": FA 3/1, 138. Goethe expresses his particulr gratitude to his "teachers" for helping him to gain a better understanding of the region (*Lehrer*, Teachers: FA 3/1, 269–79).

[17] "Einleitung": FA 3/1, 138.

[18] "Nähere Hülfsmittel" [More Related Materials for Help]: FA 3/1, 248, (249–68). The English are cited as having brought much knowledge of the Orient to Europe ("Neuere und Neueste Reisende" [Recent and Most Recent Travellers]: FA 3/1, 268).

[19] "Einleitung": FA 3/1, 138.

[20] Stephen Prickett, *Origins of Narrative: The Romantic Appropriation of the Bible* (Cambridge: Cambridge UP, 1996), 28.

[21] "Einleitung": FA 3/1, 139.

[22] Gundolf interprets this negotiation as a kind of intercultural fusion, but understands it also as a literary-political act. Friedrich Gundolf, *Goethe* (Berlin: Georg Bondi, 1922), 686.

[23] "Warnung" [Warning]: FA 3/1, 200. A recent renaissance of interest in Jones's scholarly contributions has seen a thirteen-volume collected works republished; a new biography released; selected works published; and a volume of scholarly essays. Cf: Steve Clark, "Orient knowledge not so pure," *Times Literary Supplement*, 21 March 1997, 25.

[24] "Neuere und Neueste Reisende" and "Lehrer": FA 3/1, 268–69.

[25] "Warnung": FA 3/1, 200.

[26] FA 3/1, 201.

[27] Ibid.

[28] "Lehrer" [Teachers]: FA 3/1, 270.

[29] Ibid.

[30] "Firdusi": FA 3/1, 168. Abu'l-Qasim Mansur Firdausi died in 1030 (Birus: FA 3/2, 1450).

[31] "Warnung": FA 3/1, 201. Textual examples are provided to illustrate the point.

[32] "Warnung": FA 3/1, 201–202.

[33] Charles Taylor, *The Ethics of Authenticity* (Cambridge, MA: Harvard UP, 1991; originally published in Canada [1991] as the *Malaise of Modernity*), 28.

[34] *Johann Gottfried Herder Werke*, ed. by Martin Bollacher and others, 10 vols. (Frankfurt am Main: Deutscher Klassiker Verlag, 1985–2000), vol. 1: *Frühe Schriften* 1764–1772, ed. by Ulrich Gaier (1985), 261–365 (312–13).

[35] Cf. Egmont's defense of Dutch *Eigenheit*: IV *Culenburgischer Palast*: FA 5, 528

[36] Herder, *Über die neuere deutsche Literatur* (On Newer German Literature, 1767), 367–539: FA 1, 376.

[37] Berlin, *The Crooked Timber of Humanity*, 37.

[38] "Die alte Literatur der eigenen Nation ist immer als eine fremde anzusehen" [The older literature of one's own nation is always to be considered foreign]: *Sprüche*: FA 13, 394.

[39] "Einleitung": FA 3/1, 139.

[40] "Zweifel" [Doubt]: FA 3/1, 186.

[41] "Gegenwirkung" [Reaction]: FA 3/1, 193.

[42] "Einleitung": FA 3/1, 139.

[43] "Mahmud von Gasna": FA 3/1, 165.

[44] "Vergleichung" [Comparison]: FA 3/1, 203; Jean Paul Friedrich Richter (1763–1825) was an influential German novelist.

[45] "Verwahrung": FA 3/1, 204–205.

[46] "Neuere, Neueste" [Newer, Newest]: FA 3/1, 183. Goethe had access to a French translation of these proverbs, and he also used the Persian originals; Hassan-Han was born in 1776 (Birus: FA 3/2, 1477).

[47] FA 3/1, 283.

[48] "Einleitung": FA 3/1, 139.

[49] "Silvestre De Sacy": FA 3/1, 298. Johann Gottfried Ludwig Kosegarten (1792–1860), a student of de Sacy's (1758–1838), sent him a pre-publication copy of the *Divan*. Goethe had used de Sacy's *Grammaire Arabe*. Kosegarten would replace Lorsbach as the Professor of *Orientalistik* at the University of Jena (Birus: FA 3/2, 1589).

[50] "Wir haben nun den guten Rath gesprochen . . ." [We have spoken good counsel . . .] Kosegarten translated the Arabic into German; Goethe modified it slightly (Birus: FA 3/2, 1591).

[51] "Wir haben nun den guten Rath gesprochen . . .": FA 3/1, 299. When Trunz, in the *Hamburger Ausgabe*, following the *Fest-Ausgabe*, switches Goethe's order of the two final poems he is destroying the original order and foiling Goethe's role as a cultural envoy: Cf. HA 2, 704.

[52] Qur'an Sura 5:92 as quoted in Birus: FA 3/2, 1591.

[53] "Talismane": FA 3/1, 15.

[54] "Einleitung": FA 3/1, 138. "To every thing there is a season, and a time to every purpose under the heaven . . . a time to keep silence, and a time to speak." (Ecclesiastes 3:1 and 7) Goethe's scriptural merging (Qu'ran and Ecclesiastes) blends Islam, Judaism, and Christianity.

[55] "Einleitung": FA 3/1, 139.

[56] "I am Alpha and Omega, the beginning and the ending, saith the Lord, which is, and which was, and which is to come, the Almighty" (Revelation 1:8).

[57] Birus: FA 3/2, 1570–571.

[58] "Hammer": FA 3/1, 278. Goethe used these key editions by Hammer-Purgstall: *Der Diwan von Mohammed Schemsed-din Hafis. Aus dem Persischen zum erstenmal ganz übersetzt von Joseph v. Hammer* (1812–1813; 2 vols.) and *Fundgruben des Orients, bearbeitet durch eine Gesellschaft von Liebhabern auf Veranstaltung des Herrn Grafen Wenceslaus von Rzewuski* (1809–1818; 6 vols. ed. by Hammer-Purgstall) and *Geschichte der schönen Redekünste Persiens, mit einer Blüthenlese aus zweyhundert persischen Dichtern* (1818). Goethe was not impressed with Hammer-Purgstall's poetic ability.

[59] "Diez": FA 3/1, 271. Goethe liked especially Diez's *Denkwürdigkeiten von Asien in Künsten und Wissenschaften, Sitten, Gebräuchen und Alterthümern, Religion und Regierungsverfassung aus Handschriften und eigenen Erfahrungen gesammelt von Heinrich von Diez* (1811 and 1815). Diez and Hammer disagreed about the value of each other's scholarly contributions (Birus: FA 3/2, 1568).

[60] "Olearius": FA 3/1, 267. Goethe also used Olearius's *Des Welt-berühmten Adami Olearii colligirte und viel vermehrte Reise-Beschreibungen* (Birus: FA 3/2, 1560).

[61] "Schreiben" [Writing]: FA 3/1, 284–85.

[62] Ibid.

[63] "Hammer": FA 3/1, 278. The "disturbing times" refer to the final days of Napoleon and his one-hundred day return from Elba (Birus: FA 3/2, 1571).

[64] "Einleitung": FA 3/1, 139.

[65] FA 3/1, 286–89. Goethe also interprets the poems on pages 290–94.

[66] "Schreiben": FA 3/1, 285. These poems are from *Fundgruben des Orients* (Birus: FA 3/2, 1581).

[67] FA 3/1, 287.

[68] "Endlicher Abschluss!": FA 3/1, 291.

[69] FA 3/1, 292. England was the most powerful nation in Europe after the continental liberation.

[70] "Geschichte" [History]: FA 3/1, 154. Cf. Birus: FA 3/2, 1434.

[71] "Mahmud Von Gasna": FA 3/1, 163.

[72] "Pietro Della Valle": FA 3/1, 254.

[73] "Pietro Della Valle": FA 3/1, 260–61.

[74] Ibid.

[75] Sheehan, *German History 1770–1866*, 413 fn 29; cf. 416.

[76] Maclear, *Church and State*, 6.

[77] "Tavernier und Chardin": FA 3/1, 267–68.

[78] Heinrich Düntzer as quoted in Birus: FA 3/2, 1562.

[79] Holborn, *A History of Modern Germany 1648–1840*, 89.

[80] "Tavernier und Chardin": FA 3/1, 268. Goethe appears particularly impressed by the juxtaposition of their religion (Protestant) and citizenship (French).

[81] Pamela Currie, drawing on Christian Garve, tells of the *Weltmann* who "feared no-one, always appeared at ease and made himself agreeable to all" (*Literature as Social Action*, 189).

[82] Kant, *Was ist Aufklärung?*, 60.

[83] "Einrede": FA 3/1, 189.

[84] Malcolm's original text in English as quoted in Birus: FA 3/2, 1481.

[85] "Einleitung": FA 3/1, 139–40.

[86] "Uebersetzungen" [Translations]: FA 3/1, 280.

[87] Ibid.

[88] Ibid.

[89] "Uebersetzungen": FA 3/1, 282. Goethe probably meant northwesterly, not northeasterly as Horace Hayman Wilson (1786–1860) was from England (Birus: FA 3/2, 1579).

[90] "Uebersetzungen": FA 3/1, 281.

[91] Ibid. Johann Heinrich Voß, the Elder (1751–1826) translated the *Odyssey* and the *Iliad*.

[92] Ibid.

[93] "Uebersetzungen": FA 3/1, 282.

[94] "Nachlass-Stücke"; for a planned chapter on "*Indische Dichtungen*" [Indian Poetry]: FA 3/1, 643.

[95] Bl. 61–62 "Nachlass-Stücke"; for the chapter "Hammer": FA 3/1, 640.

[96] "Uebersetzungen": FA 3/1, 283.

[97] "Den Dienstweg schritt vom Haupt zum Ende er" [His duties he completed from beginning to end]: "Auf das Ordensband" (FA 3/1, 289).

[98] "Uebergang von Tropen zu Gleichnissen" [Transition from Tropes to Allegories]: FA 3/1, 200. That Goethe exposed himself to Middle Eastern languages (especially Arabic and Persian) is evidenced by the several grammars he used and his vocabulary lists (*Nachlass-Stücke*: FA 3/1, 693–710).

[99] "Lehrer": FA 3/1, 269–70.

[100] Ibid.

[101] "Entschuldigung" [Apology]: FA 3/1, 266.

[102] "Neuere und Neuste Reisende": FA 3/1, 268.

[103] "Pietro Della Valle": FA 3/1, 260–64.

[104] "Neuere und Neuste Reisende": FA 3/1, 268.

[105] "Tavernier und Chardin": FA 3/1, 268.

[106] "Neuere und Neuste Reisende": FA 3/1, 269.

[107] "Allgemeinstes" [The Most Universal]: FA 3/1,181.

9: Religious Freedom in
Wilhelm Meisters Wanderjahre

G OETHE'S FINAL NOVEL, *Wilhelm Meisters Wanderjahre oder Die Entsagenden* (Wilhelm Meister's Journeyman Years or The Renunciants, 1829), broadly construed, is a sequel to *Wilhelm Meisters Lehrjahre* (Wilhelm Meister's Apprenticeship, 1795); many of the earlier work's characters put in appearances, and the *Turmgesellschaft* [Society of the Tower] unveils its plans in full.[1] Interwoven in the novel's narrative, which follows the protagonist Wilhelm as he lives under the conditions imposed upon him by the *Turmgesellschaft*, namely, that he must not remain in any one area for more than three days and that he remove himself at least a league each time he does move, are a series of novellas and epistles. The *Wanderjahre* has a long history of reception as a novel that presents new societal models.[2] In it, Goethe continued what he had begun in the 1770s, to hold up an Enlightenment agenda as a map for the future.

Saint Joseph

The first two chapters foreground a family whom Wilhelm comes upon while exploring a mountainous region, and his interactions with them are the basis for allegorical commentaries on the transformation of a larger religious community, Catholicism. The description of the Holy Family is humanised, akin perhaps to a Raphael painting. Joseph is described as a hale and hardy young man, and Marie, in a blue coat and sitting on a donkey, is portrayed as a beautiful burden. Their children are compared to angels as well as common messengers.[3] Wilhelm himself makes the connection between Joseph and Marie's family and the Holy Family as he admires didactic paintings in the chapel of Saint Joseph showing the apocryphal stories of the biblical family.[4] Strictly speaking Saint Joseph is a triple reference. It refers to the New Testament husband of Mary associated with the title of book 1, chapter 1 (I/1), "Die Flucht nach Ägypten" [The Flight into Egypt]; it also refers to Saint Joseph, the church spoken of in book 1, chapter 2.[5] The heading of chapter two, "Sankt Joseph der Zweite" [Saint Joseph the

Second] alludes to the caretaker of the secularised Saint Joseph monastery, husband to Marie, who feels that he leads his life under the sign
of his namesake.[6] Saint Joseph II is perhaps also an allusion to Emperor
Joseph II who secularised monasteries.

The monastery grounds of Saint Joseph are ruined. In the courtyard
a woman sells cherries to the children and the chapel itself has been
transformed into a kitchen.[7] The humanising of Catholicism by artists
was a process that continued since the Renaissance. The Enlightenment's demythologisation is here represented as accomplished. The
Holy Family is mirrored, minus the miracles, in the unspectacular lives
of Joseph the caretaker and Marie, a re-married widow with child. The
sacred space of the Catholic Church, represented by the chapel, has
been completely secularised, filled with everyday kitchen items. Later,
instead of celebrating the Sacrament of the Lord's Supper in the chapel,
family and guests eat a plain meal with ordinary utensils, brought in by
an old maid.[8] What does remain is the aesthetic-didactic overlay — the
paintings of the life of Saint Joseph — but even they only remain, the
narrative implies, because they are too high up on the walls to be destroyed.[9]

Wilhelm speculates that, rising from the ruin of Saint Joseph's, the
spirit that once inhabited it can still bring forth something vibrant:

> Es sollte mich wundern, wenn der Geist, der vor Jahrhunderten in
> dieser Bergöde so gewaltig wirkte und einen so mächtigen Körper von
> Gebäuden, Besitzungen und Rechten an sich zog, und dafür mannig-
> faltige Bildung in der Gegend verbreitete, es sollte mich wundern,
> wenn er nicht auch aus diesen Trümmern noch seine Lebenskraft auf
> ein lebendiges Wesen ausübte.[10]

> [I would be amazed if the spirit that for centuries worked so power-
> fully on this deserted mountain and attracted such a mighty body of
> buildings, possessions, and rights to itself and in return spread such
> manifold learning in the area, I would be amazed if that spirit did not
> still exercise, from the rubble, vitality on a living being.]

Wilhelm's perceptions, when examined from an Enlightenment perspective, call to mind the most significant aspects and contributions of
the Catholic Church: art, law, and education. Stefan Blessin considers
this an unmystical as opposed to a demystified view.[11]

Joseph, like his father and grandfather before him, is a keeper in the
employ of the line of princes who owned the monastery.[12] In one sense
Joseph and Marie humorously claim to overtake their model, the Holy
Family, in number of children, even as they seek to emulate their vir-

tues. They represent a kind of original Christian vitality, such that
Wilhelm nearly feels at times transported eighteen hundred years into
the past.[13] The humane Christianity that is reflected in the couple ultimately dispenses with the Catholic Church, which is shown as a ruin —
and by extension proffers a Jesus in whom humanity, not divinity, is
treasured.

The humanisation of the Holy Family and secularised monastery
outline symbolically a kind of Enlightenment that wants to reject religious orthodoxy, yet preserve the aesthetic and ethical contributions
of religion. Accepting this legacy would allow a universal and secular
claim to be staked on Church art, architecture, and music, without
worshipping the referent of the same, and would maintain a basic social
order built upon Christian ethics, yet emptied of any specific doctrinal
demands or promises. The relinquishment and rollback of Christian
moral and dogmatic hegemony in the political realm could thus be ef-
fected without rending the fabric of society. What some Enlighteners
did not envision, particularly in revolutionary France, was that a mili-
tant attempt to eradicate religion in favour of rationalist or statist ide-
ologies could backfire and cause a recrudescence of Catholicism. In
England the enthroned state religion, despite legislated tolerance,
grappled with recognising dissenting groups as well as Catholicism. The
framers of the United States Constitution, facing a polity in which religious diversity existed, initiated the separation of church and state.

By the time Goethe completed the *Wanderjahre*, the French revolutionary dismantling of religion had been discredited, but Enlightenment deism had gained a firmer footing despite the nineteenth-century
religious resurgence. The societal models presented in the *Wanderjahre*
appear to follow the pattern of tolerance established by Joseph II and
Friedrich II, that is a dispensation of tolerance by the state. But
Goethe's knowledge of the American system of religious freedom,
something different from European tolerance, finds its way into the
Wanderjahre, and a hybrid picture emerges in its model societies.[14] The
Enlightenment critique of religion in general and Goethe's awareness
of new American religious communities converge in the *Wanderjahre*.

The Uncle's District

After Wilhelm and his son Felix leave the caretaker's family they meet
Jarno, a figure first seen in *Wilhelm Meisters Lehrjahre* who now calls
himself Montan, a name that relates to his lone studies in the moun-

tains. Eventually Wilhelm and Felix are separated from Jarno and led to a spacious residence owned by a man who governs the surrounding district.[15] The bounteous and cultivated outdoor setting is matched inside the residence by instructive geographical maps and decorations. Hersilie, whose uncle owns the home, informs Wilhelm that a literary society composed of friends and family who read Europen literature meet there.[16] The geographical maps are thus mirrored by a cultural mapping of an emergent European *Weltliteratur*.[17] And this microcosm of European literary society is mirrored in the uncle's portrait gallery of European intellectual society: "Personen, die im achtzehnten Jahrhundert gewirkt hatten, eine große und herrliche Gesellschaft" [Persons who were active in the eighteenth century, a great and glorious society].[18] The eighteenth century is held up as a model period, and it appears as if Wilhelm has this century and this society in mind when he earlier reminds Felix about the "vollkommenes Jahrhundert" [perfect century] in which the boy was born:

> Welchen Weg mußte nicht die Menschheit machen, bis sie dahin gelangte, auch gegen Schuldige gelind, gegen Verbrecher schonend, gegen Unmenschliche menschlich zu sein! Gewiß waren es Männer göttlicher Natur, die dies zuerst lehrten, die ihr Leben damit zubrachten, die Ausübung möglich zu machen und zu beschleunigen.[19]

> [What road did humanity not have to go down before it arrived at the point of being gentle with even the guilty, concerned for criminals, and treating humanely the inhumane! Certainly these were men of divine nature who first taught this, who spent their lives making possible and accelerating these practices.]

This could be a description of the Enlightenment generation that Wilhelm grew up with. Certainly the names Beccaria (1738–1794) and Filangieri (1752–1788), who are invoked as the uncle's role models, fit this description.[20] Juliette, Hersilie's sister, notes that the maxim of "allgemeine Menschlichkeit" [universal humanity] was accepted in many spheres "damals" [back then].[21] This past tense may be one reason why Wilhelm tries to teach Felix, a representative of the next generation, about the achievements of the earlier. Later in the novel in a letter to Natalie, as Wilhelm contemplates studying medicine, he recalls his father's Enlightenment activities including introducing vaccination, working for the humane treatment of prisoners, and improving conditions in hospitals.[22] Wilhelm further writes that his father believed in the power of "guten Willen" [good will] and that "das Gute" [the good] was there "zu ergreifen und zu nutzen" [to seize and use].[23]

The uncle is a direct recipient of Enlightenment thought, as well as a contributor to its continuation. Wilhelm learns that this man, often referred to as "trefflich" [excellent],[24] grows the many fruits and vegetables on his expansive grounds, land normally used for personal pleasure, because he cares for those who live in the nearby mountains.[25] Furthermore, the uncle has stored many hard-to-come-by necessities such as salt and spices for those mountain dwellers.[26] His family history, which is at once an intellectual genealogy, is given by the narrator, who believes that the reader should get to know the "würdige Person" [worthy person] and "außerordentlicher Mann" [extraordinary man], and judge him.[27]

The uncle's grandfather was an active member of a legation in England and became acquainted with William Penn. Penn, a Quaker, visited Frankfurt Pietists in 1677 and invited them to New Jersey, where he wanted to settle with his persecuted co-religionists. But in 1681 King Charles II of England discharged a debt owed to Penn by giving him land in the English colonies that became known as Pennsylvania. He was able to establish a safe haven, called a "city of brotherly love" — Philadelphia — in 1683. Penn wanted the province so "that an example may be Sett up to the nations" for "an holy experiment."[28] Tolerance was fundamental to Penn's "Frame of Government" (1682) of the Province of Pennsylvania. Article XXXVI reads:

> That all persons living in this province who confess and acknowledge the one almighty and eternal God to be the creator, upholder, and ruler of the world, and that hold themselves obliged in conscience to live peaceably and justly in civil society, shall in no ways be molested or prejudiced for their religious persuasion or practice in matters of faith and worship, nor shall they be compelled at any time to frequent or maintain any religious worship, place, or ministry whatever.[29]

Penn had made a strong impression on the grandfather:

> Das hohe Wohlwollen, die reinen Absichten, die unverrückte Tätigkeit eines so vorzüglichen Mannes, der Konflikt, in den er deshalb mit der Welt geriet, die Gefahren und Bedrängnisse, unter denen der Edle zu erliegen schien, erregten in dem empfänglichen Geiste des jungen Mannes ein entschiedenes Interesse; er verbrüderte sich mit der Angelegenheit, und zog endlich selbst nach America.[30]

> [The high good will, the pure intentions, the unswerving activity of such a first-rate man, the conflict, into which he therefore came with the world, the dangers and tribulations to which the noble man had appeared to succumb, aroused in the receptive spirit of the young man

a decided interest; he felt a brotherly affinity with the affair and moved finally to America.]

William Penn is a significant marker in the tolerance discourse, to which the uncle and his father contributed: "Der Vater unseres Herrn ist in Philadelphia geboren und beide rühmten sich beigetragen zu haben, daß eine allgemein freiere Religionsübung in den Kolonien stattfand" [The father of our master was born in Philadelphia and both claimed to have assisted in bringing about a generally freer practice of religion in the colonies].[31] Philadelphia was not only where the Quakers settled, but also established itself as one of the leading centres of commerce and industry in the colonies and, as the home of Benjamin Rush, David Rittenhouse, and Benjamin Franklin (whom Goethe was reading when he wrote the *Wanderjahre*) as a centre of the American Enlightenment.[32] Goethe was aware as well of Thomas Jefferson's *Notes on the State of Virginia* (1787; German translation 1789) for he read excerpts from the *Notes* in Duke Bernhard's *Reisebericht* (Travel Report, 1828) and he also read Jefferson's *Memoir, Correspondence and private papers* (London, 1829).[33] In the *Notes,* Jefferson argues that the "legitimate powers of government extend to such acts only as are injurious to others. But it does me no injury for my neighbor to say there are twenty gods, or no god. It neither picks my pocket nor breaks my leg." And he asks his fellow Virginians to look to the model of Pennsylvania (and New York) where differing religions co-existed in "peace," "order," and "harmony" — a triple alliance esteemed highly by Enlighteners — because of "unbounded tolerance."[34] Jefferson's views on religion, as enshrined in the Virginia Statute of Religious Freedom (1779), were well known:

> no man shall be compelled to frequent or support any religious worship, place or ministry whatsoever, nor shall be enforced, restrained, molested, or burthened in his body or goods, nor shall otherwise suffer on account of his religious opinions or belief; but that all men shall be free to profess, and by argument to maintain, their opinions in matters of religion, and that the same shall in nowise diminish, enlarge, or affect their civil capacities.[35]

By highlighting the American stream of the uncle's lineage the narrator shows that ideas have consequences and histories and they must be taught and passed on through the generations if they are to continue to be effective. This genealogy is an indirect commentary on the uncle and creates expectations about religious freedom in his district. Does it exist, and if so what form will it take? The narrator shares a maxim that seems to stem from the uncle, and sheds light on his views on religion:

> daß eine in sich abgeschlossene, in Sitten und Religion herkömmlich übereinstimmende Nation vor aller fremden Einwirkung, aller Neuerung sich wohl zu hüten habe; daß aber da, wo man auf frischem Boden viele Glieder von allen Seiten her zusammen berufen will, möglichst unbedingte Tätigkeit im Erwerb, und freier Spielraum der allgemeinsittlichen und religiösen Vorstellungen zu vergönnen sei.[36]

> [that a nation closed in itself and traditionally agreeing in customs and religion ought to protect itself from all foreign influence and innovations; that however there where one wants to call together many parts from all sides on fresh ground, completely unhampered activity in trade and freer scope for universal moral and religious views is to be granted.]

This illustrates the uncle's belief that an immigrant society needs religious freedom. The uncle's father was able to purchase a large tract of land in America (a narrative detail that will prove essential to the future of the *Turmgesellschaft* and many of the mountain folk); however, the uncle decides to return to Europe. He sees how, on top of harsh pioneer conditions in the colonies, the native Americans are tricked, cheated, and beaten out of their lands.[37] However, it was not only injustice or danger that brought the uncle back to Europe, but the desire to be a part of the "kultivierte Welt" [cultivated world].[38] And he feels that even with the limitations of Europe, he can through patience and flexibility get along with king and countrymen.[39]

The narrator notes that the uncle has established a society in these more limited circumstances that is nevertheless "utopian enough."[40] This notion reflects the pragmatism of the uncle.[41] He has applied his New World experience (and wealth) to creating a better community in the Old World. Wilhelm expresses his gladness at having been an unknowing recipient of the uncle's welfare schemes, when he was able to purchase fresh fruit in the mountains where he had not expected to find any.[42]

Religious liberty is a part of this workable utopia: "Religionsfreiheit ist daher in diesem Bezirk natürlich, der öffentliche Kultus wird als ein freies Bekenntnis angesehen" [Religious freedom is therefore natural in this district, the public religion is seen as a free confession].[43] This is the first time that *Religionsfreiheit* appears in the *Wanderjahre* or in any of Goethe's writings, and it is implied, through the uncle's family history, that it is an import from Philadelphia, having originated in a real geographical place with a historical person, William Penn. Although he never receives a name in the *Wanderjahre*, the uncle is paid a high compliment by the narrator in book 3 when he is referred to as a "Welt- und Hofmann" [man of the world and court].[44] The uncle, an autocratic administrator rather than an absolutist ruler, obeys the community's laws himself.[45]

Religionsfreiheit exists in the uncles' District, yet it does not mean the same thing as religious freedom would have meant in the United States in 1791, when Congress amended the Constitution with the Bill of Rights, the first article of which legislates the separation of church and state. *Religionsfreiheit* in the uncle's district is a European-American hybrid, for while freedom of conscience exists, local land-owners have a positive responsibility to provide meeting houses for the public religion, something like the Philadelphia colonial-style Quaker meeting houses or English Methodist churches. A group of Elders teach and preside over social ceremonies and the overall ethos of the religion, to which the multi-purpose building contributes, appears to be a balanced life, with the example related that Elders could be giving instruction while young people dance under the same roof.[46]

The public religion represents a pious secularisation of Christianity. It functions as a registry office for weddings and serves the general public by sponsoring activities for edification and entertainment. Questions of appropriate moral behaviour are left up to the individual, reflecting an Enlightenment tendency to self-determination. Whereas morality is a private matter, there is a way to address concerns. Sundays are set aside as a day of rest and discussion in order to construct a way of life conducive to a regular fresh start each week. Matters with which medical practitioners, government officials, or good friends cannot assist are left to the Divine.[47] As envisioned by Enlightenment thinkers, individuals are responsible for their own actions and accountable to their consciences.[48]

The Pedagogic Province

Lenardo, the uncle's nephew, asks Wilhelm if he will find Nachodine, a tenant farmer's daughter he believes he has wronged because he did not intervene as she requested when she and her father were evicted from his uncle's property. Wilhelm is willing to oblige, but does not want to take his son Felix on the journey. Lenardo suggests that Wilhelm enrol Felix in an educational institution that he describes as "eine Art von Utopien" [a kind of utopia].[49] Wilhelm, on Lenardo's recommendation, visits an old collector and learns more about the aims of this institution that is run by wise men.[50]

Book 2 begins with Wilhelm and Felix, "die Wallfahrenden" [the pilgrims], journeying to the Pedagogic Province.[51] Wilhelm learns during this and a subsequent visit a few years later[52] that within the Pedagogic Province young boys are taught in separate regions, corresponding to their instruction in foreign languages, instrumental music, song, poetry, the visual arts, dance, crafts, farming, and horsemanship.[53] The foreign language programme of the Pedagogic Province is designed to foster contact among students who come from different countries.[54] An Enlightenment attitude is manifest in this international microcosm, because the boys learn about other cultures through a foreign language with the goal of fostering increased intercultural understanding. Wilhelm's second visit happens to fall during a market festival — which turns out to be something like a secular *Weltfest,* for buyers come from many lands. The supervisor explains that the *Marktfest* has a specific pedagogic purpose, as it is a place where the boys can practice their foreign languages.[55]

The leaders of the Pedagogic Province, one called "der Obere" [the Superior] and a group named "die Dreie" [the Three] guide Wilhelm through a special district containing "Heiligtümer" [sacred objects].[56] Wilhelm asks about the peculiar gestures and greetings that he has noticed the pupils practising. Their answer is illuminating: the movements are connected with the ethical teachings of the Province, and have to do with teaching "Ehrfurcht" [reverence].[57]

They explain that reverence itself must be comprehended in stages. The first stage is to learn reverence for those things that are above us. The accompanying gesture, crossing one's arms over the breast and looking joyfully heavenward is how they teach the "unmündige Kinder . . . daß ein Gott da droben sei, der sich in Eltern, Lehrern, Vorgesetzten abbildet und offenbart" [immature children . . . that there is a God up there who represents and reveals himself through parents, teachers, and superiors]. The next gesture, arms held behind the back with clasped hands and smiling countenance turned towards the ground, teaches the pupils to respect the earth that nourishes and provides joy as well as sorrows.[58] The final gesture is a posture whereby the pupils line up and face each other as "Kameraden," willing to face the world together. Each teaching is a stage through which the pupils pass, but a pupil passes from stage to stage only when the Three are convinced of his progress. The obvious irony in this sequence, as in most educational endeavours, is that pupils are taught to be enlightened, yet need to be told when they achieve enlightenment.[59]

One of the central plots of the *Wanderjahre* narrative is set in motion by Makarie, a symbol of reconciliation and harmony, who sends Wilhelm to look for her nephew Lenardo in the hope that he will be reunited happily with the family.[60] The novel is concluded by an array of reconciliations, and culminates in the touching reuniting of father and son, who embrace and are described as Castor and Pollux.[61] At issue in the novel is not so much the traditional nuclear family, but that people relate to each other *as* family, similar to the view of Thoas as an adopted father in *Iphigenie*, or the brotherly embrace at the end of *Egmont*, or the co-operating Protestants and Catholics in the *Sankt-Rochus-Fest zu Bingen,* or the fraternal society envisioned in the *Morgenblatt* essay. The Three therefore interpret the significance of the three reverences not in literal terms, but as yet another harmonious relationship.

The Three explain to Wilhelm that religions strive to teach reverence.[62] Later they suggest that people are beginning to accept that all religions contain something of value.[63] They present religions historically, and define the first kind of religion as the ethnic, covering all heathen religions, revering that which is above us. The next kind is the philosophical which reminds us of our commitment to humanity. And the third kind of religion, Christianity, reveres that which is beneath us, teaching us humility. When Wilhelm asks which of these religions the Three profess, they answer that they profess all three, for all are necessary to teach reverence and to attain the highest reverence, reverence for oneself.[64]

Wilhelm responds with enthusiasm that in life he has learned to look past that which divides.[65] Some critics see in Wilhelm's words a message of tolerance.[66] This assumes the Kantian postulate that it is impossible to apprehend metaphysical truth, similar to the argument in David Hume's *Natural History of Religion* (1757). These assumptions militate against positive truth claims regarding matters of salvation. The pupils are taught about "God up there" because, it appears, that the pedagogues want the pupils to believe in a well-ordered world along deistic lines, a view that would preserve enough of "God up there" to comfort the faint-hearted and encourage optimism about the benevolent progress of history.

The next morning Wilhelm views paintings with an Elder.[67] He is told that the "symphronistic" friezes show how all nations have similar religions.[68] Thus, although the history of biblical Israel dominates the gallery of ethnic/heathen religions in the province's "Hallen der Welt-geschichte" [Halls of World History], Abraham and Apollo are juxta-posed.[69] But since Christianity is based on the private life and teachings of Christ, a philosopher and wise man, its depictions are located in a different gallery.[70] The Elder explains that His teachings and ministry to the unlearned, afflicted, and poor are particularly emphasised.[71] His life is presented until the Last Supper and a veil is drawn over the final suf-ferings because they are so highly reverenced.[72]

The teachers in the Pedagogic Province instil an Enlightenment view of religion in their pupils by comparing and appreciating all relig-ions historically and implying a kind of natural religion. *Ehrfurcht*, a reverence for God, Nature, humanity, and self, or in other words the integration of vertical and horizontal accountability — much as Goethe describes the figure of Humanus in his essay on *Die Geheimnisse* — in-vites one to honour what is praiseworthy in all religions. Added to this is the international nature of the Pedagogic Province, an institution based on learning, not social class or nationality. It is a place where controlled exposure to diverse cultures occurs and the practical tools for understanding a foreign culture are taught and then practised at a multinational *Marktfest*.

The Allies

As book 3 opens, several years have passed. Wilhelm has completed his errand for Lenardo, and has found Nachodine well. Since the terms of his journeying have altered, allowing him to remain longer in one place, he has been trained as a surgeon. Felix remains at the Pedagogic Province, but eventually decides to leave the progressive boarding school and declare his love for Hersilie, with whom he exchanges letters.

Wilhelm desires to associate himself again with the "Verbündeten" [Allies] who are planning to emigrate to America, as he has been in-formed by the Abbé (a central figure in *Wilhelm Meisters Lehrjahre*).[73] The Abbé further explains to Wilhelm that their goal is to achieve a "Weltfrömmigkeit" [secular piety] and work practically to help not only their neighbours, but also "die ganze Menschheit" [all of humanity].[74]

Wilhelm eventually finds an inn, located at the foot of a hill below a mansion, where the Allies are staying, and, upon agreeing to their terms, he is granted permission to remain there.[75] After spending the night and undergoing something like an initiation,[76] Wilhelm finds he is alone and suddenly senses how still everything around him has become.

He notices that the members of the Allies attend different religious services and he concludes "daß in dieser Gesellschaft eine entschiedene Religionsfreiheit obwalte" [that in this society a decided religious freedom governs].[77] This is a critical scene because Wilhelm is observing the activities of the Allies closely. Thus, even before Lenardo's formal address to the Allies and others who wish to emigrate, in which he outlines the kind of community envisioned by himself and other leaders, Wilhelm learns that *Religionsfreiheit* will be a part of it.

The Weltbund

Lenardo, who along with Friedrich is among the leaders of the *Weltbund* [World Society], introduces his emigration vision to a general assembly attended by many of the mountain folk. He paints a persuasive picture of the restricted agricultural circumstances in Europe[78] and stresses the cultural significance that land ownership has taken on — "die Grundfeste alles Daseins" [the foundation of existence] — by connecting it to familial memory and patriotism.[79] He then asserts that one's fatherland is the place where one is useful.[80] This is a more active version of the Latin saying, "Ubi bene, ibi patria" and implies a positive answer to Iphigenie's question about whether a foreign land can become a fatherland.[81]

Next, Lenardo lists stereotypes of those who exemplify, to varying degrees, this spirit of "wandern" or journeying with a purpose, such as: students, natural scientists, tourists, craftsmen, merchants, traders, Jews, artists, musicians, dramatists, pilgrims, missionaries, diplomats, soldiers, and businessmen.[82] These categories not only resonate with, but also replicate and supplement, the journeying types that Goethe praises and holds up as enlightened role models in *Besserem Verständniss*. And it cannot be overlooked that Wilhelm himself is referred to almost interchangeably throughout the novel as "Wanderer" and "Reisender" [wanderer and traveller]. Each of the types in the *Wanderjahre* symbolises the spirit of those who are embarking on the journey to America. Lenardo is not really interested in the occupations or social status of the groups he names, but rather in the development of individuality and the opportunities for learning as one journeys.

His vision is that when people travel they cover the entire world with unseen threads, in a sense sewing it together.[83] A *Weltbund* begins to develop in which social distinctions are overcome as active members of their society will find themselves "mit Kaisern, Königen und Fürsten verbrüdert" [in brotherhood with emperors, kings, and princes].[84] This fraternal society whereby the masses and emperors meet as brothers is the fulfilment of Enlightenment aspirations: "Alle Menschen werden Brüder" [All men will become brothers].[85]

It is the threat of darkness and smallness of mind that concerns the *Weltbund*.[86] Herderian cultural anthropological assumptions are evident in their approach: "Unsere Gesellschaft aber ist darauf gegründet, daß jeder in seinem Maße nach seinen Zwecken aufgeklärt werde" [Our society is founded on this, that each be enlightened according to his ability and goals]. This is similar to the art of intercultural appreciation set forth in *Besserem Verständniss,* in which each culture is measured according to its own standard. A worldwide community of journeyers — Lenardo calls them "Weltumreiser" — have mapped many regions.[87] *Weltumreiser* are real travellers who have charted courses through the known world, and the term is also a metaphor for those who search all regions of human existence.[88] Lenardo summarises: "In solchem Sinne nun dürfen wir uns in einem Weltbunde begriffen ansehen" [In this sense we may see ourselves as part of a world society].[89] He speaks literally of their impending journey to America, and stresses that they should work together to avoid division and strife,[90] a pairing not dissimilar to that found in *Zum Reformationsfest.*[91]

Members of the *Weltbund* have two duties that feature as avowed high priorities: "jeden Gottesdienst in Ehren zu halten, denn sie sind alle mehr oder weniger im Credo verfaßt; ferner alle Regierungsformen gleichfalls gelten zu lassen" [to honour every religious service, because they are all more or less contained in the creed; furthermore, to allow all forms of government].[92] The qualification to be a *Weltumreiser* of the kind described by Lenardo, whether literally or metaphorically, appears to be not only tolerance of different religions and societies, but also an acknowledgement of, indeed an honouring of these differences. Lenardo exhorts the *Weltbund* in the closing words of his presentation to adhere to the three reverences.[93]

During a subsequent conversation about the plan, the Christian ethos of the *Weltbund* becomes apparent, as the narrator reports Friedrich's words about the future establishment of the society in America. He says that each religion searches for truth "auf ihre Weise" [in its own way].[94] And of the Christian religion, particularly of the doctrines of faith, hope, and charity, and the virtue of patience, Friedrich is reported to say: "An dieser Religion halten wir fest, aber auf eine eigne Weise" [We hold fast to this religion, but in our own way]. The *Weltbund* teaches the children a kind of Christianity, emphasising its ethical and not historical elements, in order to show reverence for the "Urheber" [originator].[95] Friedrich adds that Jews are not tolerated in their society[96] — a point that will be discussed in greater detail in the following chapter. In short, however, the *Weltbund* appears to be a community that respects other confessions and allows diversity among its members, yet demands a basic acceptance of Jesus Christ's teachings.

The European Plan

Odoardo, another leader in the *Weltbund*, presents a second colonisation plan that is connected to his role as the governor of a province on behalf of a prince. His brief speech is directed towards those who decide, as their song goes, "einzuwandern / In das feste Vaterland" [to emigrate into the firm fatherland] as opposed to travelling to America with the *Weltbund*.[97] Odoardo has made an attractive announcement to any individuals who wish to remain in Europe: an offer of job security.[98] He describes the differences between the Old World and the New, emphasising that there is room to build in both.[99] He identifies the challenges of diminishing space and inescapable tradition that exists in Europe and asserts that his isolated province provides great benefits for a society such as he envisions.[100]

He describes how he has attempted to administer the province with understanding, but felt that his neighbours did not share his views.[101] However, he now believes that history has come to his aid as younger administrators in the adjoining districts want to co-operate with him. Odoardo, like Lenardo and the *Turmgesellschaft*, has been able to join his land to that of others. Where Egmont and Don Carlos fail to convince rulers, Odoardo (a kind of enlightened administrator) succeeds.[102] His colonial initiatives have something in common with similar settlement projects of certain eighteenth-century rulers such as Maria Theresa or Friedrich II.[103]

Odoardo speaks idealistically about creating a future; nevertheless he realises that agreement on how to build this new society will not be easy to achieve.[104] What, then, is Odoardo's answer to this? Optimism. A hope in history and a faith in humanity: "Hier also haben wir zu wiederholen: das Jahrhundert muß uns zu Hülfe kommen" [Here we must repeat: the century must come to our aid].[105] He asks for three things: reason, enlarged hearts, and a united activity. Odoardo invites those who would follow his plan to look to the Enlightenment — the intellectual pantheon of persons represented in the uncle's paintings, who belong to what Wilhelm calls enthusiastically a "perfect century."[106] The recurrent praising of the eighteenth century is not a refusal to look forward, rather it is a reminder — similar to the one Goethe gives young readers in his *Morgenblatt* essay on *Die Geheimnisse* — that in order to move forward one must possess the spirit of the Enlightenment.

It is high time, announces Odoardo, to recognise the age that liberates the spirit.[107] His invitation echoes that of the Abbé to Wilhelm to journey, endure, be active, and become a "notwendigstes Glied unsrer Kette" [most indispensable link in our chain]. A similar image recurs as Odoardo envisions an individual as "ein einziges Glied . . . in einer großen Kette" [a single link . . . in a great chain].[108] This is an abstraction of the theme of brotherhood that runs throughout the novel. Odoardo describes how the future community, a "bürgerliche Welt" [civil world],[109] in the three joined provinces will function, including the initiation of a new social order, rationalised streets and villages, and an exact accounting of funds.[110]

Significantly, *Religionsfreiheit* is not mentioned in the European plan, as it is in descriptions of the uncle's district, in Wilhelm's observations of the Allies, and in the projected American community of the *Weltbund*. The synthetic approach of the Pedagogic Province encourages tolerance of and reverence for all religions, based on the Enlightenment view that they represent forms of a natural religion. Those instances where the idea of religious liberty is cited are seen as a part of the New World, a preparation for it, or an import from it. Religious freedom as such, then, may be, in Goethe's mapping of the history of ideas, more workable in an immigrant society than in Europe, although the novel shows how ideas may be transplanted or grafted. In the uncle's district, the Pedagogic Province, and the *Weltbund*, religion is viewed as an essential unifying and regulative factor in specific communities.

Throughout the novel the humane social and intellectual advances of the eighteenth century are held up as a model for the future. The *Wanderjahre* presents a series of "utopian enough" societies that venerate Enlightenment ideas, yet in one of them, the community that will be established in America, Jews are barred from participation: a puzzle and a provocation.

Notes

[1] Goethe published a version of the *Wanderjahre* in 1821; the 1829 edition was a reworked and expanded version and is the one on which the observations in this chapter are based.

[2] Gonthier-Louis Fink, Gerhart Baumann, and Johannes John review these in MA 17, 1010–1015.

[3] I/1: FA 10, 264–65.

[4] I/2: FA 10, 272.

[5] I/1: FA 10, 263 and I/2: FA 10, 270 respectively.

[6] I/2: FA 10, 274.

[7] I/2: FA 10, 270–71.

[8] I/2: FA 10, 273–74.

[9] I/2: FA 10, 271 and 275.

[10] I/2: FA 10, 273.

[11] Stefan Blessin, *Goethes Romane*, 270.

[12] I/2: FA 10, 274.

[13] I/2: FA 10, 273. An important clue to the date of the events in the novel is given, suggesting 1800.

[14] For modern discussions on intercultural tolerance: Michael Walzer, *On Toleration* (New Haven: Yale UP, 1997) and *Kulturthema Toleranz: Zur Grundlegung einer interdisziplinären und interkulturellen Toleranzforschung*, ed. by Alois Wierlacher (Munich: iudicium, 1996).

[15] I/5: FA 10, 308.

[16] I/5: FA 10, 308–309.

[17] Distributed throughout the residence and grounds are proverbs and aphorisms, some from the Qur'an (I/6: FA 10, 328). *Weltliteratur* is the subject of at least one aphorism (III/"Aus Makariens Archiv": FA 10, 770).

[18] I/6: FA 10, 325.

[19] I/4: FA 10, 306.

[20] I/6: FA 10, 327. Beccaria wrote *Dei delitti e delle pene* (On Crimes and Punishments, 1764), a work written against torture. He was among the first to support the abolition of the death penalty. Goethe calls him a "Humanitätslehrer" [teacher of humanity] and met his student, Filangieri, in Naples in 1787 (Neumann: FA 10, 1059).

[21] I/6: FA 10, 326–27.

[22] II/11: FA 10, 551.

[23] II/11: FA 10, 552.

[24] I/6: FA 10, 326 and I/7: FA 10, 342.

[25] I/6: FA 10, 327.

[26] He does not store tobacco or alcohol. The *Weltbund* also appears to be teetotal.

[27] I/7: FA 10, 342.

[28] Penn's letter of 25 August 1681 to James Harrison William in: *The Papers of William Penn*, 1680–1684, ed. by Richard S. Dunn and Mary Maples Dunn, 5 vols. (Philadelphia: U of Pennsylvania P, 1981–1987), vol. 2: 1680–1684, (1982), 108.

[29] *William Penn and the Founding of Pennsylvania: A Documentary History*, ed. by Jean R. Sunderland (Philadelphia: U of Pennsylvania P, 1983), 132.

[30] I/7: FA 10, 342. "Verbrüdern" could possibly refer to his association with the Quakers.

[31] I/7: FA 10, 342–43. Near Philadelphia is the city of Germantown, the first German settlement in America (1683). Many German religious settlements arose in Pennsylvania during the eighteenth century. Cf. Julius Friedrich Sachse, *The German Pietists of Pennsylvania, 1694–1708* (Philadelphia: Stockhausen, 1895).

[32] Goethe read Franklin's *Autobiography* from 30 December 1828 to 18 January 1829, during the time he wrote *Wanderjahre*. Gustafson also reminds us that Herder praises Franklin in the *Briefe zur Beförderung der Humanität* (Letters on the Promotion of Humanity; a work Goethe read), praises Franklin. She makes a strong case for Franklin's intellectual influence on the organisation and ethos of the *Turmgesellschaft*. Susan Gustafson, "The Religious Significance of Goethe's 'Amerikabild,'" *Eighteenth-Century Studies* 24 (1990): 69–91 (75–77).

[33] Victor Lange, "Goethes Amerikabild: Wirklichkeit und Vision," in *Amerika in der deutschen Literatur: Neue Welt – Nordamerika – USA*, ed. by Sigrid Bauschinger et al. (Stuttgart: Reclam, 1975), 63–74 (65).

[34] *Thomas Jefferson. Writings.* Edited by Merrill D. Peterson (New York: The Library of America, 1984), 285, 287.

[35] Jefferson's *Virginia Statute of Religious Freedom* (1779) in *Thomas Jefferson: In His Own Words*, ed. by Maureen Harrison and Steve Gilbert (New York: Barnes & Noble, 1993), 56–57.

[36] I/7: FA 10, 343.

[37] I/7: FA 10, 343–44.

[38] I/7: FA 10, 343. The narrator concedes that Europe could often be called a "Wildnis" [wilderness].

[39] I/7: FA 10, 343–44.

[40] Ibid.

[41] I/6: FA 10, 329.

[42] I/6: FA 10, 327.

[43] I/7: FA 10, 344.

[44] III/14: FA 10, 723.

[45] The uncle's enlightened yet autocratic ways mimic those of the so-called enlightened despots of the time (Reiss, *Goethes Romane*, 238).

[46] I/7: FA 10, 344. Pietists live in the uncle's district (I/11: FA 10, 394).

[47] I/7: FA 10, 345.

[48] I/7: FA 10, 345.

[49] I/11: FA 10, 406.

[50] I/12: FA 10, 413.

[51] I/11: FA 10, 406. One model for the Pedagogic Province is an institute for boys from the upper class founded by Philipp Emanuel Fellenberg (1771–1844) in Hofwyl near Bern. Jane Brown shows that Goethe also drew upon the ideas of Basedow and Johann Heinrich Campe (1746–1818). Jane Brown, *Goethe's Cyclical Narratives: Die Unterhaltungen deutscher Ausgewanderten and Wilhelm Meisters Wanderjahre,* University of North Carolina Studies in Germanic Languages and Literatures 82 (Chapel Hill: U of North Carolina P, 1975), 87–97.

[52] II/7–8: FA 10, 515–16.

[53] II/8: FA 10, 517–29.

[54] II/8: FA 10, 518.

[55] II/8: FA 10, 517–18.

[56] II/9: FA 10, 531.

[57] II/1: FA 10, 420.

[58] Ibid.

[59] II/1: FA 10, 421.

[60] I/11: FA 10, 392. An archetypal family is presented in book 1 through the allusion to the Holy Family. The novellas within the work also present various kinds of family relationships.

[61] III/18: FA 10, 745. Brown interprets Makarie's mediation and the string of marriages as ironic (*Goethe's Cyclical Narratives*, 67–75). *Wilhelm Meisters Lehrjahre* ends, of course, with marriages that cross class boundaries in an unrealistic way for the time.

[62] II/1: FA 10, 422.

[63] II/1: FA 10, 423.

[64] Ibid.

[65] Ibid.

[66] Fink, Baumann, and John in MA 17, 1140.

[67] Learning from paintings links Wilhelm's experiences at the Pedagogic Province with those at Saint Joseph's and at the uncle's residence.

[68] II/2: FA 10, 425. A "symphronistic" approach to religious history was taken by Hume, Voltaire, and Lessing (*Die Erziehung des Menschengeschlechts* [The Education of Mankind], 1780), and Herder (*Ideen zur Philosophie der Geschichte der Menschheit* [Ideas on the Philosophy of the History of Humanity], 1784–1791).

[69] II/2: FA, 10, 426.

[70] II/2: FA 10, 427.

[71] II/2, FA 10, 429.

[72] Ibid.

[73] II/7: FA 10, 513. Lenardo's uncle has given him a tract of land in America near the Emigration Society's land, so Lenardo and the Emigration Society decide to join forces, especially since a canal is projected in the area. The Abbé envisions that weavers, spinners, masons, carpenters, and blacksmiths will colonise the community. Lenardo is sent to certain overpopulated areas in the mountains where he seeks recruits. Meanwhile, Lothario, another leading figure of the *Turmgesellschaft* in the *Lehrjahre* and also the brother of Natalie and Friedrich, has been sent to the Pedagogic Province (with whom the Allies will remain in contact) to recruit artists (513–514).

[74] II/7: FA 10, 514.

[75] III/1: FA 10, 588.

[76] Cf. Scott Abbott, "Ritual Routes in Wilhelm Meister's Travels," in *Fictions of Freemasonry*, (59–88).

[77] III/1: FA 10, 593.

[78] III/1: FA 10, 665.

[79] Ibid.

[80] III/1: FA 10, 667.

[81] I, ii, line 76: FA 5, 557.

[82] III/9: FA 10, 667–71.

[83] III/9: FA 10, 671.

[84] Ibid.

[85] Cf. Beethoven's famous choral setting of Schiller's "An die Freude" (Ode to Joy) in the Ninth Symphony. The theme of brotherhood pervades the *Wanderjahre*, culminating in the emotional embrace of father and son who have grown into brotherhood, hence the at first sight surprising simile of Castor and Pollux, referred to above.

[86] III/9: FA 10, 671.

[87] Ibid.

[88] III/9: FA 10, 672.

[89] Ibid.

[90] Ibid.

[91] "Spaltung und Trennung" [division and separation].

[92] III/9: FA 10, 672.

[93] III/9: FA 10, 673.

[94] III/11: FA 10, 686.

[95] III/11, FA 10, 686–87.

[96] III/11: FA 10, 687.

[97] III/12: FA 10, 696.

[98] III/10: FA 10, 674.

[99] III/12: FA 10, 690.

[100] III/9: FA 10, 665.

[101] III/12: FA 10, 691–92.

[102] III/12: FA 10, 692.

[103] Neumann in FA 10, 1237.

[104] III/12: FA 10, 692.

[105] III/12: FA 10, 693.

[106] I/4: FA 10, 306.

[107] III/12: FA 10, 692.

[108] III/12: FA 10, 693–94. Odoardo's plan is in this sense similar to Faust's final vision.

[109] III/12: FA 10, 693.

[110] III/12: FA 10, 693–95.

10: Excursus: "In this sense . . . we do not tolerate Jews among us"

"AN EDOM" (To Edom), a posthumously published poem by Heinrich Heine, a nineteenth-century German-Jewish poet and writer, gives vision to one view of the relationship between Germans and Jews:

> Ein Jahrtausend schon und länger
> Dulden wir uns brüderlich;
> Du, du duldest, daß ich athme,
> Daß du rasest, dulde ich.
>
> Manchmal nur, in dunkeln Zeiten,
> Ward dir wunderlich zu Muth,
> Und die liebefrommen Tätzchen
> Färbtest du mit meinem Blut'.
>
> Jetzt wird unsre Freundschaft fester,
> Und noch täglich nimmt sie zu;
> Denn ich selbst begann zu rasen,
> Und ich werde fast wie Du![1]

[For a millennium and longer we have tolerated each other fraternally. You, you tolerate that I breathe, and I tolerate that you rave. Only sometimes, in dark moments, a weird mood came over you, and the loving pious paws you coloured with my blood. Now our friendship is becoming firmer. And even daily it increases; for I myself have begun to rave, and become almost like you!]

Given the course of German history, Heine's words carry the weight of prophecy, and lend an urgency to understanding a paradoxical moment in the *Wanderjahre*, when it seems that Jews remain, as Wilfried Barner puts it, "aus dem Idealstaat bezeichnenderweise ausgeschlossen" [significantly excluded from the ideal state].[2] Certainly critics differ regarding the reported plans of the community that will be established in America by the band of emigrants. Adolf Muschg perceives a "Hauch von Gulag" [breath of the Gulag] in the plans[3] and Ehrhard Bahr impugns what he sees as its institutionalised anti-Semitism, continuous police surveillance, deportations, and forced expropriations.[4] On the other hand, Eric Blackall observes more positively that the new community will "embody a respect for work which in turn will involve careful parcellation of one's time for activity while also leaving opportunity for reflection. Family life will be the center of communal life, and there will be a sort of police to ensure that 'no one shall be troublesome to anyone else,' with a peripatetic higher authority enforcing laws for the benefit of the whole community."[5]

Because the *Weltbund* and their emigration plans are set up in the *Wanderjahre* as a kind of utopia, paralleling that of the uncle's district and the colonists who will remain in Europe, the question arises: why are Jews barred? Some critics point out that the reader is receiving very pertinent aspects of the projected American community only second-hand, as Friedrich merely summarises the plans. Moreover, it is suggested that the narrative calls into question Friedrich's character, thereby undermining his authority as a spokesman for the community.[6] Although much of the information about the settlement in America is "distanziert dargestellt" [represented in a detached manner], and few would argue that the details of the settlement reflect the author's views,[7] suspicion nevertheless remains: "Der Ausschluß der Juden aus dem neuen Gemeinwesen ist Goethe, so bedrückend wir dies nach Auschwitz empfinden, durchaus zuzutrauen." [Goethe is well capable of the exclusion of the Jews from the new community, as oppressive as we perceive this to be after Auschwitz].[8] But before examining this exclusion in more detail, I will sketch briefly a general approach to the larger and more elusive subject of Goethe and Jews.[9]

During the Ettersburg premiere of the second version of *Jahrmarktsfest zu Plundersweilen* (Fair at Plundersweilen, 1774) Goethe played the role of Haman *and* Mordecai.[10] The range of characterisations opened up by this dual role represents, to an extent, the way much of the secondary literature describes Goethe's relationship to Jews. Curiosity about his opinion of Jews existed during his lifetime. Grüner recalled an occasion when he and Goethe explored Eger together, a town where Jews had lived and suffered for centuries, and paused to visit a former synagogue. Grüner's account is constructed to reveal Goethe's impenetrability on the subject, even given the overwhelming history literally before his eyes, under his feet, and at his fingertips. Grüner describes in detail a medieval pogrom in Eger, suggesting perhaps he and Goethe learned at least some of these details together, and concludes: "Mir lag daran, Goethes Meinung über die Juden zu erfahren. Was ich aber auch vorbringen mochte, er blieb in

Betrachtung der alten Inschriften vertieft, und äußerte sich nicht mit Bestimmtheit in Betreff der Juden" [I was interested in learning Goethe's opinion about the Jews. But whatever I presented, he remained immersed in the old inscriptions and did not express himself with certainty regarding the Jews].[11]

The visual image of Goethe straining to examine the vanishing Hebrew inscription on a Catholic church that was once a synagogue, in a town where the blood of former Jewish inhabitants ran in the streets, is powerful. One empathises with Grüner's frustration in attempting to get Goethe's response in such a setting. Yet the image also recalls that Goethe from a young age appreciated the Bible, admired the people who preserved it, and was intrigued by their language. Perhaps this accounts for his fascination with the fading Hebrew inscriptions, but maybe his silence bears witness to his ambiguous feelings about the "Contrast zwischen den Ahnherren und den Enkeln, der uns irremacht und verstimmt" [the contrast between the fathers and the grandsons, which makes us confused and disgruntled].[12] This statement suggests that Goethe felt that contemporary Jews did not measure up to their ancient ancestors.

Gustav Kars, in the subtitle of a chapter outlining the response of the German Classicists to Jews, sums it up as: "Abneigung gemildert durch Humanität" [Aversion moderated by humanity].[13] A century ago a more apologetic view was expressed in Ludwig Geiger's essay "Goethe und die Juden" [Goethe and the Jews] in his *Zeitschrift für die Geschichte der Juden in Deutschland* [Journal for the History of the Jews in Germany].[14] His paradigmatic methodology (and title) would set the tone for those that followed, a method described succinctly as quotation against quotation.[15] Naturally, quotation is used in scholarship, but the operative word here is "against" because setting one quotation against another implies "this is true, not that"; such methodology fails to see the more complex view that allows both to coexist.

Complicating matters further, in the twentieth century Goethe's relationship to Jews was ultra-politicised by anti-Semitists. Essays by Heinrich Teweles and Julius Bab, and those published in the English-speaking world by William Rose and Mark Waldman were reacting, in part at least, to the rise of National Socialism. Even Alfred Low's later work can be seen in this light.[16] Only more recently, with the essays of Wilfried Barner, Norbert Oellers, and Günter Hartung, has a more analytical and historical approach been achieved.

Generally, articles discussing Goethe's relationship to Jews follow a similar chronological and thematic pattern. They tend to rely heavily on the autobiographical *Dichtung und Wahrheit* (Poetry and Truth, 1811–1813), which contains Goethe's recollections of his early contact with the Frankfurt Jewish community. It foregrounds his admiration for the Bible, displays his opinions of Spinoza and Mendelssohn, and describes his attempts to become acquainted with Hebrew and Yiddish. His personal relationship with Jews is investigated in his documented legal acts, letters, diary entries, and reported conversations. Literary works, especially those of the 1770s, are interpreted, including the posthumously published *Judenpredigt* (Jewish Sermon, presumably 1767–1768). There is often a nod in the direction of his early biblical dramas and his never completed (and not preserved) multilingual *Roman in Briefen* (Novel in Letters, 1771), which was to include a section in Yiddish. His review of Isashar Falkensohn Behr's *Gedichte von einem Polnischen Juden* (Poems from a Polish Jew, 1772) is scrutinised. Often cited as showing a positive, humanistic, tolerant view are the essays *Brief des Pastors* and *Zwo wichtige bisher unerörtete Biblische Fragen* (Two Important Until Now Unexamined Biblical Questions, 1773). The posthumously published *Zum Reformationsfest* (1816) is also cited as evidence of Goethe's humanity vis-à-vis Jews. The so-called "Esther-spiel" (Esther Play) section of the second version of the farce, *Jahrmarktsfest zu Plundersweilen,* is said to show that Goethe knew the typical anti-Semitic arguments, while the never completed translation of the biblical *Song of Songs* (1774) is subpoenaed as evidence of Herder's influence and a growing interest in the Bible as literature. It has been said that in Goethe's version of the popular tale, *Der ewige Jude* (The Eternal Jew, 1774), he removed the anti-Jewish elements from the original story.[17] The 1797 essay *Israel in der Wüste* (Israel in the Wilderness) that eventually found its way into the *Besserem Verständniss* essay that was included in his *West-östlicher Divan* is evaluated as typical of the biblical criticism of the time. Poems in which Jews figure, like "Auf Miedings Tod" (On Miedings Death, 1782) and snippets from his proverbs and scientific works like the *Farbenlehre* (Colour Theory, 1810), are scanned for positive or negative meanings, as are the individual literary figures in, for example, *Clavigo* (1774) or *Wilhelm Meisters Lehrjahre* (1796). Obvious quotations from the *Wanderjahre* (1829) round out the theme. Perhaps it is fair to say that Goethe was "kein Freund der Juden" [no friend of the Jews] and certainly no "entschiedener Sachwalter der Juden" [decided champion of the Jews].[18] But on the other hand, as Wilfried Barner has written, "mag daran erinnert sein, daß Goethe unter den Großen seiner Zeit einer der ganz wenigen gewesen ist, die sich nicht rundheraus ablehnend über die Juden geäußert haben" [it may be remembered that Goethe, among the great ones of his time, was one of the very few who did not flatly express himself disapprovingly about the Jews].[19] The scholarly consensus appears to be, to quote again from Barner, that "ausgerechnet der wirkungsmächtigste Repräsentant der deutschen Literatur- und Bildungstradition, der große Verkünder der klassischen Humanitätsidee hat über die Juden nicht nur positive Worte gefunden" [of all people the most effective representative of the German literary and cultural tradition, the great exponent of the classical ideal of humanity, did not find only positive words about the Jews].[20] Beyond this, opinions differ on nearly everything else.

The reported conversation in book 3, chapter 11 of *Wanderjahre* revolves around "Religion und Sitte" [religion and morals], concepts the narrator defines as that which "Menschen eigentlich zusammenhält" [actually binds people together].[21] Religion and morals would be of the utmost importance in building and maintaining the new community of emigrants in America. The cohesive *sine qua non* of the new community is a shared belief not only in the Christian ideals of faith, love, hope, and patience, but also in Jesus Christ, "der Urheber" [the Originator] whom they view as holy. As Friedrich reports: "An dieser Religion halten wir fest" [We hold fast to this religion].[22] Hartung asserts that Friedrich is not speaking as a believing Christian, but that Christianity is an "Ordnungsfaktor" [factor for keeping order].[23] Unity certainly is a central facet of the emigration plans: "Einheit ist allmächtig, deshalb keine Spaltung, kein Widerstreit unter uns" [Unity is all important, therefore no division, no strife among us].[24] But Friedrich does add that they live their religion "auf eine eigne Weise" [in our own way] — a favourite phrase of Goethe's — thus suggesting that this is not a traditional Christian group. Rose calls this "a plan concerning the organisation of a new Christian community."[25] This "new Christian community," headed by a religious figure, the Abbé, is in fact similar to the many new Christian communities that dotted the United States, some of which Goethe had read about in Duke Bernhard's North American travel book,[26] in Benjamin Franklin's *Autobiography*, and in other sources. Bernhard was impressed with how religions coexisted peacefully in the United States, especially in Philadelphia. He read that twenty-two sects (including Jews) lived there: "Und alle diese Secten leben friedlich neben einander und mit einander" [And all these sects live peacefully next to and with each other]. Bernhard also visited the German-American Harmony Society in Ohio.[27] Franklin, in one section of his *Autobiography*, describes how, when it was decided to create a building for the education of poor children and occasional preachers in Philadelphia, a committee was established consisting of members of diverse Christian confessions: "it was therefore that one of each Sect was appointed, viz. one Church-of-England man, one Presbyterian, one Baptist, one Moravian, &c."[28] Kriegleder even puts forward the notion that the *Wanderjahre* emigrants are in fact going to Pennsylvania, which had a long history of German (religious) emigration.[29]

Goethe was struck by the diversity of Christian communities in the New World and by their peaceful coexistence. He used the religious pluralism of America as a metaphor to express support for similar liberty in intellectual pursuits:

> In Neuyork sind neunzig verschiedene, christliche Konfessionen, von welchen jede auf ihre Art Gott und den Herrn bekennt, ohne weiter aneinander irrezuwerden. In der Naturforschung, ja in jeder Forschung müssen wir es so weit bringen; denn was will das heißen, daß jedermann von Liberalität spricht und den andern hindern will, nach seiner Weise zu denken und sich auszusprechen.[30]

> [In New York are ninety different Christian confessions, each of which professes in its own way God and the Lord, without any friction resulting. In the pursuit of natural science, indeed in every pursuit we must get to this point; for what does it mean when everyone talks about liberality and wants to prevent others from thinking and expressing themselves in their own way.]

An especially interesting aspect of Goethe's thought in this context is that he, like the band of emigrants in the *Wanderjahre,* defines Christianity's common denominator as a belief in "God and the Lord."

Suggesting what he seems to see as a logical extension of the Christian belief upon which the new society of immigrants will be based, but also somewhat apologetically, Friedrich in the *Wanderjahre* reports: "In diesem Sinne, den man vielleicht pedantisch nennen mag, aber doch als folgerecht anerkennen muß, dulden wir keinen Juden unter uns; denn wie sollten wir ihm den Anteil an der höchsten Kultur vergönnen, deren Ursprung und Herkommen er verleugnet?" [In this sense, that one may perhaps call pedantic but must recognise as consistent, Jews are not tolerated among us; for how should we grant them a part of the highest culture whose origin and tradition they deny?][31] Jane Brown views this point as characteristic of the rigidity that permeates the entire ethos of the plan to emigrate to America, which is, ironically, in "contrast to the tolerance of the eighteenth century."[32]

Benjamin Bennett, who is also sensitive to this irony in the *Wander-jahre*, draws a somewhat different conclusion:

> If Wilhelm Meisters *Wanderjahre* were written today, in the shadow of Auschwitz, the exclusion of the Jews at the end would immediately be marked "anti-Semitic." We have forgotten how to read in that dialogical eighteenth-century manner — the manner in which Lessing and Herder read each other — which might give us time to recognize that precisely our condition as reader is reflected in those excluded Jews, and reflected *by* exactly that gesture of exclusion, which corresponds to the book's pervasive ironizing of the reader's position. The reader's relation to the Jews approaches one of identity; and the result — if a book like Goethe's could be written today — would be a response to Auschwitz, not a rebuilding of it.[33]

On different levels, both Brown's and Bennett's interpretations are sustainable. The *Wanderjahre* narrative, as Brown documents, is constructed loosely and designed to be ironic. It is not designed to reflect eighteenth-century European notions on tolerance, instead the novel attempts to introduce new ways to conceive of the relationship between the church and state, as well as explore modern meanings of religious identity. In fact, readers are to identify not only with the excluded Jews, but also with the exclusionary emigrant band as well.

In the *Wanderjahre* the reader is faced with the modern condition of fragmentation and exclusion. This moment of exclusion in the *Wanderjahre* can be read as a transformation of tolerance through recognising difference, and in this sense it is a contrast to the ideal envisioned by some Enlightenment thinkers who thought that eventually a "Glaubensvereinigung" [uniting of religions] could be achieved, thus overcoming particularism, perhaps even putting an end to religious conflicts. If religion and culture are nothing more than trappings, then finding common ground between faiths would not only bring about mutual tolerance, but might ultimately lead to the discarding of religion. "Es scheint mir zeitgemäß, einen Tugendbund zu stiften, so daß man die Guten und Tugendhaften aus allen Völkern zu einer ordentlichen Gemeinde vereinte" [It seems to me high time to found a society of virtue, so that one may unite in a regular community the good and virtuous among all peoples] reads similarly to a line from Herder's *Humanitätsbriefe* [Letters on Humanity] or Goethe's *Morgenblatt* essay. But this sentence is in fact from Benjamin Franklin as quoted in an 1830 German translation of an English book on a report on the American communities of Owen and Rapp.[34] Indeed, once tolerance began to spread, and along with the rise of higher criticism and the emergence of the state as the regulator of most public affairs, religious indifference could take root and tolerance itself could become a potential form of structural anti-religion. This has been argued, in a different context, in Bill Williams's article "The Anti-Semitism of Tolerance," which has to do with Jews in middle-class Manchester in the late nineteenth century.[35]

Ritchie Robertson suggests that Lessing's *Die Juden* [The Jews] and *Nathan the Wise* illustrate a "deceptive toleration," for

> what purports to be a neutral standpoint, intended to promote tolerance, has developed into a secular agnosticism that is hostile to religion as such. The toleration offered by such an agnosticism tends to sidestep judgement, either by interpreting other people's beliefs as being only superficially different but fundamentally the same as one's own, or by denying that any judgements of truth or value are legitimate. This conception is a pseudo-tolerance that tolerates different beliefs only on the assumption that they are not really different; masquerading as toleration of others, it actually makes the implicit claim that its own values are universal and unchallengeable.[36]

The emigrant band constitutes a religious community above all, and this is an important distinction that parallels Paul Stöcklein's view that "die Wanderjahre sind ein Sozialroman, kein Staatsroman" [the *Wanderjahre* is a novel about community, not the state].[37] This type of "new Christian community," often embracing utopian and communal ideals, was typical of the nineteenth-century United States, as Harold Bloom shows, and German emigrants constituted many of them.[38] A wide range of non-traditional German-Christian communities flourished in the early nineteenth-century United States — and not only the larger and more well-known groups that constituted the Amish, Mennonites, Moravians, Dunkards, and Hutterites, let alone German Catholics and Lutherans. La Vern J. Rippley supplies helpful examples of other German Christian communities: Johann Conrad Beissel's Ephrata community (founded in Pennsylvania, 1732); Johann Georg Rapp's Harmony Society (Pennsylvania, 1803), renamed *Harmonie* or New Harmony (Indiana, 1815); the German separatist community of Zoar (Ohio, 1817); the mystical Community of True Inspiration, founded by Christian Metz (New York, 1842), which established itself in Iowa (1855).[39] The emigrant band in the *Wanderjahre* is defined by their devotion to their "Urheber" [Originator], similar to the way in which the Elders of the Pedagogic Province define the Jews: "Es ist das beharrlichste Volk der Erde, es ist, es war, es wird sein, um den Namen Jehova durch alle Zeiten zu verherrlichen" [It is the most persistent people of the earth, it is, it was, it will be, to glorify the name of Jehovah through all times].[40] The names of Christ and Jehovah are transcendent signifiers that constitute the core beliefs of the two religions, which are traditionally held to be mutually exclusive. That Christians and Jews are excluded from the sacred spaces of each others' faiths is a necessary consequence of their difference, but this does not preclude mutual tolerance.[41] So understood, Goethe's idea in the *Wanderjahre* finds an ally in Moses Mendelssohn, who believed that a uniting of religions could lead to restrictions on freedom of conscience: "Im Grunde, kann eine Glaubensvereinigung, wenn sie je zu Stande kommen sollte, keine andere als die unseligsten Folgen fuer Vernunft und Gewissensfreyheit haben" [Basically, a uniting of religions, if it should ever come into being, would have no other then unhallowed consequences for reason and freedom of conscience].[42] In the *Wanderjahre* Judaism and Christianity have been stripped to their barest elements, as Goethe understood them. Here again the Herderian tension is explored between the particular-exclusive (unique religious identity) and the universal-inclusive (common religious denominators), tensions also felt in Goethe's *Egmont* and *Iphigenie*.

Despite the emphasis on religious exclusivity in this episode of the *Wanderjahre*, religious coexistence is the Goethean ideal.[43] This makes the question of religious identity in *Wanderjahre* even more intriguing. Readers are structurally motivated, at least at this point in the narrative, to recognise difference and exclusion as a part of modern life — they must face the condition of multiculturalism. This of course recalls Iphigenie's question, "Can a foreign land ever become for us the fatherland?"[44] The answer is again ambiguous, similar to the insufficient intercultural understanding in *Egmont*. Goethe's opposition to Church-sanctified marriages between Jews and Christians, reported by Kanzler von Müller, marks not only his discomfort "mit den Stichworten Assimilation, Akkulturation und Emanzipation" [with the key words assimilation, acculturation and emancipation],[45] but also his stance for some kind of minimum religious integrity and identity. Perhaps this is not too far from Mendelssohn's argument that Jews ought to be able to keep the "Zeremonialgesetz" [ceremonial law] — "nicht mit euch essen, nicht von euch heurathen, das, so viel wir einsehen koennen, der Stifter eurer Religion selbst weder gethan, noch uns erlaubt haben wuerde?" [not eat with you, not marry you, which, as far as we can tell, the founder of your religion neither did nor would have allowed us?].[46] Leslie Stevenson explains that, "religious belief and religiously based conceptions of culture tend to be divisive, because they involve controversial claims to truth of beliefs, and the rightness or wrongness of actions."[47]

In 1823 Grand Duke Carl August announced a new ordinance in Weimar that granted Jews the free exercise of religion, admittance to the university, and permission to marry Christians, provided that the children were raised Christians.[48] Müller reports that Goethe criticised the new "Juden-Gesetze" [Jew Laws] in a conversation on 23 September 1823, particularly the new marriage arrangements:

> Er ahnte die schlimmsten und grellsten Folgen davon, behauptete, wenn der Generalsuperintendant Charakter habe, müsse er lieber seine Stelle niederlegen als eine Jüdin in der Kirche im Namen der heiligen Dreifaltigkeit trauen. Alle sittliche Gefühle in den Familien, die doch durchaus auf den religiösen ruhten, würden durch ein solch skandalöses Gesetz untergraben.

> [He suspected the worst and most drastic consequences from it and claimed, if the General Superintendent had character, he must rather lay down his office then perform a marriage of a Jewish woman in the name of the Holy Trinity. All moral feelings in families, that rested completely on the religious, would be undermined by such a scandalous law].[49]

Foreshadowing the "Religion und Sitte" [religion and morals] passage from the *Wanderjahre*,[50] "sittliche und religiöse Gefühle" [moral and religious feelings] are seen as the basic cohesive elements of a marriage. It is telling that a modern critic can observe the following: "Die dabei auch geäußerten Zweifel an der moralisch-religiösen Substanz, an der Beständigkeit solcher Ehen mögen bis heute bedenkenswert sein" [The doubt expressed thereby about the moral and religious substance, on the cohesiveness of such marriages may be worthy of consideration even today].[51]

But, as in *Iphigenie* and *Egmont*, a tentative reason for hope is provided in the *Wanderjahre*. The political structure of religious freedom put forward throughout the novel is one that allows individual religious difference — even idiosyncrasy — and peaceful religious coexistence within a civil society. And it is also within a civil society that mutual exclusion between religious communities is possible, similar to the allegorical description of cohabiting yet separate religions in Goethe's essay on *Die Geheimnisse*. The "new Christian community" of the European emigrants in the *Wanderjahre* does not represent an "Idealstaat" [ideal state].[52] Eric Blackall stresses this point: "What is being described here is not an actual political organization but an ideal moral community."[53]

The emigrant band will be entering as a religious community into a civil society, the United States of America, where the separation of church and state forms the basis of the polity. Therefore the emigrants can secure their idiosyncratic existence as a "new Christian community" among other religious communities. In this sense, as Blackall asserts, the "most important symbol of the novel is America,"[54] a symbolic space for experimentation.[55] André Gilg puts forward the thesis, in a semiotic interpretation of the *Wanderjahre*, that the name "Juden" could be read as a sign for the "absondernden Eigenheiten" [distinguishing peculiarities][56] and hence for any separate religious identity. The idea of "Eigenheiten" will be explored in the next chapter.

Historically, the coexistence of divergent religious communities within a European nation sparked conflict and, in the sixteenth and seventeenth centuries, terrible civil and international wars. In the eighteenth century, religious toleration became a general *modus vivendi*, often granted and used as a tool by the state, to ensure *concordia* and economic prosperity. The reader is reminded, by the exclusion of Jews from the "new Christian community," that in some respects the European eighteenth-century teleology of tolerance — insofar as it meant to some the abandonment of religion altogether — has, for those who wish to maintain a religious identity, its limitations. The *Wanderjahre*, however, hints at the transformation of the negative conception of tolerance as sufferance into the more positive one of *Religionsfreiheit* within a civil society, thus allowing diverse religious communities to coexist while also expressing their unique identities. This does not resolve completely the tension between the universal and the particular; however it provides for the preservation of spiritual and cultural variety. Thus, the "new Christian community" of the *Wanderjahre* may still honour its commitment "jeden Gottesdienst in Ehren zu halten" [to revere each religious service],[57] while maintaining its religious integrity. Mendelssohn argued that a religious community could maintain its idiosyncratic commitments and yet participate in a kind of fellowship within the civil society:

> Betrachtet uns, wo nicht als Brueder und Mitbuerger, doch wenigstens als Mitmenschen und Miteinwohner des Landes. Zeiget uns Wege und gebet uns Mittel an die Hand, wie wir bessere Menschen und bessere Miteinwohner werden koennen, und lasset uns, so viel es Zeit und Umstaende erlauben, die Rechte der Menschheit mit genießen. Von dem Gesetze koennen wir mit gutem Gewissen nicht weichen, und was nuetzen euch Mitbuerger ohne Gewissen?[58]

[Consider us, if not as brothers and fellow citizens, then at least as fellow human beings and fellow residents in the land. Show us ways and give us means to become better human beings and better fellow residents and let us, insofar as time and circumstances permit, enjoy with you the rights of humanity. We cannot in good conscience budge from the law and of what use to you are fellow citizens without conscience?]

In 1783, when Mendelssohn's *Jerusalem* was published, before the United States Constitution and Bill of Rights were ratified, America was not yet the land of *Religionsfreiheit* of the 1829 *Wanderjahre*: "Leider! hoeren wir auch schon den Congreß in Amerika das alte Lied anstimmen, und von einer herrschenden Religion sprechen" [Unfortunately we already hear the Congress in America singing the old song and speaking about a dominant religion].[59]

In 1829, several months after Goethe had completed the second version of *Wanderjahre*, Steinfurt reported a conversation with the author about recent heated theological controversies in the German lands. Goethe's reply, tinged perhaps with irony, is a reminder that, while he may have touched on the perplexing modern condition of religious fragmentation and identity in his novel, his personal sentiments nevertheless lay with the inclusionary, anthropological, Enlightenment view of religion: "Am schönsten, meinte er, sei es jetzt in einer Stadt Nordamerikas, von der er neulich gelesen, daß in ihr an die sechzig Kirchen seien, in deren jeder ein anderes Glaubenssystem gepredigt werde; da könne man also an jedem Sonntag im Jahr sich in einer andern Confession erbauen."[60] [The finest thing, he opined, was now that in a city in North America about which he read recently, there were sixty churches in which each preached a different system of belief; there one could edify oneself each Sunday in the year in a different confession].

Notes

[1] *Heinrich Heine: Historisch-kritische Gesamtausgabe der Werke,* ed. by Manfred Windfuhr, 16 vols. (Hamburg: Hoffmann und Campe, 1973–1997), I/1: *Buch der Lieder* (1975), 526.

[2] Wilfried Barner, "150 Jahre nach seinem Tod: Goethe und die Juden," *Bulletin des Leo Baeck Instituts* 63 (1982): 75–82 (80).

[3] Adolf Muschg, *Goethe als Emigrant: Auf der Suche nach dem Grünen bei einem alten Dichter* (Frankfurt am Main: Suhrkamp, 1986), 114.

[4] Ehrhard Bahr, "Wilhelm Meisters Wanderjahre oder Die Entsagenden," in *Goethes Erzählwerk: Interpretationen*, ed. by Paul Michael Lützeler and James E. McLeod (Stuttgart: Reclam, 1985), 363–93 (382).

[5] Eric Blackall, *Goethe and the Novel*, 253–54.

[6] Friedrich is seen to be described with a "feiner Schalkheit" [subtle mischievousness]: Max Wundt, *Goethes Wilhelm Meister und die Entwicklung des modernen Lebensideals* (Berlin: Göschen, 1913), 434. Although Friedrich may not be a "zuverlässiger Informant" [reliable informant], Bahr feels that there is no reason for optimism about the plans of the projected America community ("Wanderjahre," 383).

[7] Degering interprets the rules governing the American settlement as those of a "Verfassung" [constitution], then attempts to explain the exclusion of the Jews as an act of the state. Thomas Degering, *Das Elend der Entsagung: Goethes "Wilhelm Meisters Wanderjahre,"* Abhandlungen zur Kunst-, Musik-, und Literaturwissenschaft 327 (Bonn: Bouvier, 1982); see: "Das Verhältnis von Staat und Religion oder 'die Judenfrage' im 'Verfassungsentwurf' des Bundes" (106–19). Cf. Henriette Herwig, *Das ewig Männliche zieht uns hinab: "Wilhelm Meisters Wanderjahre." Geschlechterdifferenz, Sozialer Wandel, Historische Anthropologie* (Tübingen: Francke, 1997), 196.

[8] Claudia Schwamborn, *Individualität in Goethes "Wanderjahren"* (Paderborn: Schöningh, 1997), 76.

[9] Significant changes occurred in the relationship between Germans and Jews during Goethe's lifetime. Cf. Michael A. Meyer, *The Origins of the Modern Jew: Jewish Identity and European Culture in Germany, 1749–1824* (Detroit: Wayne State UP, 1967); David Sorkin, *The Transformation of German Jewry, 1780–1840* (New York: Oxford UP, 1987).

[10] Gunnar Och, *Imago judaica: Juden und Judentum im Spiegel der deutschen Literatur 1750–1812* (Würzburg: Königshausen & Neumannm, 1995), 227.

[11] Conversation with Joseph Sebastian Grüner, 30 August 1821: *Goethes Gespräche*, III/1, 308.

[12] Letter to Zelter, 19 May 1812: WA IV/23, 25.

[13] Gustav Kars, *Das Bild des Juden in der deutschen Literatur des 18. und 19. Jahrhunderts* (Freiburg: Burg-Verlag, 1988), 15. Cf. Robertson, "Freedom and Pragmatism," 76: "To the Enlighteners Judaism seemed rigid, intolerant and superstitious."

[14] Ludwig Geiger, "Die Juden und die deutsche Literatur," in *Zeitschrift für die Geschichte der Juden in Deutschland* 1 (1887), see the subsection: "Goethe und die Juden," 321–65.

[15] Barner, "Goethe und die Juden," 82.

[16] Heinrich Teweles, *Goethe und die Juden* (Hamburg: Gente, 1925); Julius Bab, *Goethe und die Juden* (Berlin: Philo-Verlag, 1926); William Rose, *Men, Myths, and Movements in German Literature* (London: Allen and Unwin, 1931), see the section, "Goethe and the Jews" (157–80); Mark Waldman, *Goethe and the Jews: A Challenge to Hitlerism* (New York: Putnam's Sons, 1934). Alfred D. Low, *Jews in the Eyes of the German: From the Enlightenment to Imperial Germany* (Philadelphia: Institute for the Study of Human Issues, 1979), 67–86.

[17] Günter Hartung, "Goethe und die Juden," *Weimarer Beiträge* 40 (1994): 398–416, (409).

[18] Norbert Oellers, "Goethe und Schiller in ihren Verhältnis zum Judentum," in *Conditio Judaica: Judentum, Antisemitismus und deutschsprachige Literatur vom 18. Jahrhundert bis zum ersten Weltkrieg*, ed. by Hans Otto Horch and Horst Denkler, 2 vols. (Tübingen: Niemeyer, 1988–1989), vol. 1 (1988), 108–30, (110).

[19] Barner, "Goethe und die Juden," 78.

[20] Barner, "Goethe und die Juden," 75.

[21] II/11: FA 10, 686.

[22] Ibid.

[23] Hartung, "Goethe und die Juden," 404.

[24] III/10: FA 10, 672.

[25] Rose, "Goethe and the Jews," 175.

[26] Prince Carl Bernhard von Sachsen-Weimar, *Reise Sr. Hoheit des Herzogs Bernhard zu Sachsen-Weimar-Eisenach durch Nord-Amerika in den Jahren 1825 und 1826*, ed. by Heinrich Luden (Weimar: Wilhelm Hoffmann, 1828), 220–21 and 204–12.

[27] Cf. Walter Wadepuhl, *Goethe's Interest in the New World* (Jena: Biedermann, 1934). He lists works Goethe read about America including those he borrowed from the Grand-Ducal library.

[28] Franklin, *Autobiography*, 122.

[29] Wynfrid Kriegleder, "Wilhelm Meisters Amerika: Das Bild der Vereinigten Staaten in den Wanderjahren," *Jahrbuch des Wiener Goethe-Vereins* 95 (1991): 15–31 (26). "Pennsylvania opened its borders to many sectaries.

Mennonites from Holland, Dunkards (Baptists) from Germany, Calvinists, Lutherans, German Moravians, Amish, all made their homes there." David Christie-Murray, *A History of Heresy* (Oxford: Oxford UP, 1989), 182.

[30] *Sprüche*: FA 13, 98.

[31] III/11: FA 10, 687.

[32] Jane Brown, *Goethe's Cyclical Narratives*, 128.

[33] Benjamin Bennett, *Beyond Theory: Eighteenth-Century German Literature and the Poetics of Irony* (Ithaca: Cornell UP, 1993), 322.

[34] Ernst Ludwig Brauns, *Skizzen von America. Zu einer belehrenden Unterhaltung für gebildete Leser und mit besonderer Rücksicht auf Reisende und Auswanderer nach Amerika* (Halberstadt: Vogler, 1830), 183–84. Cf. chapter 10, a report on Owen and Rapp.

[35] Bill Williams, "The Anti-Semitism of Tolerance: Middle Class Manchester and the Jews, 1870–1900," in *City, Class and Culture: Studies of Social Policy and Cultural Production in Victorian Manchester*, ed. by Alan J. Kidd and Kenneth W. Roberts (Manchester: Manchester UP, 1985), 74–102.

[36] Robertson, "'Dies hohe Lied der Duldung?' The Ambiguities of Toleration in Lessing's *Die Juden* and *Nathan der Weise*," 108–109.

[37] Paul Stöcklein as quoted by Trunz (in HA 8, 663).

[38] Harold Bloom, *The American Religion: The Emergence of the Post-Christian Nation* (New York: Simon & Schuster, 1992).

[39] La Vern J. Rippley, *The German-Americans* (Boston: Twayne, 1976), 100–106.

[40] II/2: FA 10, 425.

[41] Cf. Ernst Cassirer, *Die Philosophie der Aufklärung*, 219.

[42] Moses Mendelssohn, *Jerusalem*, 136. Enlightenment thinkers envisioned an "unsichtbare Kirche" [invisible church] that was above confessional divisions: Stephan-Kopitzsch, *Aufklärungszeitschriften*, 57–60.

[43] Norbert Oellers, "Goethe und Schiller," 129.

[44] I, ii, line 76: FA 5, 557.

[45] Oellers, "Goethe und Schiller," 128. Cf. *Paths of Emancipation: Jews, States, and Citizenship*, ed. by Pierre Birnbaum and Ira Katznelson (Princeton: Princeton UP, 1995).

[46] Mendelssohn, *Jerusalem*, 131. Cf. David L. Schindler, *Heart of the World, Center of the Church: Communio, Ecclesiology, Liberalism, and Liberation* (Edinburgh: Clark, 1996), 43–87.

[47] Leslie Stevenson, "Religion and Cultural Identity," *Theology*, May/June (1998): 172–78 (173).

[48] Oellers, "Goethe und Schiller," 114. Cf. Reinhard Rürup, "The Tortuous and Thorny Path to Legal Equality: 'Jew Laws' and Emancipatory Legislation in Germany from the Late Eighteenth Century," *Leo Baeck Institute Yearbook* 31 (1986): 3–33. See also Volkmar Eichstädt, *Bibliographie zur Geschichte der Judenfrage* (Hamburg: Hanseatische Verlagsanstalt, 1938), vol. 1, 1750–1848.

[49] Kanzler von Müller, *Unterhaltungen mit Goethe*, ed. by Ernst Grumach with notations by Renate Fischer-Lamberg (Weimar: Hermann Böhlaus Nachfolger, 1959), 69.

[50] III/11: FA 10, 686–87.

[51] Wilfried Barner, "Goethe und die Juden," 79.

[52] Barner, "Goethe und die Juden," 80.

[53] Eric Blackall, *Goethe and the Novel*, 254.

[54] Blackall, *Goethe and the Novel*, 251.

[55] Cf. Gary Bryner and Richard Vetterli, *In Search of the Republic: Public Virtue and the Roots of American Government* (Totowa, NJ: Rowman & Littlefield, 1987); "Civil Religion and Republican Government" and "The Separation of Church and State" (89–161).

[56] André Gilg, *Wilhelm Meisters Wanderjahre und ihre Symbole*, Zürcher Beiträge zur deutschen Literatur- und Geistesgeschichte 9 (Zurich: Atlantis, 1954), 163.

[57] III/10: FA 10, 672.

[58] Mendelssohn, *Jerusalem*, 132–33.

[59] Mendelssohn, *Jerusalem*, 140 fn. Cf. David A. J. Richards, *Toleration and the Constitution* (New York: Oxford UP, 1986).

[60] Conversation with L. Löw von und zu Steinfurt, 3 October 1829: *Goethes Gespräche*, III/2, 532.

11: *Eigenheiten* and *Weltverkehr*

Le Pour et le Contre se trouvent en chaque nation; there is a balance, said he, of good and bad everywhere; and nothing but the knowing it is so can emancipate one half of the world from the prepossessions which it holds against the other — that the advantage of travel, as it regarded the *sçavoir vivre*, was by seeing a great deal both of men and manners; it taught us mutual toleration; and mutual toleration, concluded he, making me a bow, taught us mutual love.[1]

THESE THOUGHTS OF A FRENCH OFFICER, recorded by Pastor Yorick in Lawrence Sterne's *A Sentimental Journey* (1768) pay eloquent tribute to the benefits of travel and intercultural experience. In 1830 Goethe contrasts his own style with that of Sterne's and suggests that although travel descriptions since *A Sentimental Journey* had concentrated on the traveller's feelings and opinions, he had attempted to "deny himself" and focus on phenomena: "das Objekt so rein, als zu tun wäre, in mich aufzunehmen" [to absorb the object as purely as possible].[2] Goethe is here thinking about the minute operations of perception and epistemology that are at the root of intercultural relations. Several of the essays he wrote towards the end of his life explore these processes.

In *Ueber Kunst und Alterthum* (VI/1, 1827), Goethe published an essay on Sterne (1713–1768), entitled *Lorenz Sterne*. This is a significant volume of *Kunst und Alterthum* for in it Goethe uses for the first time and more than once the word *Weltliteratur*.[3] A typical critical approach has therefore been to focus on his adumbration of this important concept, one that he had on his mind at the very latest since the *Divan* (1819). This focus, valuable as it is, tends to marginalise Goethe's associated concerns. Certainly, the reader is left to organise the disparate essays in the later editions of *Ueber Kunst und Alterthum* as a part of Goethe's intended creative process that he continues in the fluid structures of *Wanderjahre* and *Faust II*. His intercultural concerns have a long genesis and grow out of his reflection on the relevance and applicability of Enlightenment ideas to new contexts.

In *Lorenz Sterne* Goethe compares one of his old ideas, "Eigenheiten" [peculiarities], to one he discovers in English thought, "ruling passion" — a particular trait that defines a person or a people generally

— and praises Sterne as a forefather of "litterarischer sowohl als humaner Bildung" [literary as well as humane education] in the eighteenth century, which Goethe calls "die große Epoche reinerer Menschenkenntniß, edler Duldung, zarter Liebe" [the great epoch of purer knowledge of humanity, noble tolerance, gentle love].[4] Only a year previously he had read *Letters from Eliza to Yorick* (1775), at that time attributed to Sterne. His journal entry for 5 January 1826 reads: "Für mich Sternes Briefe. Ruling Passion! Der Sinn dieser Worte überdacht und kommentiert" [For me, Sterne's *Letters*. Ruling Passion! Pondered and commented on the meaning of these words].[5]

Goethe describes *Eigenheiten* as that which constitutes an individual and makes specific the universal. Nevertheless he believes that even "in dem Allerwunderlichsten blickt immer noch etwas Verstand, Vernunft und Wohlwollen hindurch, das uns anzieht und fesselt" [in the most odd characteristics there peers through still something of understanding, reason, and benevolence that draws and binds us].[6] Within this context he equates *Eigenheiten* with the notion of "ruling passion," an idea he credits Sterne with developing in order to discover gently "das Menschliche im Menschen" [the humane in people].[7] Goethe understands *Eigenheiten* as that which constitutes individuality.[8]

In a review essay entitled *Irrthümer und Wahrheiten von Wilhelm Schütz* (Fallacies and Truths by Wilhelm Schütz [Schulz]), published posthumously in 1833 and related in content to *Lorenz Sterne* (some passages are identical), Goethe continues to investigate cultural differences.[9] He is particularly interested in what makes nations different from each other, especially in the role their "sittliche und religiose" [moral and religious] heritages plays in these differences.[10] He speculates anthropologically, for example, that the English and German Protestant lands need Sunday for reflection and refreshment because they are so busy during the week, whereas southern European Catholic nations have more holidays, with the result that Sunday is not as special.[11]

The essay is really less a review of Schulz's work and more a brief attempt at extending Goethe's own ideas as suggested in the first sentence, when he calls *Eigenheiten* "Phänomene der Menschheit" [phenomena of humanity].[12] In this piece Goethe weighs the difficulties of intercultural exchange. He notes that individuals and nations have *Eigenheiten*; their process of spreading he calls "Influenz," which contains associations ranging from influence to the microbiological metaphor of influenza. Goethe maintains that an unpleasant peculiarity is tolerable and should be accepted — he uses his familiar verb "geltenlassen" — if it can be interpreted as a sign of diversity.[13] *Influenzen*, however, con-

tain a potential to damage because the reaction of a local body or host
to exposure is incalculable:

> Die Influenz dagegen ist immer gefährlich, ja sie wird meist schädlich:
> denn indem sie fremde Eigenheiten über eine Masse heranführt, so
> fragt sich ja, wie diese ankommenden Eigenheiten sich mit den ein-
> heimischen vertragen, und ob sie nicht durch Vermischung einen
> krankhaften Zustand hervorbringen.[14]

> [Influence is in comparison always dangerous, indeed it becomes al-
> most always damaging: for in that it introduces foreign peculiarities
> into a mass, it is questionable how these arriving peculiarities get on
> with the local ones, and whether they do not produce a pathological
> condition through mixing.]

This echoes Margarete of Parma's fears in *Egmont* as she contemplates
apprehensively the foreign teachers and foreign religion — the "Übel"
[evil] — entering the Netherlands.[15]

Goethe illustrates his point with two microbiological examples. He
notes that when otherwise healthy groups of people crowd into an en-
closed space, such as a ship, illness often breaks out. He also cites a case
in which Hungarian and Silesian cattle herds lived healthily apart, but
the mixing of the two caused health problems in the latter.[16] Tolerance
levels break down when one set of peculiarities comes into contact with
a foreign set. Goethe thus tests the limits of tolerance, for what if, as in
his examples, exposure to *Eigenheiten* is not mutually beneficial? This
calls implicitly into question the Enlightenment idea of finding common ground and creating a brotherhood of man.

Shifting and softening his polemical stance, Goethe observes that
"Contagien" are most damaging in the initial rather than the subsequent stages. It is important to stress that by "Influenz" or "Contagien" Goethe is explaining how peculiarities spread. He recapitulates
to avoid misunderstanding: "Wir kehren dahin zurück, wo wir sagten,
daß eine Eigenheit wenigstens an sich als unschuldig und unschädlich
betrachtet werden könne" [We return again to where we said that a peculiarity can be considered at least in itself as innocent and not harm-
ful].[17] In essence, Goethe has created two poles for examining the
interaction of ideas: "das Eigene" [the native] and "das Fremde" [the
foreign]. These poles are interchangeable, depending on perspective;
elements that have not been in contact before are foreign to each other,
in a state of heterogeneity. An *Eigenheit* is nothing more or less than
das Eigene, that which is owned by, belongs or is peculiar to and suited
for an individual or nation; it is that which fits and, more strongly put

but in the same vein, that which inheres. To another individual or nation such an *Eigenheit* is *das Fremde.*

Goethe implies in another essay that fear and potential misunderstanding ought not to detract from the overall benefit of intercultural interaction: "Alle Nationen schauen sich nach uns um, sie loben, sie tadeln, nehmen auf und verwerfen, ahmen nach und entstellen, verstehen oder mißverstehen uns, eröffnen oder verschließen ihre Herzen: dies alles müssen wir gleichmütig aufnehmen, indem uns das Ganze von großem Werth ist" [All nations look at us, they praise, they criticise, accept and reject, imitate and distort, understand or misunderstand us, open or lock their hearts: we must take all of this with equanimity, in that the whole is of great value to us].[18] Colliding *Eigenheiten* challenge the notion of easy harmony in society, but it is precisely because *das Eigene* and *das Fremde* constantly engage with each other that tolerance is required, as Goethe exhorts in an 1828 essay: "nur wiederholen wir, daß nicht die Rede sein könne, die Nationen sollen überein denken, sondern sie sollen nur einander gewahr werden, sich begreifen und, wenn sie sich wechselseitig nicht lieben mögen, sich einander wenigstens dulden lernen" [we only repeat, that there can be no question of the nations becoming one, rather that they are to become aware of each other, comprehend each other and, if they cannot love each other, at least learn to tolerate each other].[19]

Goethe argues that *Influenz* can be fruitful: "Die einzige wahre Influenz ist die der Zeugung, der Geburt, des Wachsens und Gedeihens" [The only true influence is that of creation, of birth, of growth and thriving].[20] Each point of contact between *das Eigene* and *das Fremde* is a testing point. Such was the case with Yorick as he journeyed: "Seine Heiterkeit, Genügsamkeit, Duldsamkeit auf der Reise, wo diese Eigenschaften am meisten geprüft werden, finden nicht gleich ihres Gleichen" [His serenity, modesty, tolerance on the journey, where these traits are tested the most, are not soon matched].[21] Goethe was perhaps probing frontiers theoretically by weighing and calculating consequences when, less than a year after writing the Schulz essay, he referred to himself as an "ethisch-ästhetischen Mathematiker" [aesthetic-ethical mathematician]. He knew well that ideas contain the potential for tragic consequences: "in höheren Regionen ist eine falsch ergriffene Verbindung im Ästhetischen, Sittlichen, Religiosen voller Gefahr, und jedes Mißlingen von traurigen Folgen" [a falsely understood connection in the higher aesthetic, moral, religious regions is full of danger, and each failure has sorrowful consequences].[22] Hence the necessity of the cautious intellectual queries in the *Irrthümer und Wahrheiten* essay.[23]

Goethe posited that growing travel within Europe and throughout the world would bring people and nations, and hence *Eigenheiten*, into increasing contact with each other. Eckermann reported famously that Goethe admired the world travels of his friend, Alexander von Humboldt, and that he wished to live to see the completion of the Suez and Panama canals, as well as a waterway between the Danube and the Rhine.[24] He intuited and helped to create patterns for these encounters as he considered the following ideas in his writing: *Weltliteratur*, *Weltpoesie*, *Weltcultur*, *Weltbürgertum*, *Weltreligion*, *Weltfest*, *Weltfrömmigkeit*, *Weltbund*, and *Weltverkehr*.[25]

Pastor Yorick in *A Sentimental Journey* explains what has motivated him to visit foreign peoples: "to spy the *nakedness* of their hearts, and through the different disguises of customs, climates, and religion, find out what is good in them to fashion my own by — and therefore am I come."[26] This typical Enlightenment thesis, that the humane is universal, overlaps with the positions of Goethe and Herder. Yorick describes the goal of his travels not as that of the popular grand tour of the gentleman, wherein cultural knowledge is merely accumulated, but rather "a quiet journey of the heart in pursuit of . . . those affections . . . which make us love each other — and the world, better than we do."[27] This broadening of sympathies is reflected in Goethe's *Divan*, where the poet views himself as a traveller, and in his praise of the cosmopolitan and tolerant *Weltmann* in *Besserem Verständniss*. In the *Wanderjahre* it is the sensible and charitable *Weltmann*, the uncle, who learns from his Philadelphia experience and undertakes to improve life in a European mountain community.

In *Ueber Kunst und Altherthum* (VI/1, 1827) Goethe published his own translation of an article that had appeared in the French newspaper *Le Globe*. It attracted him because it championed his *Faust*. The article also contains the idea that the nations, instead of attempting to dominate each other, must recognise that they belong to a community of similar interests.[28] Goethe related to Eckermann that the "enger Verkehr" [intensive commerce] between the French, English, and Germans, including the development of *Weltliteratur*, would allow these nations to learn from each other.[29]

Goethe's recognition and reception of both European and non-European literatures are well documented in the final issues of *Ueber Kunst und Alterthum*.[30] Although he appreciated the differences between the various national literatures, he also felt that there was a tendency in the writing of his contemporaries to capture common human experience, the general as it was revealed in the particular, the specifics of nationality and personality.[31] In fact, Goethe pointed to current international influences in literature as a way to get to know the peculiarities of a nation and as a preparation for closer relations: "denn die Eigenheiten einer Nation sind wie ihre Sprache und ihre Münzsorten, sie erleichtern den Verkehr, ja sie machen ihn erst vollkommen möglich" [for the peculiarities of a nation are like its language and its coins, they make commerce easier, indeed they are what makes it perfectly possible in the first place].[32] The metaphor of foreign language and currency obtains, as the difficulties of living in a foreign environment without the knowledge of either are obvious — as are the advantages of learning a foreign language.

Goethe saw that the interacting of the particular and the universal helped to develop tolerance: "Eine wahrhaft allgemeine Duldung wird am sichersten erreicht, wenn man das Besondere der einzelnen Menschen und Völkerschaften auf sich beruhen läßt, bei der Ueberzeugung jedoch festhält, daß das wahrhaft Verdienstliche sich dadurch auszeichnet, daß es der ganzen Menschheit angehört" [A truly universal tolerance will most surely be reached when one considers the particular qualities of a single individual or nation, yet maintains the conviction that what is truly meritorious distinguishes itself in that it belongs to all of humanity].[33]

In a review of Thomas Carlyle's *German Romance*, Goethe claims that the foreign individual who is familiar with the German language finds himself "auf dem Markte wo alle Nationen ihre Waren anbieten, er spielt den Dolmetscher, indem er sich selbst bereichert" [in the marketplace where all nations are offering their wares, he plays the translator while also enriching himself]. And one way to begin this process is through "wechselseitige Anerkennung" [mutual recognition].[34] These images link with those of the *Wanderjahre* market festival and the *Divan* messenger image, for Goethe seems to mean that whatever nation will open itself up to the ideas of others will benefit. His translator metaphor sparks associations with his discussion of translation in *Besserem Verständniss* for the processes of *Weltverkehr* are related closely to that of translation. A translator, understood in these terms, is engaged in crucial cultural commerce. Goethe calls a translator a "Vermittler" [mediator] of intellectual trade: "Denn was man auch von der Unzulänglichkeit des Übersetzens sagen mag, so ist und bleibt es doch eines der wichtigsten und würdigsten Geschäfte in dem allgemeinen Weltverkehr" [For whatever one may say about the inadequacy of translating, it surely is and remains one of the most important and worthiest businesses in the universal exchanges of the world].[35] Goethe envisions a *Weltverkehr* that requires mediators who are prepared and able to embrace and engage with the cultural products of the entire world.

He concludes *German Romance* by suggesting that the Qur'an testifies: "Gott hat jedem Volke einen Propheten gegeben in seiner eigenen Sprache" [God has given each nation a prophet in its own language]. He praises each translator as, in this sense, a prophet, and puts forward Luther's translation of the scriptures and the efforts of Bible societies as examples of bringing the gospel to peoples in their own language.[36]

Goethe envisioned that *Weltliteratur* would become a secular gospel available to the entire world, informed by but not limited to creed, culture, or nationality, and nurtured in an environment of tolerance. To this community — and we have seen the theme of fraternity in his writings — Goethe belonged and contributed:

> Wie es die Welt jetzt treibt, muß man sich immer und immerfort sagen und wiederholen: daß es tüchtige Menschen gegeben hat und geben wird, und solchen muß man ein schriftlich gutes Wort gönnen, aussprechen und auf dem Papier hinterlassen. Das ist die Gemeinschaft der Heiligen, zu der wir uns bekennen.[37]

> [The way things are going in the world, one must say again and always repeat: there have been and will be virtuous men and to these we must dedicate a good word, say something and leave a written legacy. That is the community of saints to which we confess.]

Notes

1 Laurence Sterne, *A Sentimental Journey through France and Italy*, ed. by Graham Petrie with an introduction by A. Alvarez (London: Penguin Classics, 1986), 84; vol. 1, "The Rose." For a brief description of Goethe's reception of Sterne, see: Lawrence Marsden Price, *Reception of English Literature in Germany*, 240–47. Cf. Terence James Reed, "Englische Literatur," in *Goethe-Handbuch*, ed. by Bernd Witte et al., 4 vols. (Stuttgart: Metzler, 1996–1998), 4/1: *Personen, Sachen, Begriffe* (A-K), ed. by Hans-Dietrich Dahnke and Regine Otto (1998), 259–64.

2 *Tag- und Jahreshefte* (Annual Journals) 1789: FA 17, 17.

3 Cf. Peter J. Brenner, "'Weltliteratur.' Voraussetzungen eines Begriffs in Goethes Literaturkritik," *Goethe Jahrbuch* 89 (1981): 25–42.

[4] FA 22, 338–39.

[5] WA III/10, 144. The *Letters* are now viewed as not by Sterne, and "ruling passion" actually occurs in *Tristram Shandy* (1759–1767; FA 22, 1163–164).

[6] FA 22, 339.

[7] Ibid.

[8] FA 22, 339.

[9] On 12 January 1826 Goethe again read Schulz's book (WA III/10, 147). In 1819 Schulz (1797–1860) was relieved of military duty in Hessen due to his liberal ideas. After he was arrested for political reasons, he fled to Straßburg (1834). Two years later he settled in Zurich and became friends with Georg Büchner, Gottfried Keller, and Ferdinand Freiligrath (Gisela Henckmann: MA 13.1, 915).

[10] FA 22, 665.

[11] Ibid. Goethe's observations anticipate Max Weber's 1904–1905 analysis in *Die protestantische Ethik und der Geist des Kapitalismus* (The Protestant Ethic and the Spirit of Capitalism).

[12] FA 22, 663.

[13] FA 22, 663.

[14] FA 22, 663.

[15] I "Palast der Regentin": FA 5, 468.

[16] FA 22, 664.

[17] FA 22, 664.

[18] FA 22, 356–57: *Le Tasse* in *Ueber Kunst und Alterthum* (VI/1, 1827).

[19] FA 22, 491: *Edinburgh Reviews* in *Ueber Kunst und Alterthum* (VI/2, 1828). Cf. Goethe's letter to Zelter of 7 November 1816 (WA IV/27, 220) and his similar charge.

[20] FA 22, 666.

[21] *Sprüche*: FA 13, 305.

[22] Letter to Sulpiz Boisserée, 3 November 1826: WA IV/41, 221.

[23] Cf. Reinhart Koselleck, "Aufklärung und die Grenzen ihrer Toleranz," in *Glaube und Toleranz: Das theologische Erbe der Aufklärung,* ed. by Trutz Rendtorff (Gütersloh: Mohn, 1982), 256–71.

[24] 21 February 1827: FA 39, 580.

[25] World literature, poetry, culture, citizenship, religion, festival, piety, society, commerce.

[26] Sterne, *A Sentimental Journey*, vol. 2, page 108, "The Passport: Versailles."

[27] Ibid.

[28] FA 22, 324.

[29] 15 July 1827: FA 39, 257. Cf. Fritz Strich, *Goethe und die Weltliteratur* (Bern: Francke, 1946). Cf. the collection of quotations in "Goethe: Über Weltliteratur und Nationalliteratur," *Jahrbuch der Goethe-Gesellschaft* 33 (1971): xiii–xvi.

[30] See, for example, Goethe's essays: *Chinesisches* (Chinese, 1827) or the nine reviews in *Nationelle Dichtkunst* (1828, National Poetry). Cf. Wenqiao Dong, "Goethe und der Kulturaustausch zwischen dem chinesischen und dem deutschen Volk," *Goethe Jahrbuch* 107 (1990): 314–26.

[31] Review of Thomas Carlyle's *German Romance* in *Ueber Kunst und Alterthum* (VI/2, 1828): FA 22, 433.

[32] FA 22, 434.

[33] FA 22, 434. "Verdienst" [merit] is a sign of Goethe's particular approbation. Cf. Hellmut Sichtermann, "'Verdienst' als ästhetischer Wert im Klassizismus," *Goethe Jahrbuch* 25 (1963), 283–98.

[34] FA 22, 434.

[35] FA 22, 434. Birus includes poets, critics, university teachers, etc. as a part of this cultural trade: Hendrik Birus, "Am Schnittpunkt von Komparatistik und Germanistik: Die Idee der Weltliteratur heute," in *Germanistik und Komparatistik: DFG-Symposion 1993,* ed. by Hendrik Birus, Germanistische Symposien Berichtsbände 16 (Stuttgart: Metzler, 1993), 439–57 (452).

[36] Ibid.

[37] Letter to Zelter, 18 June 1831: WA IV/48, 241.

Conclusion

ACH NATION IS USUALLY ASSIGNED its piece of the Enlightenment: to England Locke, France Voltaire, the United States Franklin, Italy Beccaria, and so forth. It is generally accepted and — given the twentieth-century disasters in German history — celebrated, that Lessing, the author of *Nathan der Weise*, bore the torch of tolerance and Enlightenment for his people too. Yet the debt owed by Goethe's thought to the Enlightenment — and his development of Enlightenment ideas — is still not generally acknowledged in intellectual history. It is hoped that this book takes a step in that direction.

Goethe was detached enough from his intellectual forebears to recognise that certain "enlightened" ideas could be flawed. When he noticed that Voltaire, in his zeal to undermine the notion of a biblical deluge, was willing in his *Dictionnaire philosophique* (1764) to reject the fossil record, Goethe dismissed the philosopher.[1] With great curiosity he read d'Holbach's *Système de la nature* (1770), a book forbidden by the clergy, but found it to be grey, primitive, and deadening.[2] Goethe respected Diderot and d'Alembert's *Encyclopédie* (1751–1772), but saw its pitfalls too, likening it, specifically the famous entry on weaving — to an incomprehensible and confusing mechanism.[3] Perhaps he sensed that such attempts to achieve totality could run amok.[4] Moreover, his writings forecast recent re-evaluations of the Enlightenment along multicultural and religious lines.[5] Krippendorff, putting it another way, suggests that Goethe's method is that of a "sanfte Aufklärung," a gentle Enlightenment, which, it could be argued, mitigates if not opposes the strict rationality, mechanistic systems, and the religious and cultural prejudices of some Enlightenment thinkers.[6]

One of the most tangible proofs that an Enlightenment legacy remained with Goethe throughout his life is contained in the essay *Plato als Mitgenosse einer christlichen Offenbarung* (Plato as a Co-Recipient of a Christian Revelation), a piece he had written in 1795–1796, but did not publish until 1826. His opening salvo contains a nearly palpable sense of exasperation: "Niemand glaubt genug von dem ewigen Urheber erhalten zu haben, wenn er gestehen müßte, daß für alle seine Brüder eben so wie für ihn gesorgt wäre" [Nobody believes he has received enough from the eternal Originator, if he had to confess that all of his brothers were equally, like himself, provided for].[7]

Goethe had his frontiers, his clearly demarcated borders, but he recognised that it was precisely at the margins that he had to evaluate carefully and respond with tolerance and recognition. In 1792 Goethe accompanied Duke Carl August of Weimar in observing the Prussian-Austrian operations against the French revolutionary forces. During this campaign Goethe visited with a Catholic group that has been known since then as the Münster Circle.[8] He acknowledged their kindness and participated gladly in cultivated conversation, something he had missed sorely while on military duty. At the end of Goethe's stay, the leader of the group, Princess Adelheid Amalia, confronted him with two things: first, that she had been asked whether he is a Catholic; second, that she had been warned that he could act insincerely so as to appear Catholic. Placed in this awkward position, Goethe answered his host kindly and frankly — his friendliness and understanding should not be confused as either agreement with a religion he does not embrace or dissembling of any kind, but as his attempt to live and let live:

> Was mir widersteht, davon wend' ich den Blick weg, aber manches, was ich nicht gerade billige, mag ich gern in seiner Eigentümlichkeit erkennen; da zeigt sich denn meist, daß die andern ebenso recht haben, nach ihrer eigentümlichen Art und Weise zu existieren, als ich nach der meinigen.

> [That which I detest I turn away from, but much which I do not exactly condone, I am happy to perceive in its peculiarity; it often becomes apparent that the others have as much right in existing according to their particular way, as I do according to mine.][9]

One year before his death, Goethe described in a letter an ancient religion that he had learned about and felt sympathy with. This group sought to honour goodness and perfection wherever they were to be found, so long as these qualities brought its members closer to Deity.[10] And only days before his passing, Eckermann observed Goethe musing on how the love and teachings of Jesus alleviate denominational differences among Christians. Moreover, Goethe praised the divinely inspired men who had lived among the Chinese, Indians, Persians, Jews, and Greeks.[11] This represents Goethe's Enlightenment inheritance, a heritage that pervades a lifetime of thought and writing, an appreciation of religious and cultural diversity and more specifically an uncompromising esteem for all that is praiseworthy. Goethe inspired the

English historian Thomas Carlyle "to new effort in appropriating what is Beautiful and True, wheresoever and howsoever it is to be found."[12]

Goethe's writings lifted both spatial and temporal barriers as he attempted to clarify how, despite "fremde Tracht" [foreign dress] and "ferner Himmel" [distant heaven], "das allgemein Menschliche wiederholt sich in allen Völkern" [the universally human repeats itself in all peoples].[13] He compared the nations of various ages and places to a tremendous chorus performing a hymn of humanity featuring mixed harmonies and individual voices that develop as a fugue and then join in a glorious canto.[14] In this sense Iphigenie's question, "Can a foreign land become for us the fatherland?" is answered positively by Goethe: "The wide world, expansive as it is, is always only an extended fatherland."[15]

Goethe was consciously striving to find ways to improve societal conditions in Europe. He recognised that the nations had suffered together through terrifying wars, and that this closer contact created a chance for "freyen geistigen Handelsverkehr" [free intellectual trade], which he compared to trade in goods, the wealth of nations indeed.[16] He thought that intellectual exchange could help to refine sentiments, and although he knew that such cultural traffic would not bring about a universal cessation of hostilities, he did hope that it could create an atmosphere of mildness, so that war would become less horrific and victory less arrogant.[17] And Goethe knew what the necessary catalyst had to be: "Tolerance is the only mediator of a peace that will free all our powers and potential."[18]

Notes

[1] DuW III/11: FA 14, 529. Cf. Gonthier L. Fink, "Goethe und Voltaire," *Goethe Jahrbuch* 101 (1984): 74–111.

[2] DuW III/11: FA 14, 534.

[3] DuW III/11: FA 14, 531.

[4] Cf. Max Horkheimer and Theodor W. Adorno, *Dialektik der Aufklärung* (New York: Social Studies Association, 1944).

[5] Cf. *Race and the Enlightenment: A Reader*, ed. by Emmanuel Chukwudi Eze (Oxford: Blackwell, 1991) and Leslie Stevenson, "Religion and Cultural Identity," *Theology* May/June (1998): 172–78.

[6] Ekkehart Krippendorff, *Goethe: Politik gegen den Zeitgeist* (Frankfurt am Main: Insel, 1999), 125.

[7] FA 22, 235. This essay was published in *Ueber Kunst und Alterthum* (V/3).

[8] Cf. Siegfried Sudhof, "Goethe und der 'Kreis von Münster,'" *Goethe Jahrbuch* 89 (1981): 72–85.

[9] *Campagne in Frankreich 1792* (Campaign in France 1792, 1822): *Münster, November 1792*: FA 16, 552.

[10] Letter to Boisserée, 22 March 1831: WA IV/48, 156. Cf. Kurt Mauch, "Goethe, der Hypsistarier," *Die Bruderschaft* 15 (1959): 14–16.

[11] FA 39, 745–50.

[12] Letter to Goethe, 20 August 1827: *Briefe an Goethe*, ed. by Karl Mandelkow, 2 vols. (Hamburg: Wegner, 1965–1969), vol. 2 (1969), 456.

[13] *Serbische Lieder* (Serbian Songs) in *Ueber Kunst und Alterthum* (V/2, 1825): FA 22, 125.

[14] *Sprüche*: FA 13, 328.

[15] "Die weite Welt, so ausgedehnt sie auch sei, ist immer nur ein erweitertes Vaterland." This is contained in a posthumously published excerpt, "Ferneres über Weltliteratur" (More on *Weltliteratur*): FA 22, 866.

[16] Goethe's 1830 foreword to the German edition of Carlyle's *Life of Schiller*: FA 22, 870.

[17] Goethe's review of Thomas Carlyle's *German Romance* in *Ueber Kunst und Alterthum* (VI/2, 1828): FA 22, 433.

[18] "Duldung ist die einzige Vermittlerin eines in allen Kräften und Anlagen thätigen Friedens." *Varrenhagen* [Varnhagen] *von Ense's Biographien* published in *Ueber Kunst und Alterthum* (VI/1, 1827): FA 22, 359.

Works Consulted

Collected Editions of Goethe's Writings

Goethes Werke. Weimarer Ausgabe. Edited under the auspices of Großherzogin Sophie von Sachsen. 143 vols. Weimar: Böhlau, 1887–1919.

Johann Wolfgang Goethe: Sämtliche Werke. Briefe, Tagebücher und Gespräche. Frankfurter Ausgabe. Edited by Hendrik Birus et al. 40 vols. Frankfurt am Main: Deutscher Klassiker Verlag, 1987–1999.

Johann Wolfgang Goethe: Sämtliche Werke nach Epochen seines Schaffens. Münchner Ausgabe. Edited by Karl Richter in collaboration with Herbert G. Göpfert, Norbert Miller, and Gerhard Sauder. 21 vols. Munich: Hanser, 1985–1998.

Goethes Werke. Hamburger Ausgabe. Edited by Erich Trunz. 14 vols. Munich: Deutscher Taschenbuch Verlag, 1988.

Briefe an Goethe. Edited by Karl Mandelkow. 2 vols. Hamburg: Wegner, 1965–1969.

Goethes Gespräche: Eine Sammlung zeitgenössischer Berichte aus seinem Umgang auf Grund der Ausgabe und des Nachlasses von Flodoard Freiherrn von Biedermann. Edited and supplemented by Wolfgang Herwig. 4 vols. Zurich and Stuttgart: Artemis, 1965–1984.

Primary Sources

Adelung, Johann Christoph. *Versuch eines vollstaendigen grammatisch-kritischen Woerterbuches der Hochdeutschen Mundart mit bestaendiger Vergleichung der uebrigen Mundarten.* 5 vols. Leipzig: Bernhard Christoph Breitkopf und Sohn, 1774–1786.

Arnold, Gottfried. *Gottfrid Arnolds Unparteyische Kirchen- und Ketzer-Historie / von Anfang des Neuen Testament biß auff das Jahr Christi 1688.* 2 vols. Frankfurt am Main: Thomas Fritsch, 1699–1700.

Benad, Matthias. *Toleranz als Gebot christlicher Obrigkeit: Das Büdinger Patent von 1712.* Studia Irenica 27. Hildesheim: Gerstenberg, 1983.

Brauns, Ernst Ludwig. *Skizzen von America. Zu einer belehrenden Unterhaltung für gebildete Leser und mit besonderer Rücksicht auf Reisende und Auswanderer nach Amerika.* Halberstadt: Vogler, 1830.

Burns, James MacGregor, et al., editors. *Government by the People.* 16th ed. Englewood Cliffs, NJ: Prentice Hall, 1995. Insert: complete text of the Constitution of the United States of America.

Carl, Bernhard, Prince of Sachsen-Weimar. *Reise Sr. Hoheit des Herzogs Bernhard zu Sachsen-Weimar-Eisenach durch Nord-Amerika in den Jahren 1825 und 1826.* Edited by Heinrich Luden. Weimar: Wilhelm Hoffmann, 1828.

Dunn, Richard S., and Mary Maples Dunn, editors. *The Papers of William Penn, 1680–1684.* 5 vols. Philadelphia: U of Pennsylvania P, 1981–1987.

Eckermann, Johann Peter. *Gespräche mit Goethe in den letzten Jahren seines Lebens 1823–1832 von Johann Peter Eckermann* in Johann Wolfgang Goethe: *Sämtliche Werke. Briefe, Tagebücher und Gespräche.* Frankfurter Ausgabe. Edited by Hendrik Birus et al. 40 vols. Frankfurt am Main: Deutscher Klassiker Verlag, 1987–1999: vol. 39.

Ehler, Sidney Z., and John B. Morrall, editors and translators. *Church and State Through the Centuries: A Collection of Illustrative Documents.* London: Burns and Oates, 1954.

Eze, Emmanuel Chukwudi, editor. *Race and Enlightenment: A Reader.* Oxford: Blackwell, 1991.

Franklin, Benjamin. *Autobiography and Other Writings.* Edited by Ormond Seavey. Oxford: Oxford UP, 1993.

Goldsmith, Oliver. *The Vicar of Wakefield.* Edited by Stephen Coote. London: Penguin, 1986.

Heine, Heinrich. *Historisch-kritische Gesamtausgabe der Werke.* Edited by Manfred Windfuhr. 16 vols. Hamburg: Hoffmann and Campe, 1973–1997.

Herder, Johann Gottfried. *Werke.* Edited by Martin Bollacher, et al. 10 vols. Frankfurt am Main: Deutscher Klassiker Verlag, 1985– .

Hildebrandt, Horst, editor. *Die deutschen Verfassungen des 19. und 20. Jahrhunderts.* Paderborn: Schöningh, 1975.

Humboldt, Wilhelm von. *Gesammelte Schriften.* Edited by Albert Leitzmann. Königliche Preussische Akademie der Wissenschaften. Berlin: Behr, 1903–1936; repr. Berlin: De Gruyter, 1968.

Hume, David. *Essays: Moral, Political and Literary.* Edited by Eugene F. Miller, rev. ed. Indianapolis, IN: Liberty Fund, 1985.

Jefferson, Thomas. *Thomas Jefferson: In His Own Words.* Edited by Maureen Harrison and Steve Gilbert. New York: Barnes & Noble, 1993.

———. *Thomas Jefferson. Writings.* Edited by Merrill D. Peterson. New York: The Library of America, 1984.

Kant, Immanuel. *Werke.* Edited by Wilhelm Weischedel. 6 vols. Frankfurt am Main: Insel, 1960–1964.

Lessing, Gotthold Ephraim. *Werke und Briefe.* Edited by Wilfried Barner et al. 12 vols. Frankfurt am Main: Deutscher Klassiker Verlag, 1985– .

Lindberg, Carter, editor. *The European Reformations Sourcebook.* Oxford: Blackwell, 2000.

Locke, John. *A Letter Concerning Toleration.* Trans. from the Latin by William Popple. Second edition corrected. London: Awnsham Churchill, 1690.

Maclear, J. F., editor. *Church and State in the Modern Age: A Documentary History.* New York: Oxford UP, 1995.

Mann, Thomas. *Gesammelte Werke.* 12 vols. 2nd ed. Oldenburg: Fischer, 1960.

Mendelssohn, Moses. *Jerusalem: Oder ueber die religiöse Macht und Judentum.* Berlin: Friedrich Maurer, 1783.

Morley, Edith J., editor. *Crabb Robinson in Germany 1800–1805: Extracts from his Correspondence.* London: H. Milford, Oxford UP, 1929.

Müller, Kanzler von. *Unterhaltungen mit Goethe.* Edited by Ernst Grumach with notations by Renate Fischer-Lamberg. Weimar: Hermann Böhlaus Nachfolger, 1959.

Schiller, Friedrich. *Sämtliche Werke.* Edited by Helmut Koopman. 5 vols. Munich: Winkler, 1968.

Sterne, Laurence. *A Sentimental Journey through France and Italy.* Edited by Graham Petrie with an introduction by A. Alvarez. London: Penguin, 1986.

Voltaire. *Traité sur la tolérance.* Geneva: Cramer, 1763.

Zedler, Johann Heinrich. *Grosses Vollstaendiges Universal Lexikon aller Wissenschaften und Kuenste welche durch menschliche Verstand und Witz erfunden worden.* 64 vols. [in 32] Leipzig and Halle: Johann Heinrich Zedler, 1737–1750.

Secondary Sources

Abbott, Scott. *Fictions of Freemasonry and the German Novel.* Detroit: Wayne State UP, 1991.

Adorno, Theodor W. "Zum Klassizismus von Goethes Iphigenie." In *Gesammelte Schriften,* edited by Rolf Tiedemann. 20 vols. Frankfurt am Main: Suhrkamp, 1970–1986; vol. 11, 1974.

Altmann, Alexander. *Die trostvolle Aufklärung: Studien zur Metaphysik und politischen Theorie Moses Mendelssohns.* Stuttgart: Fromann-Holzboog, 1982.

Anderson, M. S. *Europe in the Eighteenth Century 1713–1783.* 3rd ed. London: Longman, 1991.

Arndt, Karl J. R. *Georg Rapp's Harmony Society 1785–1847.* Philadelphia: U of Pennsylvania P, 1965.

Bab, Julius. *Goethe und die Juden.* Berlin: Philo-Verlag, 1926.

Bahr, Ehrhard, editor. *"Was ist Aufklärung?": Thesen und Definitionen.* Stuttgart: Reclam, 1989.

———. "Wilhelm Meisters Wanderjahre oder Die Entsagenden." In *Goethes Erzählwerk: Interpretationen,* edited by Paul Michael Lützeler and James E. McLeod. Stuttgart: Reclam, 1985.

Barner, Wilfried. "150 Jahre nach seinem Tod: Goethe und die Juden." *Bulletin des Leo Baeck Instituts* 63 (1982): 75–82.

Baur, Jörg. "Martin Luther im Urteil Goethes." *Goethe-Jahrbuch* 113 (1996): 11–22.

Beatty, Edward Corbyn Obert. *William Penn as Social Philosopher.* New York: Columbia UP, 1939.

Bell, Matthew. *Goethe's Naturalistic Anthropology: Man and other Plants.* Oxford: Clarendon Press, 1994.

Bennett, Benjamin. *Beyond Theory: Eighteenth-Century German Literature and the Poetics of Irony.* Ithaca, NY: Cornell UP, 1993.

———. *Modern Drama and German Classicism: Renaissance from Lessing to Brecht.* Ithaca, NY: Cornell UP, 1986.

Berlin, Isaiah. *The Crooked Timber of Humanity: Chapters in the History of Ideas.* London: Fontana, 1991.

Berman, Antoine. *The Experience of the Foreign: Culture and Translation in Romantic Germany.* Translated from the French by S. Heyvaert. Albany: State University of New York, 1992.

Bernard, Paul P. *Joseph II.* New York: Twayne, 1968.

Besier, Gerhard. "Toleranz." *Geschichtliche Grundbegriffe: Historisches Lexikon zur politisch-sozialen Sprache in Deutschland.* Edited by Otto Brunner et al. 8 vols. Stuttgart: Klett-Cotta, 1972–1997. Vol. 6 (1990): 495–523.

Bielefeldt, Heiner. "Toleranz und Menschenrechte." *Jahrbuch Deutsch als Fremdsprache* 20 (1994): 177–84.

Birnbaum, Pierre, and Ira Katznelson, editors. *Paths of Emancipation: Jews, States, and Citizenship.* Princeton, NJ: Princeton UP, 1995.

Birus, Hendrik. "Am Schnittpunkt von Komparatistik und Germanistik: Die Idee der Weltliteratur heute." In *Germanistik und Komparatistik: DFG-Symposion 1993*, edited by Hendrik Birus. Germanistische Symposien Berichtsbände 16. Stuttgart: Metzler, 1993. 439–57.

———. *Hermeneutische Positionen: Schleiermacher – Dilthey – Heidegger – Gadamer.* Kleine Vandenhoeck-Reihe 1479. Göttingen: Vandenhoeck & Ruprecht, 1982.

Blackall, Eric A. *Goethe and the Novel.* Ithaca, NY: Cornell UP, 1976.

Blanckmeister, Franz. *Goethe und die Kirche seiner Zeit.* Dresden: Sturm, 1923.

Blessin, Stefan. *Goethes Romane: Aufbruch in die Moderne.* Paderborn: Schöningh, 1996.

Bloom, Harold. *The American Religion: The Emergence of the Post-Christian Nation.* New York: Simon & Schuster, 1992.

———. *The Anxiety of Influence: A Theory of Poetry.* London: Oxford UP, 1973.

Bohn, Ursula. "Moses Mendelssohn und die Toleranz." In *Toleranz heute: 250 Jahre nach Mendelssohn und Lessing*, edited by Peter von der Osten-Sacken. Berlin: Veröffentlichungen aus dem Institut Kirche und Judentum bei der Kirchlichen Hochschule Berlin, 1979. 26–36.

Boorstin, Daniel J. *The Americans: The Colonial Experience.* New York: Random House, 1958.

Borchmeyer, Dieter. "Iphigenie auf Tauris," in *Goethes Dramen: Interpretationen*, ed. by Walter Hinderer. Stuttgart: Reclam, 1992. 111–57.

———. *Weimarer Klassik: Porträt einer Epoche.* Weinheim: Beltz/Athenäum, 1994.

———. "Wie aufgeklärt ist die Weimarer Klassik? Eine Replik auf Beiträge von John A. McCarthy und Gottfried Willems." *Jahrbuch der deutschen Schiller-Gesellschaft* 36 (1992): 434–40.

Boyd, James. *Goethe's Iphigenie auf Tauris.* Oxford: Blackwell, 1942.

———. *Goethe's Knowledge of English Literature.* Oxford: Clarendon Press, 1932.

Boyle, Nicholas. *Goethe: The Poet and the Age.* Vol. 1, *The Poetry of Desire: 1749–1790.* Rev. ed. Oxford: Oxford UP, 1992– .

Brecht, Martin. "'Ob ein weltlich Oberkait Recht habe, in des Glaubens Sachen mit dem Schwert zu handeln': Ein unbekanntes Nürnberger Gutachten zur Frage der Toleranz aus dem Jahre 1530." *Archiv für Reformationsgeschichte* 60 (1969): 65–75.

Brenner, Peter J. "'Weltliteratur.' Voraussetzungen eines Begriffs in Goethes Literaturkritik." *Goethe Jahrbuch* 89 (1981): 25–42.

Brown, Jane K. *Goethe's Cyclical Narratives: "Die Unterhaltungen deutscher Ausgewanderten" and "Wilhelm Meisters Wanderjahre."* University of North Carolina Studies in Germanic Languages and Literatures 82. Chapel Hill: U of North Carolina P, 1975. 87–97.

Bruford, W. H. *Germany in the Eighteenth Century: The Social Background of the Literary Revival.* Cambridge: Cambridge UP, 1965.

Brunner, Otto, et al., editors. *Geschichtliche Grundbegriffe: Historisches Lexikon zur politisch-sozialen Sprache in Deutschland.* 8 vols. Stuttgart: Cotta, 1972–1997.

Bryner, Gary, and Richard Vetterli. *In Search of the Republic: Public Virtue and the Roots of American Government.* Totowa, NJ: Rowman & Littlefield, 1987.

Burdach, Konrad. *Die älteste Gestalt des West-östlichen Divans.* Sitzungsberichte der königlich preussischen Akademie der Wissenschaften 27. Berlin: Reichsdruckerei, 1904.

Bürgel, Johann Christoph. *Drei Hafis-Studien: Goethe und Hafis, Verstand und Liebe bei Hafis, Zwölf Ghaselen, übertragen und interpretiert* [by Johann Christoph Bürgel]. Europäische Hochschulschriften, Reihe 1, Deutsche Literatur und Germanistik 113. Bern: Lang, 1975.

Butterfield, Herbert. "Toleration in Early Modern Times." *Journal of the History of Ideas* 38 (1977): 573–84.

Carr, William. *A History of Germany 1815–1990.* London: Arnold, 1991.

Cassirer, Ernst. *Die Philosophie der Aufklärung.* Tübingen: Mohr, 1932.

———. *Goethe und die geschichtliche Welt: Drei Aufsätze.* Berlin: Bruno Cassirer, 1932.

Christie-Murray, David. *A History of Heresy.* Oxford: Oxford UP, 1989.

Clark, Robert T. Jr. "The Noble Savage and the Idea of Tolerance in Herder." *Journal of English and Germanic Philology* 33 (1934): 46–56.

Clark, Steve. "Orient knowledge not so pure." *Times Literary Supplement,* 21 March 1997, 25.

Craig, Gordon. *The Politics of the Unpolitical: German Writers and the Problem of Power.* New York: Oxford UP, 1995.

Crick, Bernard. "Toleration." *Government and Opposition* 6 (1971): 144–71.

Currie, Pamela. *Literature as Social Action: Modernist and Traditionalist Narratives in Germany in the Seventeenth and Eighteenth Centuries.* Columbia, SC: Camden House, 1995.

Daemmrich, Horst S., and Ingrid Daemmrich. *Themes & Motifs in Western Literature: A Handbook.* Tübingen: Francke, 1987.

Dahnke, Hans-Dietrich. "Die Geheimnisse." In *Goethe-Handbuch,* edited by Bernd Witte et al. 4 vols. Stuttgart: Metzler, 1996–1998; vol. 1, edited by Regine Otto and Bernd Witte (1996), 546–52.

Damrosch, Leo. "Generality and Particularity." In *The Cambridge History of Literary Criticism,* edited by H. B. Nisbet and Claude Rawson. 8 vols. Cambridge: Cambridge UP, 1989–. Vol. 4: *The Eighteenth Century* (1997). 381–93.

Davis, Garold N. *German Thought and Culture in England 1700–1770: A Preliminary Survey including a Chronological Bibliography of German Literature in English Translation.* University of North Carolina Studies in Comparative Literature 47. Chapel Hill: U of North Carolina P, 1969.

Degering, Thomas. *Das Elend der Entsagung: Goethes "Wilhelm Meisters Wanderjahre."* Abhandlungen zur Kunst-, Musik-, und Literaturwissenschaft 327. Bonn: Bouvier, 1982.

Dietrich, Wofgang. "Die Geheimnisse, Achilles, Das Tagebuch." In *Goethes Erzählwerk,* edited by Paul Michael Lützeler and James E. McLeod. Stuttgart: Reclam, 1985. 268–90.

Dong, Wenqiao. "Goethe und der Kulturaustausch zwischen dem chinesischen und dem deutschen Volk." *Goethe-Jahrbuch* 107 (1990): 314–26.

Ebbinghaus, Julius. "Über die Idee der Toleranz: Eine staatsrechtliche und religionsphilosophische Untersuchung." *Archiv für Philosophie* 4 (1950): 1–34.

Eichstädt, Volkmar. *Bibliographie zur Geschichte der Judenfrage.* Hamburg: Hanseatische Verlagsanstalt, 1938. Vol. 1: 1750–1848.

Ersparnen, Peter R. *The Elusiveness of Tolerance: The "Jewish Question" from Lessing to the Napoleonic Wars.* University of North Carolina Studies in the Germanic Languages and Literatures 117. Chapel Hill: U of North Carolina P, 1997.

Evans, Robert J. W. *The Making of the Habsburg Monarchy 1550–1700.* Oxford: Clarendon Press, 1991.

Fink, Gonthier L. "Goethe und Voltaire." *Goethe Jahrbuch* 101 (1984): 74–111.

Fischer, Bernd. *Das Eigene und das Eigentliche: Klopstock, Herder, Fichte, Kleist: Episoden aus der Konstruktionsgeschichte nationaler Intentionalitäten.* Philologische Studien und Quellen 135. Berlin: Schmidt, 1995.

Fischer, Bernhard. "Das Ende der Kunst und die Krise der Aufklärung: Zur Entwicklung der spätaufklärischen Geschichtsphilosophie Johann Gottfried Herders." *Jahrbuch des Freien Deutschen Hochstifts* (1991): 68–89.

Frank, Isnard Wilhelm, editor. *Toleranz am Mittelrhein: Referate der 35. Jahrestagung der Gesellschaft für mittelrheinische Kirchengeschichte vom 12. und 13. April 1983 in Worms.* Quellen und Abhandlungen zu mittelrheinische Kirchengeschichte 50. Mainz: Selbstverlag der Gesellschaft für mittelrheinische Kirchengeschichte, 1984.

Freimark, Peter, et al., eds. *Lessing und die Toleranz: Beiträge der vierten internationalen Konferenz der Lessing Society im Hamburg vom 27. bis 29. Juni 1985.* Sonderband zum *Lessing Yearbook.* Munich: edition + kritik; Detroit: Wayne State UP, 1986.

Fulbrook, Mary, editor. *German History since 1800.* London: Arnold, 1997.

Gampl, I. "Toleranz(-patent)." In *Handwörterbuch zur deutschen Rechtsgeschichte,* edited by Adalbert Erler et al. 5 vols. Berlin: Schmidt, 1971–1998. Vol. 5 (1998), 270–73.

Ganz, Peter. "Sankt-Rochus-Fest zu Bingen." *Oxford German Studies* 10 (1979): 110–120.

Gay, Peter. *The Enlightenment: An Interpretation.* 2 vols. New York: Norton, 1995–1996.

Geiger, Ludwig. "Die Juden und die deutsche Literatur." *Zeitschrift für die Geschichte der Juden in Deutschland* 1 (1887): sub-section on "Goethe und die Juden," 321–65.

Gilg, André. *Wilhelm Meisters Wanderjahre und ihre Symbole.* Zürcher Beiträge zur deutschen Literatur- und Geistesgeschichte 9. Zurich: Atlantis, 1954.

Götting, Franz. *Die Bibliothek von Goethes Vater.* Nassauische Annalen 64. Wiesbaden: Verlag des Vereins für Nassauische Altertumskunde und Geschichtsforschung, 1953.

Gould, Stephen Jay. *The Mismeasure of Man.* New York: Norton, 1981.

Green, Vivian. *The European Reformation.* Phoenix Mill: Sutton, 1998.

Grell, Ole Peter, and Bob Scribner, editors. *Tolerance and Intolerance in the European Reformation.* With an introduction by Ole Peter Grell. Cambridge: Cambridge UP, 1996.

Grimminger, Rolf, editor. *Hansers Sozialgeschichte der deutschen Literatur.* Vol. 3, Deutsche Aufklärung bis zur Französischen Revolution 1680–1789. Munich: Hanser, 1980.

Grossmann, Walter. "Toleration – 'exercitium religionis privatum.'" *Journal of the History of Ideas* 40 (1979): 129–34.

Guggisberg, "Wandel der Argumente für religiöse Toleranz und Glaubens-freiheit im 16. und 17. Jahrhundert." In *Zur Geschichte der Toleranz und Religionsfreiheit,* ed. by Heinrich Lutz. Wege der Forschung 246. Darm-stadt: Wissenschaftliche Buchgesellschaft, 1977.

Güldner, Gerhard. *Das Toleranz-Problem in den Niederlanden im Ausgang des 16. Jahrhunderts.* Historische Studien 403. Lübeck: Matthiesen, 1968.

Gundolf, Friedrich. *Goethe.* Berlin: Bondi, 1922.

Gustafson, Susan. "The Religious Significance of Goethe's 'Amerikabild.'" *Eighteenth-Century Studies* 24 (1990): 69–91.

Haag, Norbert. *Predigt und Gesellschaft: die lutherische Orthodoxie in Ulm 1640–1740.* Veröffentlichungen des Instituts für Europäische Geschichte Mainz, Abteilung Religionsgeschichte 145. Mainz: Philipp von Zabern, 1992.

Haase, Erich. "Das Literarhistorische Interesse an den Toleranzkontroversen am Ende des Grand Siècle." *Germanisch-romanische Monatsschrift* 35 (1954): 138–49.

Hahn, H.-J. *German Thought and Culture: From the Holy Roman Empire to the Present Day.* Manchester: Manchester UP, 1995.

Hall, Edith. *Inventing the Barbarian: Greek Self-Definition through Tragedy.* Oxford: Clarendon Press, 1989.

Hamilton, J. Taylor, and Kenneth G. Hamilton. *History of the Moravian Church: The Renewed Unitas Fratrum 1722–1957.* 2nd ed. Bethlehem, PA: Moravian Church in America, 1983.

Hampson, Norman. *The Enlightenment: An Evaluation of its Assumptions, At-titudes and Values.* London: Penguin, 1990.

Harrison, Peter. *"Religion" and the Religions in the English Enlightenment.* Cambridge: Cambridge UP, 1990.

Hartung, Günter. "Goethe und die Juden." *Weimarer Beiträge* 40 (1994): 398–416.

Helmstadter, Richard, editor. *Freedom and Religion in the Nineteenth Cen-tury.* Stanford: Stanford UP, 1997.

Henkel, Hermann. *Goethe und die Bibel.* Leipzig: Biedermann, 1890.

Henriques, Ursula Ruth Quixano. *Religious Toleration in England, 1787–1833.* London: Routledge and Kegan Paul, 1961.

Herr, Richard, and Harold T. Parker, editors. *Ideas in History: Essays pre-sented to Louis Gottschalk by his former students.* Durham, NC: Duke UP, 1965.

Herwig, Henriette. *Das ewig Männliche zieht uns hinab: "Wilhelm Meisters Wanderjahre." Geschlechterdifferenz, Sozialer Wandel, Historische Anthropologie.* Tübingen: Francke, 1997.

Heyd, David, editor. *Toleration an Elusive Virtue.* Princeton: Princeton UP, 1996.

Hill, David. "Lessing: Die Sprache der Toleranz." *Deutsche Vierteljahresschrift für Literaturwissenschaft und Geistesgeschichte* 64 (1990): 218–46.

Hoffmann, Heinrich. *Die Religion des Goetheschen Zeitalters.* Tübingen: Mohr, 1917.

Hoffmann, Hermann. *Friedrich II. von Preussen und die Aufhebung der Gesellschaft Jesu.* Bibliotheca Instituti Historici, S. I., 30. Rome: Institutum Historicum, S. I., 1969.

Holborn, Hajo. *A History of Modern Germany 1648–1840.* Princeton: Princeton UP, 1982.

Horacek, Blanka. "Goethe und das Christentum." *Jahrbuch des Wiener Goethe-Vereins* 77 (1973): 88–104.

Horkheimer, Max, and Theodor W. Adorno. *Dialektik der Aufklärung.* New York: Social Studies Association, 1944.

Horton, John, and Susan Mendus, editors. *Aspects of Toleration: Philosophical Studies.* London: Methuen, 1985.

Howard, Elizabeth Fox. "Goethe und Luke Howard." *Der Quäker* 9 (1932): 207–211.

Huch, Ricarda. *Das Zeitalter der Glaubenspaltung.* Frankfurt am Main: Weisbecker, 1954.

Im Hof, Ulrich. *Das Europa der Aufklärung.* 2nd ed. Munich: Beck, 1995.

Irmscher, Hans Dietrich. "Goethe und Herder im Wechselspiel von Attraktion und Repulsion." *Goethe-Jahrbuch* 106 (1989): 22–52.

Jellinek, Max Hermann. *Geschichte der Neuhochdeutschen Grammatik von den Anfängen bis auf Adelung.* Germanische Bibliothek 7. 2 vols. Heidelberg: Carl Winter, 1913–1914.

Jens, Walter. "'Nathans Gesinnung ist von jeher die meinige gewesen.'" In *Dichtung und Religion,* edited by Walter Jens and Hans Küng. Munich: Kindler, 1985. 102–118.

Jordan, Wilbur Kitchener. *The Development of Religious Toleration in England.* 4 vols. London: Unwin, 1932.

Kamen, Henry Arthur Francis. *The Rise of Toleration.* London: Weidenfeld and Nicolson, 1967.

Kann, Robert. *A History of the Habsburg Empire 1526–1918*. Berkeley: U of California P, 1980. 45–53.

Karniel, Josef. *Die Toleranzpolitik Kaiser Joseph II*. Translated from the Hebrew by Leo Koppel. Schriftenreihe für Deutsche Geschichte, Universität Tel Aviv 9. Gerlingen: Bleicher, 1986.

Kars, Gustav. *Das Bild des Juden in der deutschen Literatur des 18. und 19. Jahrhunderts*. Freiburg: Burg-Verlag, 1988.

Katz, Jacob. "Aufkärung und Toleranz." In *Toleranz heute: 250 Jahre nach Mendelssohn und Lessing,* edited by Peter von der Osten-Sacken. Berlin: Veröffentlichungen aus dem Institut Kirche und Judentum bei der Kirchlichen Hochschule Berlin, 1979. 6–14.

Kiesel, Helmut. "Problem und Begründung der Toleranz im 18. Jahrhundert." In *Festgabe für Ernst Walter Zeeden,* edited by Horst Raabe et al. Münster: Aschendorf, 1976. 370–85.

King, Preston. *Toleration*. London: Allen & Unwin, 1976.

Klaus, Georg, and Manfred Buhr, editors. *Philosophisches Wörterbuch*. 2nd ed. 2 vols. Leipzig: VEB Bibliographisches Institut Leipzig, 1976.

Kohn, Hans. *The Mind of Germany: The Education of a Nation*. New York: Harper & Row, 1965.

Kommers, Donald P. *The Constitutional Jurisprudence of the Federal Republic of Germany*. Durham, NC: Duke UP, 1989.

Kondylis, Panajotis. *Die Aufklärung im Rahmen des neuzeitlichen Rationalismus*. Munich: Deutscher Taschenbuch Verlag, 1986.

Koopmann, Helmut. "Brief des Pastors zu *** an den neuen Pastor zu ***. Aus dem Französischen." In *Goethe-Handbuch,* edited by Bernd Witte et al. 4 vols. Stuttgart: Metzler, 1996–1998. Vol. 3 (1997), 526–32.

Kopitzsch, Franklin. "Lessing und seine Zeitgenossen im Spannungsfeld von Toleranz und Intoleranz." *Jahrbuch des Instituts für Deutsche Geschichte* 3 (1980): 29–85.

Köpke, Wulf. "Johann Gottfried Herder: Der Ruf nach Vernunft und Billigkeit." *Jahrbuch Deutsch als Fremdsprache* 20 (1994): 237–55.

Korff, H. A. *Die Liebesgedichte des West-östlichen Divans*. Zurich: Hirzel, 1949.

Koselleck, Reinhart. "Aufklärung und die Grenzen ihrer Toleranz." In *Glaube und Toleranz: Das theologische Erbe der Aufklärung,* edited by Trutz Rendtorff. Gütersloh: Mohn, 1982. 256–71.

Krauss, R. "Schubart und Goethe." *Goethe-Jahrbuch* 23 (1902): 118–29.

Krauss, Werner. "Goethe und die Französische Revolution." *Goethe Jahrbuch* 94 (1977): 127–36.

Krieger, Leonard. *The German Idea of Freedom: History of a Political Tradition*. Chicago: U of Chicago P, 1972.

Kriegleder, Wynfrid. "Wilhelm Meisters Amerika: Das Bild der Vereinigten Staaten in den *Wanderjahren*." *Jahrbuch des Wiener Goethe-Vereins* 95 (1991): 15–31.

Krippendorff, Ekkehart. *Goethe: Politik gegen den Zeitgeist*. Frankfurt am Main: Insel, 1999.

Kuschel, Karl-Josef. *Vom Streit zum Wettstreit der Religionen: Lessing und die Herausforderung des Islam*. Weltreligionen und Literatur 1. Düsseldorf: Patmos, 1998.

Lamport, Francis John. *German Classical Drama: Theatre, Humanity and Nation 1750–1870*. Cambridge: Cambridge UP, 1992.

———. *Lessing and the Drama*. Oxford: Clarendon Press, 1981.

Lange, Victor. "Goethes Amerikabild: Wirklichkeit und Vision." In *Amerika in der deutschen Literatur: Neue Welt – Nordamerika – USA,* edited by Sigrid Bauschinger et al. Stuttgart: Reclam, 1975. 63–74.

Lea, Charlene. "Tolerance Unlimited: 'The Noble Jew' on the German and Austrian Stage (1750–1805)." *The German Quarterly* 64 (1991): 166–77.

Lecler, Josef S. J.. *Histoire de la tolérance au siècle de la Réforme*. 2 vols. Théologie 31. Paris: Aubier, 1955.

Lemmel, Monika. *Poetologie in Goethes west-östlichem Divan*. Reihe Siegen 73. Heidelberg: Carl Winter, 1987.

Lentz, Wolfgang. *Goethes Noten und Abhandlungen zum West-östlichen Divan*. Hamburg: Augustin, 1958.

Limm, Peter. *The Dutch Revolt 1559–1648*. London: Longman, 1997.

Livingstone, David N., and Charles W. J. Withers, editors. *Geography and Enlightenment*. London: U of Chicago P, 1999.

Lohner, Edgar, editor. *Interpretationen zum West-östlichen Divan Goethes*. Wege der Forschung 288. Darmstadt: Wissenschaftliche Buchgesellschaft, 1973.

Low, Alfred D. *Jews in the Eyes of the Germans: From the Enlightenment to Imperial Germany*. Philadelphia: Institute for the Study of Human Issues, 1979.

Lutz, Heinrich, editor. *Zur Geschichte der Toleranz und Religionsfreiheit*. Wege der Forschung 246. Darmstadt: Wissenschaftliche Buchgesellschaft, 1977.

MacCormack, John R. "Religion and Freedom." In *Faith & Reason,* edited by John A. Howard. Belfast: Christian Journals Limited, 1981. 87–107.

MacCulloch, Diarmaid. *Groundwork of Christian History*. London: Epworth Press, 1987.

McCarthy, John A. "Politics and Morality in Eighteenth-Century Germany" *Deutsche Vierteljahresschrift für Literaturwissenschaft und Geistesgeschichte* 68 (1994): 77–98.

McLeod, Hugh. *Secularisation in Western Europe, 1848–1919*. European Studies Series. London: Macmillan, 2000.

Mattenklott, Gert. "Die Leiden des jungen Werthers." In *Goethe-Handbuch*, edited by Bernd Witte et al. 4 vols. Stuttgart: Metzler, 1996–1998. Vol. 3 (1997), 51–100.

Mauch, Kurt. "Goethe, der Hypsistarier." *Die Bruderschaft* 15 (1959): 14–16.

Maurer, Michael. *Aufklärung und Anglophilie in Deutschland*. Göttingen: Vandenhoeck & Ruprecht, 1987.

Mensching, Gustav. *Toleranz und Wahrheit in der Religion*. Heidelberg: Quelle & Meyer, 1955.

Meyer, Michael A. *The Origins of the Modern Jew: Jewish Identity and European Culture in Germany, 1749–1824*. Detroit: Wayne State UP, 1967.

Möbus, Gerhard. *Die Christus-Frage in Goethes Leben und Werk*. Osnabrück: Fromm, 1964.

Möller, Horst. *Fürstenstaat oder Bürgernation. Deutschland 1763–1815*. Berlin: Sielder, 1998.

Molnár, Géza von. *Goethes Kantstudien*. Schriften der Goethe-Gesellschaft 64. Weimar: Böhlau, 1994.

Mommsen, Katharina. *Goethe und unsere Zeit*. Sonderduck. Frankfurt am Main: Suhrkamp, 1999.

———. "West-östlicher Divan" und "Chinesisch-deutsche Jahres- und Tageszeiten" *Goethe-Jahrbuch* 108 (1991): 169–78.

———. *Goethe und die arabische Welt*. Frankfurt am Main: Insel, 1988.

———. "Der unbequeme Goethe." *Publications of the English Goethe Society* 37 (1968):12–42.

———, ed. *Goethe — Warum? Eine repräsentative Auslese aus Werken, Briefen und Dokumenten*. Insel Taschenbuch 759. Frankfurt am Main: Insel, 1984.

Morgan, Peter. *The Critical Idyll: Traditional Values and the French Revolution in Goethe's Hermann und Dorothea*. Studies in German Literature, Linguistics, and Culture 54. Columbia, SC: Camden House, 1990.

Müller, Ulrich. "Toleranz im Mittelalter? Eine Skizze zu den Beziehungen zwischen dem christlich-lateinischen Okzident und dem islamischen Orient." *Jahrbuch Deutsch als Fremdsprache* 20 (1994): 209–236.

Munck, Thomas. *The Enlightenment: A Comparative Social History 1721–1794.* London: Arnold, 2000.

Muschg, Adolf. *Goethe als Emigrant: Auf der Suche nach dem Grünen bei einem alten Dichter.* Frankfurt am Main: Suhrkamp, 1986.

Niewöhner, Friedrich. *Veritas Sive Varietas: Lessings Toleranzparabel und das Buch Von den drei Betrügern.* Bibliothek der Aufklärung 5. Heidelberg: Schneider, 1988.

Niggl, Günter. *"Fromm" bei Goethe: Eine Wortmonographie.* Hermaea: Germanistische Forschungen 21. Tübingen: Niemeyer, 1967.

Nipperdey, Thomas. *Deutsche Geschichte 1800–1866. Bürgerwelt und starker Staat.* Munich: Beck, 1998.

Nisbet, Hugh Barr. "Lessing and Pierre Bayle." In *Tradition and Creation: Essays in Honour of Elizabeth Mary Wilkinson,* edited by C. P. Magill et al. Leeds: Maney & Sons, 1978. 13–29.

———. "Goethes und Herders Geschichtsdenken." *Goethe-Jahrbuch* 110 (1993): 115–33.

Nye, Russel B. "History and Literature: Branches of the Same Tree." In *Essays on History and Literature,* edited by Robert H. Bremner. Columbus, OH: Ohio State UP, 1966: 123–59.

O'Brien, Charles H. "The Ideas of Religious Toleration at the Time of Joseph II: A Study of the Enlightenment among Catholics in Austria." *Transactions of the American Philosophical Society* 59 (1969): 1–77.

Och, Gunnar. *Imago judaica: Juden und Judentum im Spiegel der deutschen Literatur 1750–1812.* Würzburg: Königshausen & Neumann, 1995.

Oellers, Norbert. "Goethe und Schiller in ihrem Verhältnis zum Judentum." In *Conditio Judaica: Judentum, Antisemitismus und deutschsprachige Literatur vom 18. Jahrhundert bis zum ersten Weltkrieg,* edited by Hans Otto Horch and Horst Denkler. 2 vols. Tübingen: Niemeyer, 1988–1989. Vol. 1, 1988.

Outram, Dorinda. *The Enlightenment.* New Approaches to European History 7. Cambridge: Cambridge UP, 1997.

Pasley, Malcolm, editor. *Germany: A Companion to German Studies.* 2nd ed. London: Routledge, 1988.

Pennington, D. H. *Seventeenth-Century Europe.* London: Longman, 1970.

Pfeifer, Wolfgang, editor. *Etymologisches Wörterbuch des Deutschen.* Berlin: Akademie-Verlag, 1989.

Pfund, Harry W. "Goethe and the Quakers." *The Germanic Review* 14 (1939): 258–69.

Porter, Roy. *The Enlightenment.* Studies in European History. London: Macmillan, 1990.

Price, Lawrence Marsden. *The Reception of English Literature in Germany.* Berkeley: U of California P, 1932.

Prickett, Stephen. *Origins of Narrative: The Romantic Appropriation of the Bible.* Cambridge UP: Cambridge, 1996.

Pullan, Leighton. *Religion since the Reformation.* Oxford: Clarendon Press, 1923.

Pütz, Peter. *Die deutsche Aufklärung.* Erträge der Forschung 81. Darmstadt: Wissenschaftliche Buchgesellschaft, 1978.

Quedenbaum, Gerd. *Der Verleger und Buchhändler Johann Heinrich Zedler 1706–1751: Ein Buchunternehmer in den zwängen seiner Zeit. Ein Beitrag zur Geschichte des deutschen Buchhandels im 18. Jahrhundert.* Hildesheim: Olms, 1977.

Ramm, Agatha. *Europe in the Nineteenth Century 1789–1905.* 7th ed. London: Longman, 1984.

Rasch, Wolfdietrich. *Goethes "Iphigenie auf Tauris" als Drama der Autonomie.* Munich: Beck, 1979.

Ratz, Alfred E. "C. M. Wieland: Toleranz, Kompromiß und Inkonsequenz. Eine kritische Betrachtung." *Deutsche Vierteljahresschrift für Literaturwissenschaft und Geistesgeschichte* 42 (1968): 493–514.

Reardon, Bernard M. G. *Religion in the Age of Romanticism.* Cambridge: Cambridge UP, 1989.

Reed, Terence James. "Englische Literatur." In *Goethe-Handbuch,* edited by Bernd Witte et al. 4 vols. Stuttgart: Metzler, 1996–1998. Vol. 4/1 (1998), 259–64.

———. "Iphigenie auf Tauris." In *Goethe-Handbuch,* edited by Bernd Witte et al. 4 vols. Stuttgart: Metzler, 1996–1998. Vol. 2 (1996).

———. "Talking to Tyrants: Dialogues with Power in Eighteenth-Century Germany." *The Historical Journal* 33 (1990): 63–79.

———. "Die Geburt der Klassik aus dem Geist der Mündigkeit." *Jahrbuch der deutschen Schiller-Gesellschaft* 32 (1988): 367–74.

———. *The Classical Centre: Goethe and Weimar 1775–1832.* Oxford: Oxford UP, 1986.

———. "Iphigenies Unmündigkeit: Zur weiblichen Aufklärung." In *Germanistik: Forschungsstand und Perspektiven: Vorträge des Deutschen Germanistentages 1984*, edited by Georg Stötzel. Berlin: De Gruyter, 1985. 505–24.

———. "Ecclesia Militans: Weimarer Klassik als Opposition." In *Unser Commercium: Goethe und Schillers Literaturpolitik*, edited by Wilfried Barner et al. *Veröffentlichungen der Deutschen Schillergesellschaft* 42 (Stuttgart: Cotta, 1984).

Reill, Peter Hans, and Ellen Judy Wilson, editors. *Encyclopedia of the Enlightenment*. New York: Book Builders, 1996.

Reinhardt, Hartmut. "Egmont." In *Goethes Dramen: Interpretationen*, edited by Walter Hinderer. Stuttgart: Reclam, 1992. 158–98.

———. "Egmont." In *Goethes Dramen: Neue Interpretationen*, ed. by Walter Hinderer. Stuttgart: Reclam, 1980. 122–43.

Reinhardt, Kurt F. *Germany: 2000 Years. The Rise and Fall of the "Holy Empire."* New York: Ungar, 1988.

Reischer, Franz. *Die Toleranzgemeinden Kärntens nach einem Visitationsbericht im Jahre 1786*. Archiv für vaterländische Geschichte und Topographie 60. Klagenfurt: Verlag des Geschichtsvereines für Kärnten, 1965.

Reiss, Hans Siegbart. "Sozialer Wandel in Goethes Werk." *Goethe-Jahrbuch* 113 (1996): 66–83.

———. "Goethe, Möser and the Aufklärung: The Holy Roman Empire in 'Götz von Berlichingen' and 'Egmont.'" *Deutsche Vierteljahresschrift für Literaturwissenschaft und Geistesgeschichte* 60 (1986): 609–644.

———. *Goethes Romane*. Bern: Francke, 1963.

Rendtorff, Trutz. *Vielspältige: Protestantische Beiträge zur ethischen Kultur*. Stuttgart: Kohlhammer, 1991.

Richards, David A. J. *Toleration and the Constitution*. New York: Oxford UP, 1986.

Riemann, Carl. "Goethes Gedanken über Kunst und Religion." *Jahrbuch der Goethe-Gesellschaft* 24 (1962): 109–134.

———. "Goethes Gedanken über Toleranz." *Jahrbuch der Goethe-Gesellschaft* 21 (1959): 230–54.

———. "Verhältnismässige Aufklärung: Zur bürgerlichen Ideologie am Ende des 18. Jahrhunderts." *Jahrbuch der Jean-Paul-Gesellschaft* 9 (1974): 103–26.

Rippley, La Vern J. *The German-Americans*. Boston: Twayne, 1976.

Roberts, Julian. *German Philosophy: An Introduction*. Oxford: Polity Press, 1990.

Robertson, Ritchie. "Freedom and Pragmatism: Aspects of Religious Toleration in Eighteenth-century Germany." *Patterns of Prejudice* 32 (1998): 69–80.

———. "'Dies hohe Lied der Duldung?' The Ambiguities of Toleration in Lessing's *Die Juden* and *Nathan der Weise.*" *Modern Language Review* 93 (1998): 105–120.

———. "Joseph Rohrer and the Bureaucratic Enlightenment." *Austrian Studies* 2 (1990): 23–42.

Rogge, Christian. "Goethe und die Predigt." Separatabdruck aus der Monatsschrift *Der Türmer* 3 (1900): 1–13.

Rose, William. *Men, Myths, and Movements in German Literature.* London: Allen and Unwin, 1931.

Rothe, Wolfgang. *Der politische Goethe. Dichter und Staatsdiener im deutschen Spätabsolutismus.* Göttingen: Vandenhoeck & Ruprecht, 1998.

Rürup, Reinhard. "The Tortuous and Thorny Path to Legal Equality: 'Jew Laws' and Emancipatory Legislation in Germany from the Late Eighteenth Century." *Leo Baeck Institute Yearbook* 31 (1986): 3–33.

Sachse, Julius Friedrich. *The German Pietists of Pennsylvania 1694–1708.* Philadelphia: Stockhausen, 1895.

Sagarra, Eda. *An Introduction to Nineteenth Century Germany.* Essex: Longman, 1980.

———. *A Social History of Germany 1648–1914.* London: Methuen, 1977.

Sagarra, Eda, and Peter Skrine. *A Companion to German Literature: From 1500 to the Present.* Oxford: Blackwell, 1997.

Saine, Thomas P. *Black Bread — White Bread: German Intellectuals and the French Revolution.* Studies in German Literature, Linguistics, and Culture 36. Columbia, SC: Camden House, 1988.

———. *Von der Kopernikanischen bis zur Französischen Revolution: Die Auseinandersetzung der deutschen Frühaufklärung mit der neuen Zeit.* Berlin: Schmidt, 1987.

———. "'Was ist Aufklärung?': Kulturgeschichtliche Überlegungen zu neuer Beschäftigung mit der deutschen Aufklärung." *Zeitschrift für deutsche Philologie* 93 (1974): 522–45.

Sauder, Gerhard. "Der junge Goethe und das religiöse Denken des 18. Jahrhunderts." *Goethe-Jahrbuch* 112 (1995): 97–110.

———. "Aufklärung des Vorurteils — Vorurteile der Aufklärung?" *Deutsche Vierteljahrsschrift für Literaturwissenschaft und Geistesgeschichte* 57 (1983): 259–77.

Schindler, David. *Heart of the World, Center of the Church: Communio, Ecclesiology, Liberalism, and Liberation.* Edinburgh: Clark, 1996.

Schings, Hans-Jürgen. "Freiheit in der Geschichte: Egmont und Marquis Posa im Vergleich." *Goethe-Jahrbuch* 110 (1993): 61–76.

Schlüter, Gisela. *Die französische Toleranzdebatte im Zeitalter der Aufklärung: Materiale und formale Aspekte.* Untersuchungen zu den romanischen Literaturen der Neuzeit 15. Tübingen: Niemeyer, 1992.

Schmidt, Georg. "Goethe: politisches Denken und regional orientierte Praxis im Alten Reich." *Goethe-Jahrbuch* 112 (1995): 197–212.

Schmidt, James, ed. "What is Enlightenment?": Eighteenth-Century Answers and Twentieth-Century Questions. *Philosophical Traditions* 7. Berkeley: U of California P, 1996.

Schneiders, Werner. *Die wahre Aufklärung: Zur Aufklärung der deutschen Aufklärung.* Munich: Alber, 1974.

Schoeps, Hans Joachim. "Über Toleranz." *Tradition und Leben* 14 (1962): 13–15.

Schottlaender, Rudolf. "Der Gedanke der Toleranz und seine Geschichte." *Studium Generale* 6 (1949): 307–314.

Schreiner, Klaus. "Toleranz." *Geschichtliche Grundbegriffe: Historisches Lexikon zur politisch-sozialen Sprache in Deutschland.* Edited by Otto Brunner et al. 8 vols. Stuttgart: Klett-Cotta, 1972–1997. Vol. 6 (1990): 445–94; 524–605.

Schultze, Harald. *Lessings Toleranzbegriff: Eine theologische Studie.* Göttingen: Vandenhoeck & Ruprecht, 1969.

Schulz, Georg-Michael. "Egmont." In *Goethe-Handbuch,* edited by Bernd Witte et al. 4 vols. Stuttgart: Metzler, 1996–1998. Vol. 2 (1996), 154–72.

Schulze, Winfried. "Concordia, Discordia, Tolerantia: Deutsche Politik im konfessionellen Zeitalter." *Zeitschrift für historische Forschung* 3 (1987): 43–79.

Schütz, Hans. *Juden in der deutschen Literatur: eine deutsch-jüdische Literaturgeschichte im Überblick.* Serie Piper 1520. Munich: Piper, 1992.

Schwamborn, Claudia. *Individualität in Goethes "Wanderjahren."* Paderborn: Schöningh, 1997.

Schwarz, Karl. "Die Toleranz im Religionsrecht des Heiligen Römischen Reiches Deutscher Nation, in Brandenburg-Preussen und in Österreich." *Österreichisches Archiv für Kirchenrecht* 3 (1985): 258–81.

Seager, Richard H. *The World's Parliament of Religions: The East/West Encounter, Chicago, 1893.* Bloomington, IN: Indiana UP, 1995.

Sheehan, James J. *German History 1770–1866.* Oxford: Clarendon Press, 1993.

Sichtermann, Hellmut. "'Verdienst' als ästhetischer Wert im Klassizismus." *Jahrbuch der Goethe-Gesellschaft* 25 (1963): 283–98.

Simonutti, Luisa. "Between Political Loyalty and Religious Liberty: Political Theory and Toleration in Huguenot Thought in the Epoch of Bayle." *History of Political Thought* 17 (1996): 523–54.

Sorkin, David. *The Transformation of German Jewry, 1780–1840.* New York: Oxford UP, 1987.

Speyer, Wolfgang. *Die literarische Fälschung im Heidnischen und Christlichen Altertum: Ein Vesuch Ihrer Deutung.* Munich: Beck, 1971.

Stahl, E. L. *Goethe: Iphigenie auf Tauris.* Studies in German Literature 7. London: Arnold, 1961.

Staiger, Emil. *Goethe.* 3 vols. Zurich: Atlantis, 1952–1959.

Steer, A. G. "Sankt-Rochus-Fest zu Bingen: Goethes politische Anschauungen nach den Befreiungskriegen." *Jahrbuch des Freien Deutschen Hochstifts* (1965): 186–236.

Steiner, George. *Real Presences.* London: Faber and Faber, 1990.

Stephan-Kopitzsch, Ursula. *Die Toleranzdiskussion im Spiegel überregionaler Aufklärungszeitschriften.* Europäische Hochschulschriften, Reihe 3, Geschichte und ihre Hilfswissenschaften, 382. Frankfurt am Main: Lang, 1989.

Stevenson, Leslie. "Religion and Cultural Identity." *Theology* May/June (1998): 172–78.

Strich, Fritz. *Goethe und die Weltliteratur.* Bern: Francke, 1946.

Strohbach, Margrit. *Johann Christoph Adelung: Ein Beitrag zu seinem germanistischen Schaffen mit einer Bibliographie seines Gesamtwerkes.* Berlin: Walter de Gruyter, 1984.

Sudhof, Siegfried. "Goethe und der 'Kreis von Münster.'" *Goethe Jahrbuch* 89 (1981): 72–85.

Sunderland, Jean R., editor. *William Penn and the Founding of Pennsylvania: A Documentary History.* Philadelphia: U of Pennsylvania P, 1983.

Swales, Martin. *Goethe: The Sorrows of Young Werther.* Cambridge: Cambridge UP, 1987.

———. "A Questionable Politician: A Discussion of the Ending of Goethe's 'Egmont.'" *Modern Language Review* 66 (1971): 832–40.

Taylor, Charles. *The Ethics of Authenticity.* Cambridge, MA: Harvard UP, 1991.

Teweles, Heinrich. *Goethe und die Juden*. Hamburg: Gente, 1925.

Thorp, Malcolm R., and Arthur J. Slavin, editors. *Politics, Religion and Diplomacy in Early Modern Europe: Essays in Honor of De Lamar Jensen*. Sixteenth Century Essays and Studies 27. Kirksville, MO: Northeast Missouri State University, 1994.

Vaget, Hans Rudolf. "Die Leiden des jungen Werthers." In *Goethes Erzählwerk: Interpretationen*, ed. by Paul Michael Lützeler and James E. McLeod. Stuttgart: Reclam, 1985. 37–72.

Vierhaus, Rudolf. "Aufklärung." In *Goethe-Handbuch*, edited by Bernd Witte et al. 4 vols. Stuttgart: Metzler, 1996–1998. Vol. 4/1 (1998), 85–88.

Viëtor, Karl. *Goethe the Thinker*. Cambridge, MA: Harvard UP, 1950.

Voelcker, Heinrich. "Kirche und religiöses Leben in Frankfurt am Main." In *Die Stadt Goethes: Frankfurt am Main im XVIII. Jahrhundert*, edited by H. Voelcker Frankfurt am Main: Werner u. Winter Universitätsdrückerei, 1932.

Wach, Joachim. *Das Verstehen: Grundzüge einer Geschichte der hermeneutischen Theorie im 19. Jahrhundert*. 3 vols. Tübingen: Mohr, 1926–1933.

Wadepuhl, Walter. *Goethe's Interest in the New World*. Jena: Biedermann, 1934.

Waldman, Mark. *Goethe and the Jews: A Challenge to Hitlerism*. New York: Putnam's Sons, 1934.

Walker, Michael. *The Salzburg Transaction. Expulsion and Redemption in Eighteenth-Century Germany*. Ithaca: Cornell UP.

Walker, Williston. *A History of the Christian Church*. 3rd ed. Edinburgh: Clark, 1970.

Walzer, Michael. *On Toleration*. New Haven: Yale UP, 1997.

Ward, W. R. *Faith and Faction*. London: Epworth, 1993.

Wertheim, Ursula. *Von Tasso zu Hafis: Probleme von Lyrik und Prosa des "West-östlichen Divans."* Berlin: Rütten & Loening, 1965.

Whaley, Joachim. *Religious Toleration and Social Change in Hamburg, 1529–1819*. Cambridge: Cambridge UP, 1985.

White, Hayden. *Metahistory: The Historical Imagination in Nineteenth-Century Europe*. Baltimore: Johns Hopkins UP, 1973.

Wierlacher, Alois, editor. *Kulturthema Toleranz: Zur Grundlegung einer interdisziplinären und interkulturellen Toleranzforschung*. Munich: iudicium, 1996.

———. "Was ist Toleranz? Zur Rehabilitation eines umstrittenen Begriffs." *Jahrbuch Deutsch als Fremdsprache* 20 (1994): 115–37.

———. "Ent-fremdete Fremde: Goethes Iphigenie auf Tauris als Drama des Völkerrrechts." *Zeitschrift für deutsche Philologie* 102 (1983): 161–80.

Wilkinson, Elizabeth Mary, editor. *Goethe Revisited*. London: Calder, 1984.

———. *Goethe: Poet and Thinker*. London: Arnold, 1962.

Willems, Gottfried. "Von der ewigen Wahrheit zum ewigen Frieden: 'Aufklärung' in der Literatur des 18. Jahrhunderts, insbesondere in Lessings 'Nathan' und Wielands 'Musarion.'" *Wieland-Studien* 3 (1996): 10–46.

———. "Goethe—ein 'Überwinder der Aufklärung'? Thesen zur Revision des Klassik-Bildes." *Germanisch-romanische Monatsschrift* 40 (1990): 22–40.

Williams, Bill. "The Anti-Semitism of Tolerance: Middle Class Manchester and the Jews, 1870–1900." In *City, Class and Culture: Studies of Social Policy and Cultural Production in Victorian Manchester*, edited by Alan J. Kidd and Kenneth W. Roberts. Manchester: Manchester UP, 1985.

Williams, John R. *The Life of Goethe. A Critical Biography*. Oxford: Blackwell, 1998.

Witte, Bernd, et al. *Goethe Handbuch*. 4 vols. Stuttgart: Metzler, 1996–1998. Vol. 1: *Personen, Sachen, Begriffe (A–K)*, edited by Hans Dietrich Dahnke and Regine Otto (1998).

Wohlleben, Joachim. "Des Divans Poesie und Prose: Ein Blick auf den 'West-östlichen Divan' im allgemeinen und die 'Noten und Abhandlungen' im besonderen." *Goethe-Jahrbuch* 111 (1994): 111–23.

Woesler, Winfried. "Möser und Goethe." *Goethe-Jahrbuch* 113 (1996): 23–36.

Woloch, Isser. *Eighteenth-Century Europe: Tradition and Progress, 1715–1789*. New York: Norton, 1982.

Wundt, Max. *Goethes Wilhelm Meister und die Entwicklung des modernen Lebensideals*. Berlin: Göschen, 1913.

Yolton, John W., editor. *The Blackwell Companion to the Enlightenment*. Oxford: Blackwell, 1995.

Zagari, Luciano. "Goethe und die europäische Romantik in ihrer Wirkung und Gegenwirkung?" *Goethe-Jahrbuch* 112 (1995): 213–26.

Index